The Supremacy Clause

Recent Titles in
Reference Guides to the United States Constitution
Jack Stark, Series Editor

The Right to the Assistance of Counsel
James J. Tomkovicz

Prohibited Government Acts
Jack Stark

State Sovereign Immunity
Melvyn R. Durchslag

Constitutional Remedies
Michael Wells and Thomas A. Eaton

Privileges and Immunities
David Skillen Bogen

Searches, Seizures, and Warrants
Robert M. Bloom

The Supremacy Clause

A Reference Guide to the United States Constitution

Christopher R. Drahozal

Foreword by Carter G. Phillips

REFERENCE GUIDES TO THE
UNITED STATES CONSTITUTION, NUMBER 7
Jack Stark, *Series Editor*

PRAEGER

Westport, Connecticut
London

Library of Congress Cataloging-in-Publication Data

Drahozal, Christopher R.
The supremacy clause : a reference guide to the United States Constitution / Christopher R. Drahozal; foreword by Carter G. Phillips.
p. cm.—(Reference guides to the United States Constitution, ISSN 1539-8986; no. 7)
Includes bibliographical references and index.
ISBN 0-313-31447-0 (alk. paper)
1. Exclusive and concurrent legislative powers—United States. I. Title. II. Series.
KF4612.D73 2004
342.7302—dc22 2004041572

British Library Cataloguing in Publication Data is available.

Library of Congress Catalog Card Number: 2004041572
ISBN: 0-313-31447-0
ISSN: 1539-8986

First published in 2004

Praeger Publishers, 88 Post Road West, Westport, CT 06881
An imprint of Greenwood Publishing Group, Inc.
www.praeger.com

Printed in the United States of America

The paper used in this book complies with the Permanent Paper Standard issued by the National Information Standards Organization (Z39.48-1984)

10 9 8 7 6 5 4 3 2 1

For Stephanie

Contents

Series Foreword

JACK STARK

One can conceive of the United States Constitution in many ways. For example, noting the reverence in which it has been held one can think of it as equivalent to a sacred text. Unfortunately, most of its devotees have had less knowledge and even less understanding of the document than they have had reverence for it. Sometimes it is treated as primarily a political document and on that basis has been subjected to analysis, such as Charles Beard's *An Economic Interpretation of the Constitution of the United States*. One can plausibly argue that the Constitution seems most astounding when seen in light of the intellectual effort that has been associated with it. Three brief but highly intense bursts of intellectual energy produced, and established as organic law, most of the Constitution as it now exists. Two of those efforts, sustained over a long period of time, have enabled us to better understand the document.

The first burst of energy occurred at the Constitutional Convention. Although some of the delegates' business, such as the struggle between populous and non-populous states about their representation in Congress, was political, much of it was about fundamental issues of political theory. A few of the delegates had or later achieved international eminence for their intellects. Among them are Benjamin Franklin, Alexander Hamilton, and James Madison. Others, although less well known, had first-rate minds. That group includes George Mason and George Wythe. Many of the delegates contributed intelligently. Although the Convention's records are less than satisfactory, they indicate clearly enough that the delegates worked mightily to constitute not merely a polity—but a rational polity that would rise to the standards envisioned by the delegates' intellectual ancestors. Their product, though brief, is amazing. William Gladstone called it "the most wonderful work ever struck off."

Despite the delegates' eminence and the Constitution's excellence as seen from our place in history, its ratification was far from certain. That state of affairs necessitated the second burst of intellectual energy associated with that document: the debate over ratification. Soon after the convention adjourned, articles and speeches (some supporting the Constitution and some attacking it) began to proliferate. A national debate commenced—not only about the document itself but also about the nature of the polity that ought to exist in this country. Both sides included many writers and speakers who were verbally adroit and steeped in the relevant political and philosophical literature. The result was an accumulation of material that is remarkable for both its quantity and its quality. At its apex is the *Federalist Papers*, a production of Alexander Hamilton, James Madison, and John Jay that deserves a place among the great books of Western culture.

Another burst, although not as impressive as the first two but highly respectable, occurred when the Bill of Rights was proposed. Some delegates to the Constitutional Convention had vigorously asserted that such guarantees should be included in the original document. George Mason, the principal drafter of the Virginia Declaration of Rights, so held, and he walked out of the convention when he failed to achieve his purpose. Even those who had argued that the rights in question were implicit recognized the value of adding protection of them to the Constitution. The debate was thus focused on the rights that were to be explicitly granted, not on whether any rights ought to be explicitly granted. Again many writers and speakers entered the fray, and again the debate was solidly grounded in theory and was conducted on a high intellectual level.

Thus, within a few years a statement of organic law and a vital coda to it had been produced. However, the meaning and effect of many of that document's provisions were far from certain; the debates on ratification of the Constitution and the Bill of Rights had demonstrated that. In addition, the document existed in a vacuum, because statutes and actions had not been assessed by its standards. The attempt to resolve these problems began after Chief Justice John Marshall, in Marbury v. Madison, asserted the right of the U.S. Supreme Court to interpret and apply the Constitution. Judicial interpretation and application of the Constitution, beginning with the first constitutional case and persisting until the most recent, is one of the sustained exertions of intellectual energy associated with the Constitution. The framers would be surprised by some of the results of these activities. References in the document to "due process," which seems to refer only to procedures, have been held also to have a substantive dimension. A right to privacy has been found lurking among the penumbras of various parts of the text. A requirement that states grant the same "privileges and immunities" to citizens of other states that they granted to their own citizens, which seemed to guarantee important rights, was not held to be particularly important. The corpus of judicial interpretations of the Constitution is now as voluminous as that document is terse.

As judicial interpretations multiplied, another layer (interpretations of interpretations) appeared, and also multiplied. This layer, the other sustained intellectual effort associated with the Constitution, consists of articles, most of them published in law reviews, and books on the Constitution. This material varies in quality and significance. Some of these works of scholarship result from meticulous examination and incisive thought. Others repeat earlier work, or apply a fine-tooth comb to matters that are too minute even for such a comb. Somewhere in that welter of tertiary material is the answer to almost every question that one could ask about constitutional law. The problem is finding the answer that one wants. The difficulty of locating useful guidance is exacerbated by the bifurcation of most constitutional scholarship into two kinds. In "Two Styles of Social Science Research," C. Wright Mills delineates macroscopic and molecular research. The former deals with huge issues, the latter with tiny issues. Virtually all of the scholarship on the Constitution is of one of those two types. Little of it is macroscopic, but that category does include some first-rate syntheses such as Jack Rakove's *Original Meanings*. Most constitutional scholarship is molecular and, again, some fine work is included in that category.

In his essay, Mills bemoans the inability of social scientists to combine the two kinds of research that he describes to create a third category that will be more generally useful. This series of books is an attempt to do for constitutional law the intellectual work that Mills proposed for social science. The author of each book has dealt carefully and at reasonable length with a topic that lies in the middle range of generality. Upon completion, this series will consist of thirty-seven books, each on a constitutional law topic. Some of the books, such as the book on freedom of the press, explicate one portion of the Constitution's text. Others, such as the volume on federalism, treat a topic that has several anchors in the Constitution. The books on constitutional history and constitutional interpretation range over the entire document, but each does so from a single perspective. Except for a few of the books, the special circumstances of which dictate minor changes in format, each book includes the same components—a brief history of the topic, a lengthy and sophisticated analysis of the current state of the law on that topic, a bibliographical essay that organizes and evaluates scholarly material in order to facilitate further research, a table of cases, and an index. The books are intellectually rigorous (in fact, authorities have written them) but, due to their clarity and to brief definitions of terms that are unfamiliar to laypersons, each is comprehensible and useful to a wide audience, one that ranges from other experts on the book's subject to intelligent non-lawyers.

In short, this series provides an extremely valuable service to the legal community and to others who are interested in constitutional law, as every citizen should be. Each book is a map of part of the U.S. Constitution. Together they map all of that document's territory that is worth mapping. When this series is complete, each book will be a third kind of scholarly work that combines the macroscopic and the molecular. Together they will explicate all of the important constitutional topics. Anyone who wants assistance in understanding either a topic in constitutional law or the Constitution as a whole can easily find it in these books.

Foreword

CARTER G. PHILLIPS*

Professor Christopher Drahozal has succeeded in accomplishing something I frankly did not believe could be done. He has made the Supremacy Clause—which dryly states that "[t]his Constitution, and the Laws of the United States which shall be made in Pursuance thereof; and all Treaties made, or which shall be made, under the Authority of the United States, shall be the supreme Law of the Land . . ."—come alive with relevance to people who ordinarily would not care about that provision of the United States Constitution. Professor Drahozal's book relies upon compelling real-life situations to illustrate vividly the clashes between federal and state power that are inherent in "Our Federalism" and that the Supremacy Clause must resolve. Beginning with South Carolina Governor Jim Hodges' attempt to halt the federal government's transportation of radioactive waste into his state for storage and ending with the shooting by an FBI agent of one of the participants in the standoff at Ruby Ridge, Idaho, Professor Drahozal masterfully weaves these compelling historical and contemporary events into a thorough analysis of the history and current legal thinking about the Supremacy Clause in its myriad applications.

The reader might wonder why anyone would ask a practicing lawyer who primarily represents businesses to introduce a scholarly treatment of the Supremacy Clause, but the explanation is not all that obscure. With the exception, perhaps, of the dormant Commerce Clause, there is no provision in the Constitution that provides greater protection on a more consistent basis for business interests than the Supremacy Clause. In particular, the preemption doctrine, which identifies when federal law conflicts with state law and how to resolve that conflict, frequently

*Mr. Phillips is the Managing Partner of the Washington, D.C. office of Sidley Austin Brown & Wood. He first appeared in the Supreme Court in 1981 and has argued more than forty cases since then. He received his B.A. summa cum laude from the Ohio State University in 1973, an M.A. from Northwestern University in 1975, and a J.D. magna cum laude from Northwestern University in 1977.

protects business interests against overreaching (at least in the view of the businesses) regulation by state and local entities. In addition, preemption doctrine has resulted in increasing uniformity and consistency in business regulation, as federal law displaces state law in areas traditionally regulated by states.

As Professor Drahozal notes, preemption cases have been a staple of the Supreme Court's docket for more than thirty years. Indeed, but for Congress's decision almost a decade ago to eliminate appellate jurisdiction in situations where state courts uphold state law against federal constitutional challenges, it seems quite likely that the Court would have decided far more preemption cases than it has. What is striking is that despite the fact that the Court's review of preemption cases is now purely discretionary, the Court still decides several such cases every Term.

Because the Supremacy Clause is the cornerstone of "Our Federalism," it is difficult to think of a better time to undertake a comprehensive and scholarly review of this single provision of the Constitution. Federalism has been the jurisprudential doctrine that has almost single-handedly dominated most of the major decisions of the United States Supreme Court during Chief Justice Rehnquist's tenure. What is surprising is Professor Drahozal's finding that states do not uniformly succeed in litigation arising under the Supremacy Clause. In preemption cases where the Court presumes that traditional state law regulation is permissible and requires a clear expression of congressional intent to preempt, the Court has struck down state laws more often than not.

Given the Court's consistently pro-states' rights approach to litigation under the Eleventh Amendment and the Commerce Clause, it may seem curious that the Court has been less protective of the states' prerogatives in the face of arguably conflicting federal law. Professor Drahozal does not directly address the issue, but it is implicit in his careful exposition of the preemption doctrine. There are crosscutting currents of legal reasoning at work in the preemption area. The touchstone of preemption is congressional (or sometimes executive branch) intent. Thus, at bottom, the issues are really matters of statutory construction. In that context, plain language and structure of the statute may lead to but one conclusion and, if so, those who tend to favor state interests still will feel constrained to implement Congress' manifest intent. Thus, it really should come as no surprise that the Court is as likely as not to find preemption in any given case.

To the extent the states and localities actually appear to have improved their winning percentage some in more recent years, I would be inclined to attribute that to better lawyering. It is clear that organizations like the National Association of Attorneys General and the State and Local Legal Center have improved dramatically the quality of the advocacy on behalf of states and localities and thus there is not an inherent advantage owned by either the federal government or large corporations in their ability to develop persuasive arguments before the Supreme Court.

For obvious reasons, I particularly focused on the portion of the Supremacy Clause that creates the analytical underpinnings of the preemption doctrine. But the reader will do him- or herself a disservice by focusing only on that portion of this book. The analysis of federal immunity provides a careful exposition of how the immunity doctrine arose in the taxation context and has expanded into state civil and criminal regulatory activities. Professor Drahazol makes a compelling showing that the principles derived from the state tax cases can readily be applied to the broader issues and ensure some consistency in approach.

Finally, Professor Drahozal takes up the complicated issues posed by applying various international law sources of law as the "supreme law of the land." In this context he concludes his powerful presentation with a provocative look at the potential impact of international law norms that condemn the use of the death penalty in cases involving juveniles. This issue, which has been left open by the Supreme Court, poses an exquisitely difficult and controversial application of the Supremacy Clause with implications that every reader can fully appreciate.

At the end of the day, this is a book that provides such a thorough treatment of the Supremacy Clause that every practitioner who litigates on behalf of private entities against states and localities should keep it close at hand. Without doubt, it is the most comprehensive analysis of the history and application of the Supremacy Clause ever undertaken. As a practicing lawyer, I, for one, owe a huge debt of thanks to Professor Drahozal for making this subject as understandable and user-friendly as the topic will permit.

Acknowledgments

I wish to thank the University of Kansas School of Law, particularly Dean Steve McAllister and Associate Deans Sid Shapiro and Webb Hecker, for their support of this project, both financial and otherwise. Thanks also to the University of Kansas and the University of Kansas General Research Fund for sabbatical leave and summer research support. Discussions with and comments from my colleagues, in particular John Head, Laura Hines, Rick Levy, Ellen Sward, and Steve Ware, have been invaluable, as has been the research assistance of Eric Aufdengarten, Chris Confer, and Matt Geary. And thanks especially to my family for their patience and understanding.

Introduction

This Constitution, and the Laws of the United States which shall be made in Pursuance thereof; and all Treaties made, or which shall be made, under the Authority of the United States, shall be the supreme Law of the Land; and the Judges in every State shall be bound thereby, any Thing in the Constitution or Laws of any State to the Contrary notwithstanding.

In April 2002, the United States Department of Energy ("DOE") announced that it would transport six tons of surplus plutonium from the Rocky Flats Environmental Technology Site (in Colorado) to its Savannah River Site (in South Carolina) for long-term storage.[1] The decision was part of DOE efforts to clean up and close the Rocky Flats facility. It also was designed to help the United States fulfill its commitment to Russia to dispose of surplus weapons-grade plutonium. DOE was to make the first shipment as early as May 15, 2002, although it eventually agreed to defer the shipments until June 22, 2002, at the earliest.

Transport and storage of radioactive materials is highly controversial in the best of times. The September 11 terrorist attacks and the arrest of a suspect for an alleged plot to construct a "dirty bomb" (a bomb made with conventional explosives and surrounded with radioactive material) made the transport and storage of plutonium at the Savannah River Site even more sensitive than it otherwise would have been.

Political opposition in South Carolina was intense, at least in part because of fears that the plutonium once brought into the state would not be removed. The governor of South Carolina, Jim Hodges, who was facing a fierce reelection campaign (which he ultimately lost), publicly opposed shipment of the plutonium into South Carolina and filed a lawsuit challenging DOE's decision. On June 13, 2002, the United States District Court for the District of South Carolina rejected the

Governor's lawsuit, ruling that "DOE has adequately considered and disclosed the environmental impact of its actions and its decision is not arbitrary or capricious" (Hodges. v. Abraham, D.S.C. 2002).

Governor Hodges was not willing to concede defeat. First, as permitted, he took an appeal from the district court's decision to the United States Court of Appeals for the Fourth Circuit, challenging the district court's holding that DOE's action was authorized by federal law.[2] Second, he issued an Executive Order blockading the Savannah River Site to keep out the plutonium.[3] After describing DOE's actions and reciting the "legitimate threat of theft, diversion, or use of plutonium by terrorists," the Executive Order stated:

> I hereby declare that an emergency exists and order that the transportation of plutonium on South Carolina roads and highways is prohibited; that any persons transporting plutonium shall not enter the State of South Carolina; and that any persons nevertheless attempting or intending to transport plutonium along the public thoroughfares of the State of South Carolina shall give notice of such intention and to cease and desist from such action until further direction is given.

The Governor previously had been quoted in the press as saying: "If it is necessary for me to lie down in front of the trucks [carrying the plutonium], I'll do that. We're going to do whatever it takes."[4] Immediately after issuance of the Executive Order (although before the earliest date the plutonium shipments might begin), state police blockaded the Savannah River Site and searched at least two vehicles seeking to enter.

The United States filed an action with the same federal court seeking an injunction against the blockade. Although Governor Hodges defensively asserted in the press that DOE had broken a promise not to store plutonium in South Carolina, he offered no defense to the lawsuit brought by the United States, essentially conceding that his action was unlawful. In open court the district judge stated: "It is a sad day for South Carolina when a governor, who has taken an oath as an officer of the state and as an attorney to uphold the state and United States constitutions, must be ordered to obey it."[5]

The reason Governor Hodges could offer no defense to the federal government's action was Article VI, clause 2 of the United States Constitution—the Supremacy Clause—which makes federal law the "supreme Law of the Land." The district court found the case "easily resolved by reference to" McCulloch v. Maryland (1819), in which the Supreme Court stated that "the states have no power . . . to retard, impede, burden, or in any manner control, the operations of the constitutional laws enacted by congress to carry into execution the powers vested in the general government." Following *McCulloch*, the district court held that Governor Hodges' Executive Order and his attempt physically to block the plutonium shipments into South Carolina were "null and void as a violation of the Supremacy Clause" (Abraham v. Hodges, D.S.C. 2002).

Governor Hodges' dispute with the federal government—which Hodges recognized was so one-sided he could not even offer a defense—hardly seems worth mentioning. Direct confrontations between state officials and the federal government are rare, particularly ones involving a "nonracial, nonemotional issue" such as this one.[6] But the case is noteworthy precisely because it is so unusual. State officials may grumble about a bloated federal bureaucracy or complain about unfunded federal mandates, but in the vast majority of cases no one questions that federal law overrides state law and must be followed. The guiding principle of the Supremacy Clause—that federal law controls over state law—is so central to the American system of government, and so ingrained into day-to-day life, that most of the time no one even thinks about it.

This book examines in detail the history of the Supremacy Clause and the legal doctrines that have developed under it. The Supremacy Clause plays an essential role in defining America's system of government as a *federal* one, with two tiers (state governments and the federal government) that have overlapping areas of competency. In those areas, when state law and federal law conflict, the Supremacy Clause provides that federal law is controlling. In the event of a confrontation between a state and the federal government, as happened in South Carolina, so long as the federal government is acting within its delegated powers, the Supremacy Clause dictates that the federal government will prevail.

Thus, the central theme of the book is federal supremacy: Federal law is the supreme law and overrides conflicting state constitutions, state statutes, and state common-law doctrines. A secondary theme, however, is not supremacy, but equality. In a number of substantive areas, the Supreme Court's Supremacy Clause jurisprudence requires the states to treat the federal government no worse than other groups in the state—that is, it invalidates state laws that discriminate against the federal government or federal law. State legislatures cannot discriminate against the federal government or those who deal with it by imposing higher taxes or more stringent regulations. State courts cannot discriminate against federal law by refusing to hear federal law claims when they would hear similar state law claims. Not only the Supreme Court but also the United States Congress, when enacting a statute that will preempt conflicting state law, sometimes enacts a nondiscrimination standard, forbidding states to treat the federally protected interest differently from others in the state. The theory behind such a nondiscrimination standard—a standard of equal treatment, rather than special treatment—is that it creates a "political check" against abusive state regulation. States may only subject the federal government to a law when they are willing to impose the same law on others in the state, others who can use the political process to change the law if it is too stringent. Under the Supremacy Clause, the Supreme Court adopts nondiscrimination rules as default standards when Congress itself has not adopted a more protective standard.

Part I details the history of the Supremacy Clause. After briefly discussing the colonies' struggles against the supremacy of the British Parliament, it examines the Articles of Confederation, under which the supremacy of federal law was unclear. This failing was highlighted by conflicts between state laws and the Treaty of Peace ending the Revolutionary War and was among the reasons a convention was called in Philadelphia to consider amendments to the Articles. This Part then considers at length the evolution of the Supremacy Clause at the Constitutional Convention (which went well beyond amending the Articles). The origins of the Supremacy Clause were in the "congressional negative" in the Virginia Plan, which would have permitted Congress to veto state laws that conflicted with the Constitution. The delegates ultimately rejected the congressional negative and replaced it with the Supremacy Clause, making federal law the supreme law of the land and binding state court judges to follow federal law, without regard to contrary state laws. The Supremacy Clause was widely criticized in the debates on ratification of the Constitution as likely to abolish the states altogether, or at least to override the protections of state bills of rights. Part I then examines early Supreme Court decisions construing the Supremacy Clause, which found (albeit not without limitation) in favor of a strong national government and laid the foundation for the doctrinal role of the Supremacy Clause today. Finally, Part I concludes by examining the role of the Supremacy Clause in critical confrontations between states and the federal government—during the nullification crisis of 1832, the secession of eleven Southern states giving rise to the Civil War, and attempts at the "interposition" of state law to resist Supreme Court decisions requiring the desegregation of the public schools in the 1950s and 1960s.

Part II then analyzes current Supremacy Clause doctrine, focusing on four topics. The first topic is the Supremacy Clause and the courts, which covers the doctrine of judicial review and the duty of state courts to apply federal law. Next, it discusses preemption doctrine, perhaps "the most frequently used doctrine of constitutional law in practice."[7] Federal law invalidates (preempts) conflicting state law, either expressly (when a provision in the statute itself defines the scope of preemption) or impliedly (when the federal statute occupies an entire field, when compliance with both federal law and state law is impossible, or when state law is an obstacle to accomplishing Congress' purposes in enacting the federal law). The third topic is federal immunity from state law: the extent to which the Supremacy Clause protects the federal government and those who deal with it from state taxes, regulations, and even criminal law. Finally, this Part examines the role of treaties and other international agreements as the supreme law of the land.

As with this introduction, the discussion of each doctrinal topic begins with a recent controversy that implicates the particular aspect of Supremacy Clause doctrine. The subjects are varied: from the confrontation over a monument to the Ten Commandments in the Alabama State Judicial Building ("The Supremacy Clause and the Courts") to the growing use of arbitration clauses in consumer contracts ("Federal Preemption of State Law") to a shooting by an FBI agent at Ruby Ridge, Idaho ("Federal Immunity from State Law") to the juvenile death penalty ("Treaties as the Supreme Law of the Land"). The hope is to illustrate the practical as well as theoretical relevance of the Supremacy Clause today.

ENDNOTES

1. Most of the background facts that follow come from the opinion of the United States Court of Appeals for the Fourth Circuit in Hodges v. Abraham (4th Cir. 2002).
2. The Fourth Circuit ultimately affirmed the District Court's order (Hodges v. Abraham, 4th Cir. 2002), and the Supreme Court denied review.
3. S. Car. Exec. Order 2002-14 (June 14, 2002), at www.state.sc.us/governor/2002-14.html.
4. "Tussle Brews Over Plutonium Hauls," CBSNews.com (Aug. 11, 2001), at www.cbsnews.com/stories/2001/08/11/national/printable306053.shtml.
5. Sammy Fretwell, "Hodges Ordered Not to Block Plutonium Shipments to S.C.," *The State* (June 19, 2002), at www.thestate.com/mld/state/3498421.htm.
6. Joey Holleman, "Governor Took on the Feds, Earning Kudos from Some, Censure from Others," *The State* (June 19, 2002), at www.thestate.com/mld/state/3498414.htm (quoting University of South Carolina Professor Dan Carter).
7. Stephen A. Gardbaum, "The Nature of Preemption," 79 *Cornell L. Rev.* (1994) 767, 768.

PART I

History

From Independence to Ratification of the Constitution

PROLOGUE: SOVEREIGNTY AND SUPREMACY BEFORE INDEPENDENCE

[I]n every Common-wealth and government there be found some rights of Soveraignty, unless Custome, or the provisional ordinance of that State doe otherwise dispose of them: which Soveraigne power is *potestas suprema*, a power that can controule all other powers, and cannot be controuled but by itself.

Sir James Whitelocke, 1610[1]

The accepted view of sovereignty, as it developed from Whitelocke's time through the American Revolution, was that it could not be divided. Alexander Hamilton illustrates the view, writing in 1775 that "[i]n every civil society there must be a supreme power, to which all the members of that society are subject; for otherwise, there could be no supremacy, or subordination, that is no government at all."[2] From the British perspective, parliamentary supremacy over the King led to what historian John Phillip Reid calls the "imperial truism" of parliamentary supremacy over the colonies.[3] Thus, the Declaratory Act of 1766 merely restated "an axiom of eighteenth-century English political thought"[4]: "That the said colonies and plantations in America have been, are, and of right ought to be, subordinate unto, and dependent upon the imperial crown and parliament of Great Britain"; and that Parliament "had, hath, and of right ought to have, full power and authority to make laws and statutes of sufficient force and validity to bind the colonies and people of America, subjects of the crown of Great Britain, in all cases whatsoever."[5] Because of the belief that sovereignty could not be divided, there was no middle ground: Either Parliament was supreme as to all things or the colonies effectively were independent. As Massachusetts Governor Thomas

Hutchinson stated to the Massachusetts General Court in 1773: "I know of no line that can be drawn between the supreme authority of Parliament and the total independence of the colonies: it is impossible there should be two independent Legislatures in one and the same state. . . ."[6]

Although this "concept of supremacy threatened to make federalism impossible in the eighteenth-century British empire,"[7] in fact the origins of the American federal system of government can be traced to the colonies' experience with empire. According to Professor Martin Flaherty, "Historians have done much to show that a model of divided authority was at the core of the patriots' case against Great Britain."[8] The colonists began from the premise that even supreme power was subject to limits. Professor Reid quotes Henry Goodricke: "Supremacy meant 'nothing more,—than that it is *absolutely supreme* in command; that there is no *civil* or *legal* power in the state *superior* to it, and that its acts can not be controlled or annulled by any other *authority*. This does not preclude in the least its being limited, as to the extent of its power, either by laws of Nature, or by rules and principles of the Constitution.' "[9] Relying on this theory of supreme but limited power, the colonists accepted Parliament's power to regulate trade generally; but they argued that the English Constitution limited Parliament's power to regulate the colonies' domestic affairs.[10] In effect, the colonies were arguing for a federal structure, with two tiers of government and divided sovereignty (Parliament supreme as to some matters and the colonial legislatures supreme as to others).[11]

The argument failed, however, giving way to the British theory of undivided sovereignty. But the colonists turned the theory against the British by asserting that the colonial legislatures and not Parliament were supreme.[12] The colonies resisted the ever increasing incursions by Parliament into their domestic affairs. Resistance turned into revolution and then independence, leaving the newly independent country to face its own questions of sovereignty and supremacy.

THE ARTICLES OF CONFEDERATION

According to historian Gordon Wood, "When the Americans came in 1776 to erect their own confederated empire, most did so with an overwhelming conviction, as Samuel Adams told the Carlisle Commission in 1778, 'that in every kingdom, state, or empire there must be, from the necessity of the thing, one supreme legislative power, with authority to bind every part in all cases the proper object of human laws.' "[13] This view of undivided sovereignty lingered from colonial days and influenced the drafting of the Articles of Confederation, which created a weak national government and left open serious questions about federal supremacy. After the end of the Revolutionary War, the supremacy of federal law under the Articles was put to the test. Numerous conflicts between state laws and the Treaty of Peace with Great Britain starkly presented the question of federal supremacy: Did the treaty override the state laws, or did state legislatures first have to implement the treaty by repealing the conflicting state laws? The uncertainty of federal supremacy under the Articles of Confederation was among the failings that the Framers sought to remedy in the Constitutional Convention in Philadelphia in 1787.

Federal Supremacy Under the Articles of Confederation

On June 12, 1776, the day after appointing a committee to draft a Declaration of Independence, Congress appointed another committee to prepare draft Articles of Confederation. The committee, headed by John Dickinson, reported to Congress on July 12, 1776, the initial draft of what ultimately became the Articles of Confederation. This draft, known as the Dickinson draft, gave Congress broad powers and limited the states to powers that did not conflict with the powers of Congress.[14] Thus, Article III of the draft reserved to each of the colonies "the sole and exclusive Regulation and Government of its internal police, *in all matters that shall not interfere with the Articles of Confederation*" (emphasis added). Similarly, Article VIII permitted each colony to tax imports and exports, "provided such Imposts or Duties do not interfere with any Stipulations in Treaties hereinafter entered into by the United States assembled." Article XII required that "[e]very Colony shall abide by the Determinations of the United States assembled, concerning the Services performed and Losses or Expenses incurred by every Colony for the common Defence or general Welfare." At the same time, the Dickinson draft gave broad powers to Congress, excluding, however, the power to tax (except to support the post office). As summarized by Merrill Jensen: "The Dickinson draft, while by no means as explicit as the Constitution of 1787, made the constitution of the central government the standard by which the rights, powers, and duties of the states were to be measured. Congress was theoretically, if not practically, the supreme authority."[15]

When Congress resumed consideration of the Articles, the strong central government in the Dickinson draft did not survive. Attempts to establish precedents for federal supremacy had managed to stir up supporters of states' rights.[16] Thomas Burke proposed an amendment to the Articles providing that "all sovereign power was in the States separately, and that particular acts of it, which should be expressly enumerated, would be exercised in conjunction, and not otherwise; but that in all things else each State would exercise all the rights and power of sovereignty, uncontrolled."[17] Congress approved Burke's amendment by a vote of 11 to 1, with one state divided. Burke wrote that he "was much pleased to find the opinion of accumulating powers to Congress so little supported."[18] The draft Articles thus shifted strongly back in the direction of preserving state sovereignty.

The Articles of Confederation as approved and ratified created just that—a confederation of the thirteen states. Each state retained its "sovereignty, freedom, and independence, and every power, jurisdiction, and right . . . not . . . expressly delegated to the United States, in Congress assembled"—the final version of the Burke amendment.[19] The Articles delegated to Congress only limited powers (although Article IX did grant Congress the "sole and exclusive right and power" to declare war and to make treaties). Moreover, Congress largely was dependent on the states for carrying out its directives. It had no power to tax, and instead relied on the state legislatures to raise money to fund its operations. Indeed, it may be an overstatement to call the national government under the Articles a "government" at all. As stated by Edward Corwin: "The essential defect of the Articles of Confederation . . . consisted in the fact that the government established by them operated not upon the individual citizens of the United States but upon the states in their corporate capacity—that, in brief, it was not a government at all, but rather the central agency of an alliance."[20]

The Articles of Confederation as ratified contained no provision expressly declaring federal law supreme to state law. Article VI prohibited imposts or duties that interfered with federal treaties, but, in a variation from Article VIII of the Dickinson draft, was limited to stipulations "in pursuance of any treaties already proposed by Congress to the courts of France and Spain."[21] Further, Article XIII of the Articles (the equivalent of Article XII of the Dickinson draft) provided that "[e]very state shall abide by the determinations of the united states in congress assembled, on all questions which by this confederation are submitted to them. And the Articles of this confederation shall be inviolably observed by every state . . . ." The directive that each state "shall abide by the determinations" of Congress might be read as making federal law supreme to state law: States were to do what Congress determined, even if state law was to the contrary. Likewise, the requirement that the Articles "be inviolably observed by every state" seems to give supreme status to the Articles of Confederation themselves. For these reasons, Article XIII is sometimes referred to as the "supremacy clause" of the Articles of Confederation.

But Article XIII was limited in several important ways that undercut its effectiveness in making federal law supreme to state law. First, the provision was unclear whether congressional determinations had any effect in the absence of state implementing legislation. A state law enacted to carry out Congress' determination certainly would be binding in state court. But there was a serious question whether a congressional determination had any effect without being enacted into state law by the state legislature. In general, Congress acted through state legislatures, and Article XIII does not clearly indicate otherwise.

Second, nothing in Article XIII provided an enforcement mechanism if a state failed to implement the congressional determination. No sanction was imposed on states that did not "abide" by congressional actions or "observe[ ]" the Articles of Confederation. Indeed, Congress could not even enforce its requisitions to state legislatures for money, much less other determinations it made. Nor was there any direction to state courts that they must treat the determination as binding in the absence of state legislation.

Third, Article XIII did not address the effect of subsequent state legislation on the obligation of states to follow determinations of Congress. Even if a subsequent congressional determination could override a prior state law (which itself was questionable), nothing in Article XIII ruled out the possibility that a state could override a congressional determination by enacting a new state law. The states ratified the Articles of Confederation, not by calling a constitutional convention in the state or requiring a vote of their citizens, but by enacting a state statute that authorized the state's delegates to sign. Arguably, the Articles and congressional determinations adopted under the Articles had no higher status than any other enactment of the state legislature. Although some states incorporated the Articles into their state constitutions, giving them higher authority than ordinary state law, other states did not. "[I]f the authority of federal law within a state rested entirely on an ordinary state statute," Professor Caleb Nelson explains, "and if courts applied the normal rule that later statutes trump earlier ones in the event of contradiction, then a subsequently enacted state statute could conceivably prevent the application of federal law."[22]

James Madison cited these weaknesses in his *Vices of the Political System of the United States*, written in Spring 1787 in preparation for the Constitutional Convention.[23] In *Vices*, Madison explained that the Articles of Confederation were "nothing more than a treaty of amity of commerce and of alliance, between so many independent and Sovereign States," and that it was unrealistic to expect the "unanimous and punctual obedience" of all the states to congressional decisions. Although acts of Congress were "nominally authoritative," they were "in fact recommendatory only," as they "depend[ed] for their execution on the will of state legislatures." Madison also argued that in some states a state law might prevail over a previous federal enactment, particularly because a state court would "be most likely to lean on the side of the State." In short, although it might appear that Article XIII made federal law supreme over state law, in reality there was serious question whether that was the case.

It might have been different had a proposed amendment to the Articles, prepared by a committee headed by Madison, been adopted.[24] The memorandum setting out the amendment recognized that nothing in Article XIII expressly granted Congress the power to take actions against states that failed to comply with congressional directives, although the memorandum asserted that Congress had a "general and implied power" to do so. Accordingly, it recommended an amendment to the Articles authorizing Congress "to employ the force of the United States as well by sea as by land to compel such State or States to fulfill their federal engagements." Indeed, the amendment would have authorized Congress to act directly against the vessels and goods of individuals in the state, as well to impose an embargo against the state until it complied. The proposed amendment never made it through Congress, however, being referred to various committees and ultimately dying a quiet death.[25]

Supremacy and the Treaty of Peace

The uncertainty about the supremacy of federal law under the Articles of Confederation manifested itself most clearly in the dispute between Great Britain and the United States over compliance with the Treaty of Peace (also referred to as the Treaty of Paris) that ended the Revolutionary War. Provisional articles were agreed to on November 30, 1782, and the definitive Treaty signed on September 5, 1783.[26] In the treaty, Great Britain recognized the United States as "free, sovereign, and independent states," and renounced all claims to its territory. The Treaty specified the boundaries of the United States, and required the British to "withdraw all . . . armies, garrisons and fleets from the said United States, and from every post, place and harbour within the same." Article IV of the Treaty provided that "creditors on either side, shall meet with no lawful impediment to the recovery of the full value in sterling money, of all bona fide debts heretofore contracted." Because the creditors at issue were mostly British subjects, Article IV in practical effect imposed obligations almost exclusively on the United States. Other articles of the Treaty forbid future confiscations of property (again, likely the property of British loyalists) and required Congress to "recommend it to the legislatures of the respective states" to restore properties already confiscated from British subjects and loyalists.

In December 1785, the United States complained to the British Secretary of State that Great Britain had not yet withdrawn all of its troops from the United States as required by Article VII of the Treaty of Peace. Although more than two years had passed since the definitive Treaty had been signed, John Adams wrote, "the posts of Oswegatchy, Oswego, Niagara, Presqueisle, Sandusky, Detroit, Michillimackinac," among others, were "still held by British garrisons, to the loss and injury of the said United States."[27] He demanded that the British withdraw all troops from the United States.

Great Britain justified its failure to remove its troops on the ground that the United States itself was in violation of the Treaty of Peace. The British response, set out in a letter from the British Secretary of State to Adams dated February 28, 1786,[28] cited various state laws alleged to be "lawful impediment[s]" to British collection of debts. Attached to the letter was a list of grievances asserted by British subjects, in varying amounts of detail, alleging violations of Article IV.

Secretary for Foreign Affairs John Jay investigated the British complaints. In his report to Congress, Jay documented numerous violations of the Treaty of Peace by the United States. The vast majority were violations of Article IV, as the British had alleged. Jay further rejected any argument that the individual states had the right to disregard or interpret for themselves the provisions of the Treaty of Peace. In so doing, he asserted in strong terms the supremacy of the federal treaty over conflicting state laws:

> When therefore a treaty is constitutionally made, ratified and published by Congress, it immediately becomes binding on the whole nation, and superadded to the laws of the land, without the intervention, consent or fiat of state legislatures. It derives its obligation from its being a compact between the sovereign of this, and the sovereign of another nation; but laws or statutes derive their force from being acts of a legislature competent to the passing of them. Hence it is clear, that treaties must be implicitly received and observed by every member of the nation; for as state legislatures are not competent to the making of such compacts or treaties, so neither are they competent, in that capacity, authoritatively to decide on or ascertain the construction and sense of them.[29]

Jay recommended that Congress pass resolutions declaring the supremacy of the Treaty of Peace as federal law and urging the states to repeal all laws inconsistent with the Treaty.

John Jay's report was not the first assertion of the supremacy of the Treaty of Peace under the Articles of Confederation. Indeed, Professor Corwin contends that Jay's position on federal supremacy "was suggested in the first instance by [Alexander] Hamilton's argument in" Rutgers v. Waddington (N.Y. City Mayor's Ct. 1784).[30] The *Rutgers* case also arose out of an alleged conflict between state law and the Treaty of Peace. Elizabeth Rutgers abandoned her brewery when the British captured New York City in 1776. The British commandeered the building, and it was occupied by Waddington until 1780 under an order by the British commissary-general, and thereafter until 1783 under an order by the British military commander. In 1784, Rutgers sued Waddington seeking to recover back rent for the brewery. Waddington defended against the rent action for the latter period on the ground that he was authorized to occupy the property by the British military commander. But the New York Trespass Act (which also gave Mrs. Rutgers a claim in trespass against Waddington) precluded such a defense. The case was highly controversial at the time, both because of continued tensions from the war and because of possible implications of the case for the availability of judicial review (the power of courts to invalidate statutes).

Among other arguments, Alexander Hamilton, Waddington's attorney, contended that the Trespass Act was invalid because it conflicted with the Treaty of Peace. (In his report to Congress, John Jay later identified the Act as one of the state laws that violated the treaty.) Hamilton's notes in preparation for his appellate argument in the case (which may reflect the argument he made at trial) state that "[a] breach of the treaty is a violation of [Congress'] constitution[al] authority & a breach of the Confederation," and "[w]hile the Confederation exists a law of a particular state derogating from its constitutional authority *is no law*." He further cited the "golden rule" of Cicero that "'when two or more laws clash that which relates to the most important concerns ought to prevail.' "[31] The *Rutgers* court avoided the supremacy issue by construing the Trespass Act narrowly. As explained by Julius Goebels: The court ruled that, "in effect, an invalid order from the Commissary General could not be pleaded under the statute while an order from the Commander-in-Chief, valid under the law of nations, could be pleaded, because the statute did not apply to it. The result, therefore, was that the case was decided without application of the prohibition of the Trespass Act, which consequently became irrelevant."[32] Nonetheless, Hamilton had raised the supremacy issue. To the extent his argument influenced Jay's report, it soon would influence Congress as well.

On March 21, 1787, the Continental Congress unanimously passed the resolutions Jay recommended in his report. In the first resolution, Congress declared plainly the supremacy of treaties as a part of federal law:

> That the legislatures of the several States cannot of right pass any act or acts for . . . restraining, limiting or in any manner impeding, retarding or counteracting the operation and execution of [a national treaty or any part or clause of it] for that on being constitutionally made ratified and published they become in virtue of the confederation part of the law of the land and are not only independent of the will and power of such legislatures but also binding and obligatory on them.[33]

The letter by which the congressional resolutions were transmitted to the states repeated the language used in Jay's report asserting the supremacy of federal law: "When therefore a treaty is constitutionally made ratified and published by us, it immediately becomes binding on the whole nation and superadded to the laws of the land, without the intervention of State Legislatures."[34] Thus, Congress asserted strongly that a federal treaty was supreme to state law.

In the remaining resolutions, however, Congress undercut much of the force of the first resolution. The second resolution urged the states to repeal any statutes that conflicted with the Treaty of Peace, in part to avoid continued treaty violations but in part "to avoid the disagreeable necessity there might otherwise be of raising and discussing their validity and obligation." In a third resolution, Congress further recommended that the repealing legislation be general in form (rather than listing individually every conflicting statute), and that it direct state courts to apply the treaty "according to the tenor, true intent and meaning of the same anything in the said Acts or parts of Acts to the contrary thereof in any wise notwithstanding." In answer to questions about the need for the second and third resolutions, James Madison explained that repeal of the laws by the states "was expedient and even necessary to free the Courts from the bias of their oaths which bound the Judges more strongly to the State than the federal authority."[35] Further, repeal would avoid the "delicate question" of the "foundation of the federal authority." Anticipating his argument in *Vices*, Madison explained that the legislative ratification of the Articles in some states meant that a federal treaty might override only state laws enacted before the treaty took effect; laws enacted after the treaty arguably would remain in force. In sum, Congress' action was equivocal as to the supremacy of the federal treaty: It asserted that supremacy, but just in case asked the states to implement the treaty obligations themselves.

Most states, although not all, responded to the resolutions by enacting legislation repealing all statutes that conflicted with the Treaty of Peace.[36] In support of such legislation in New York, Alexander Hamilton reiterated his arguments in favor of federal supremacy from Rutgers v. Waddington.[37] Hamilton's speech emphasized the benefits of the Treaty of Peace to New York (thus appealing to the self-interest of New York legislators), but also argued that the Treaty prevailed over state law. He rejected the argument that the resolutions would give too much power to judges: Hamilton "insisted that their powers would be the same, whether this law was passed or not. For, that as all treaties were known by the constitution as the laws of the land, so must the judges act on the same, any law to the contrary notwithstanding." He again cited Cicero for the proposition that the more important of two conflicting laws controls. According to Hamilton, "[i]f this rule prevails, who can doubt what would be the conduct of the judges, should any laws exist inconsistent with the treaty of peace . . . . [T]he full operation of the bill, would be no more than merely to declare the treaty the law of the land. And that the judges viewing it as such, shall do away all laws that may appear in direct contravention of it."

Thus, while the Articles of Confederation themselves only ambiguously gave supreme authority to federal law, they provided precedent for such a view. Hamilton's arguments in Rutgers v. Waddington and before the New York legislature, John Jay's report to Congress, and Congress' resolutions addressing conflicts between the Treaty of Peace and state law, all served as the intellectual foundation for the Supremacy Clause.

THE CONSTITUTIONAL CONVENTION

On February 21, 1787, Congress called for a convention to be held in Philadelphia later that year "for the sole and express purpose of revising the Articles of Confederation."[38] Although Congress did not identify the "defects in the present confederation" that prompted its action, James Madison described what he viewed as the Confederation's defects in *Vices of the Political System of the United States*.[39] Madison identified two broad categories of defects: what might be called external defects—state interferences with other states and the national government; and internal defects—abuses within a state of minorities by the majority. With respect to the first category, Madison asserted that under the Articles of Confederation, the states had failed to comply with requisitions by Congress; usurped federal powers (such as by entering into treaties and raising troops); violated federal treaties (specifically citing the Treaty of Peace with Great Britain); trespassed on the rights of other states (particularly in the commercial field); and so on. As to the second category, Madison faulted the Confederation for failing to protect minorities against the "multiplicity," "mutability," "injustice," and "impotence" of state laws. In Madison's view, a strong national government was necessary to deal with many such "evils . . . which are found within the States individually, as well as those which directly affect the States collectively."

When the delegates to the Constitutional Convention met in Philadelphia in May 1787, they quickly abandoned any attempt to amend the Articles of Confederation (which would have required the unanimous agreement of all the states). Instead, despite Congress' directive that the "sole and exclusive purpose" of the Convention was to suggest amendments to the Articles, the delegates began working on a proposal for an entirely new government. To resolve conflicts between state law and federal law, the delegates considered a variety of options. According to Madison (in an 1831 letter to N.P. Trist), "[t]he modes presenting themselves, were 1. A Veto on the passage of the State laws. 2. a Congressional repeal of them, 3 a Judicial annulment of them."[40] Another possibility the delegates considered was the use of military force against states that refused to follow federal law—thus bringing all three branches of government (legislative, judicial, and executive) under consideration. Nor were the options mutually exclusive: The different plans that would come before the Convention included various combinations of the options.[41]

The delegates quickly tabled the option of military force. The veto, or negative, of state laws by Congress, a favorite idea of Madison's, ultimately was rejected. In the end, the delegates settled on a clause declaring federal law supreme to state law, thus facilitating repeal by Congress and, more importantly, annulment of the state law in court. Indeed, the Supremacy Clause as finally adopted by the Convention not only declared federal law to be supreme, but it made federal law binding on state court judges, regardless of anything in state law—including state constitutions—to the contrary. Ironically, Madison, who staunchly supported the Constitution in the ratification debates in the states, believed that this solution was inadequate and that as a result the Constitution would fail.

Negative on State Laws

The Virginia delegation to the Convention (Madison, Edmund Randolph, John Blair, George Mason, James McClurg, George Washington, and George Wythe) arrived before there was a quorum of delegates from the other states.[42] They used the time to prepare a plan for a new government, which became known as the Virginia Plan. The plan, which plainly was influenced by Madison's views, provided for a much stronger national government than existed under the Articles of Confederation (although not as strong as Madison favored).

On May 29, 1787, once a quorum of delegates had arrived, Edmund Randolph introduced the Virginia Plan to the Convention. He began by identifying what he saw as the characteristics essential for a new government, including that it "be able to defend itself against incroachment" and that it "be paramount to the state constitutions."[43]* The Articles of Confederation, according to Randolph, were defective in both of these respects. Thus, under the Articles of Confederation, the national government could not defend itself against encroachment by the states: "In every State assembly there has been a party opposed to federal measures. The States have been therefore delinquent. To What expedient can congress resort, to compel delinquent States to do what is right? If force, this force must be drawn from the States, and the States may or may not furnish it" (1 Farrand 26). Likewise, the Articles were "[*i*]*nferior to State constitutions*," as Randolph explained:

> *State constitutions* formed at an early period of the war, and by persons *elected by the people* for that purpose. . . . The *confederation* was formed long after this, and had its ratification not by an *special appointment* from the people, but from the several assemblies. No judge will say that the *confederation* is paramount to a State constitution. (1 Farrand 26)

As the remedy for these (and other) failings of the Confederation government, Randolph proposed a new form of government outlined in the Virginia Plan.

The Virginia Plan contained no language making federal law supreme to state law. Instead, it dealt with conflicts between state law and federal law in two ways. First, the Virginia Plan listed among the powers of the legislature that "the National Legislature ought to be impowered . . . to negative all laws passed by the several States, contravening in the opinion of the National Legislature the articles of Union" (1 Farrand 21). Using this power, Congress could veto an unconstitutional state law after it was enacted by the state legislature and prevent it from taking effect. Second, the Plan gave the national legislature the power to use military force against recalcitrant states, that is, "to call forth the force of the Union agst. any member of the Union failing to fulfill its duty under the articles thereof" (1 Farrand 21). Using this power—admittedly an extreme one—Congress could use troops to enforce compliance with federal law.

The negative on state laws originated (albeit in a broader form) in Madison's writings. In separate letters to Thomas Jefferson, George Washington, and Edmund Randolph, written in the months leading up to the Convention, Madison identified the congressional negative as perhaps the central pillar in his vision of a new national government.[44] Indeed, Madison supported a broader congressional veto (not limited to laws contrary to the Constitution) that Congress could exercise "*in all cases whatsoever*." Madison explained the need for the congressional negative in a letter to Washington in April 1787:

---

*Citations hereafter to Farrand will be in parentheticals in the text.

Without this defensive power, every positive power that can be given on paper will be evaded & defeated. The States will continue to invade the national jurisdiction, to violate treaties and the law of nations & to harrass each other with rival and spiteful measures dictated by mistaken views of interest. Another happy effect of this prerogative would be its controul on the internal vicisitudes of State policy; and the aggressions of interested majorities on the rights of minorities and individuals.[45]

Madison thus had high hopes for the congressional negative. As Madison wrote to Jefferson (after the close of the Convention), in his view the negative was essential to address the failings of the Articles of Convention that he had identified in *Vices*. The negative would permit the national government to protect itself from interference by the states and to protect minorities within the states from abuse by the majority.[46] Indeed, in Madison's view the congressional negative was "essential and the least possible abridgement of the State Soveriegnties."[47]

As a political matter, Madison's preferred congressional negative was highly sensitive. Madison based the negative on the "Kingly prerogative" to veto colonial legislation.[48] For obvious reasons, this model was unpopular and had been harshly criticized by Thomas Jefferson in the Declaration of Independence. Moreover, the broad reach of Madison's proposal—"in all cases whatsoever"—echoed the language of the Declaratory Act of 1766, by which Great Britain declared that Parliament "had, hath, and of right ought to have, full power and authority to make laws and statutes of sufficient force and validity to bind the colonies and people of America, subjects of the crown of Great Britain, *in all cases whatsoever*."[49] According to Professor Jack Rakove, Madison's willingness to link his proposal to these unpopular reminders of British rule shows the "depth of Madison's attachment to this proposal."[50]

Thomas Jefferson, for one, was skeptical of the congressional negative. In responding to Madison's March 1787 letter to him, Jefferson stated: "Primâ facie I do not like it." Jefferson's main objection was that the negative (as described in Madison's letters) was overbroad:

It fails in an essential character, that the hole & the patch should be commensurate. But this proposes to mend a small hole by covering the whole garment. Not more than 1. out of 100. state-acts concern the confederacy. This proposition then, in order to give them 1. degree of power which they ought to have, gives them 99. more which they ought not to have, upon a presumption that they will not exercise the 99.[51]

Instead, Jefferson favored permitting "an appeal from the state judicatures to a federal court," which in Jefferson's words, would be "exactly commensurate to the defect."

The moderating influence of other members of the Virginia delegation resulted in a constrained version of the negative in the Virginia Plan. Rather than a negative in all cases whatsoever, as favored by Madison, the version in the Virginia

Plan was limited to state laws "contravening in the opinion of the National Legislature the articles of Union." The Convention would later consider and reject the broader negative favored by Madison, shortly before it rejected even the narrower version in the Virginia Plan.

On May 31, the Committee of the Whole (consisting of all delegates to the Convention) approved the congressional negative (1 Farrand 54). Previously, on motion of Benjamin Franklin, the clause had been amended without debate or dissenting vote to add "or any treaties subsisting under the authority of the Union" (1 Farrand 54). At the same time, Madison expressed second thoughts about authorizing the use of force against recalcitrant states. According to Madison, "[a] Union of the States (containing such an ingredient) seemed to provide for its own destruction" because "[t]he use of force agst. a State, would . . . probably be considered by the party attacked as a dissolution of all previous compacts by which it might be bound" (1 Farrand 54). Instead, Madison expressed the hope that the government might be structured so as to make the use of force unnecessary. His motion to postpone consideration of the use of military force was approved by the Committee of the Whole.

Charles Pinckney of South Carolina moved on June 8 to replace the negative on state laws in the Virginia Plan with a broader one, providing "that the National Legislature shd. have authority to negative all Laws which they shd. judge to be improper" (1 Farrand 162, 164). This "universal negative" would replace the narrower one limited to state acts "contravening in the opinion of the National Legislature the articles of Union." In support of his amendment, Pinckney argued that "the States must be kept in due subordination to the nation"; otherwise, states would continue to interfere with acts of Congress and treaties with foreign nations. He cited as precedent "the negative of the Crown," which "under the British Govt. . . . had been found beneficial."

Madison seconded Pinckney's motion. In Madison's view, such "an indefinite power to negative legislative acts of the States" was "absolutely necessary to a perfect system" (1 Farrand 164). He listed the weaknesses of the Articles of Confederation: "a constant tendency in the States to encroach on the federal authority; to violate national Treaties, to infringe the rights & interests of each other; to oppress the weaker party within their respective jurisdictions." In Madison's view, "[a] negative was the mildest expedient that could be devised for preventing these mischiefs." The only alternative, according to Madison, was military force. But "[a]ny Govt. for the U. States formed on the supposed practicability of using force agst. The (unconstitutional proceedings) of the States, wd. prove as visionary & fallacious as the Govt. of Congs." He concluded using astronomical imagery:

> In a word, to recur to the illustrations borrowed from the planetary System, This prerogative of the General Govt. is the great pervading principle that must controul the centrifugal tendency of the States; which, without it, will continually fly out of their proper orbits and destroy the order & harmony of the political system. (1 Farrand 165)

Other delegates opposed the amendment. Elbridge Gerry of Massachusetts (who later would refuse to sign the Constitution) complained that "[t]he Natl. Legislature with such a power may enslave the States" and that the states would never agree to it. He also feared that conflicting interests among the states would lead to abuse of the negative. Gunning Bedford of Delaware asserted that the negative would "strip the small States of their equal right of sufferage": "Will not these large States crush the small ones whenever they stand in the way of their ambitions or interested views" (1 Farrand 167). He also questioned the practicality of the negative, asking whether state laws were to be suspended while they were carried to Congress for review and whether that the national legislature would have to be continually in session. Pierce Butler of South Carolina "was vehement agst. the Negative in the proposed extent, as cutting off all hope of equal justice to the distant States" (1 Farrand 168).

Madison responded that the practical concerns could be taken care of, perhaps by establishing an authority in each state that could give temporary approval to emergency measures. To avoid having the House (with more members) constantly be in session, the veto power could be vested in the Senate. As for the small states, Madison asserted that their fears were unfounded: "If the large States possessed the Avarice & ambition with which they were charged, would the small ones in their neighbourhood, be more secure when all controul of a Genl. Govt. was withdrawn" (1 Farrand 168).

In the end, the small states prevailed and the Committee rejected the motion to extend the negative on a vote of 7 to 3, with one state (Delaware) divided (1 Farrand 163, 168). Only large states—Virginia, Pennsylvania, and Massachusetts—voted in favor of the motion.[52] Among the Virginia delegates, Edmund Randolph and George Mason voted against the proposal, suggesting that the narrower negative in the original Virginia Plan was due to their influence.[53]

Although the motion to extend the veto was rejected, the narrower version of the congressional negative remained in the Virginia Plan. On June 13, the Committee of the Whole reported to the Convention the Virginia Plan as revised, which included the congressional negative in the following terms: "Resolved. that the national Legislature ought to be empowered . . . to negative all laws passed by the several States contravening, in the opinion of the national legislature, the articles of union, or any treaties subsisting under the authority of the union" (1 Farrand 229).

Introduction of the Supremacy Clause

On June 15, William Paterson of New Jersey proposed an alternative plan for a new government, known as the New Jersey Plan. The New Jersey Plan contained the earliest version of what was to become the Supremacy Clause. Resolution 6 proposed by Paterson stated:

Resd. that all Acts of the U. States in Congs. made by virtue & in pursuance of the powers hereby & by the articles of confederation vested in them, and all Treaties made & ratified under the authority of the U. States shall be the supreme law of the respective States so far forth as those Acts or Treaties shall relate to the said States or their Citizens, and that the Judiciary of the several States shall be bound thereby in their decisions, any thing in the respective laws of the Individual States to the contrary notwithstanding . . . . (1 Farrand 245)

(For a complete timeline of the Supremacy Clause, see Figure 1 in the Appendix to Part I.) In addition, the New Jersey Plan reintroduced language authorizing the use of force against noncomplying states: "the federal Executive shall be authorized to call forth ye power of the Confederated States . . . to enforce and compel an obedience to such Acts, or an Observance of such Treaties" (1 Farrand 245).

Unlike the congressional negative, which the Virginia Plan listed among the powers of the legislature, the Supremacy Clause in the New Jersey Plan did not purport to be a source of federal power.[54] Moreover, this early version of the Supremacy Clause provided only for limited supremacy of federal law. It did not make the Constitution supreme, merely federal statutes and treaties (although that may have been an oversight). Nor did it make clear that state constitutions—as opposed to state statutes—were subject to federal law (although it may have had that effect). Moreover, federal law was only the "supreme law of the respective States," not the supreme law of the land, and the directive was to the "Judiciary of the several States," not state judges personally. According to James Liebman and William Ryan: "Although subtle, these last two distinctions are important: The New Jersey version brought federal law into the corpus of state law, thereby obliging state institutions to treat federal law as their own."[55] The state judges were to remain in their "local institutional roles," however, and to continue to apply state law, albeit state law that now would include federal law.

Over the next several days, the delegates debated the New Jersey Plan at length. One delegate, John Lansing of New York, took the opportunity to argue further against the congressional negative, contending that "[t]he States will never feel a sufficient confidence in a general Government to give it a negative on their laws. The Scheme is itself totally novel. There is [no] parallel to it to be found" (1 Farrand 250). Edmund Randolph and Alexander Hamilton challenged the provision in the New Jersey Plan authorizing the use of force. Randolph found such military coercion "to be *impracticable, expensive, cruel to individuals*. It tended also to habituate the instruments of it to shed the blood & riot in the spoils of their fellow Citizens, and consequently trained them up for the service of Ambition" (1 Farrand 256). Hamilton argued that the use of military force against a state "amounts to a war between the parties." Foreign countries likely would intervene, with the result that "the confusion will increase, and a dissolution of the Union ensue" (1 Farrand 285). At the end of his lengthy speech, Hamilton offered his own thoughts on a plan for government, not "as a proposition to the Committee," but instead to indicate the amendments he "probably" would offer to the Virginia Plan. Included were both a supremacy clause and a negative of state laws, but with the veto power held by federally appointed governors in each state: "X All laws of the particular States contrary to the Constitution or laws of the United States to be utterly void; and the better to prevent such laws being passed, the Governour or president of each state shall be appointed by the General Government and shall have a negative upon the laws about to be passed in the State of which he is Governour or President" (1 Farrand 293).

Madison, not surprisingly, found the New Jersey plan wholly inadequate. His evaluation drew upon the failings of the Articles of Confederation he had identified in *Vices*. He asked of the New Jersey Plan: "Will it prevent those violations of the law of nations & of Treaties which if not prevented must involve us in the calamities of foreign wars?" "Will it prevent encroachments on the federal authority?" "Will it prevent trespasses of the States on each other?" "Will it secure the internal tranquility of the States themselves?" "Will it secure a good internal legislation & administration to the particular States?" "Will it secure the Union agst. the influence of foreign powers over its members?" (1 Farrand 316–319). In each case he answered no, thus condemning the New Jersey Plan with the same failings as the Articles of Confederation.

Two particular points of Madison's remarks are noteworthy. First, as in *Vices*, Madison emphasized not only conflicts among the states, but weaknesses of the political systems within the states. He argued that "it is proper to take into view those which prevail within the States individually as well as those which affect them collectively: Since the former indirectly affect the whole; and there is great reason to believe that the pressure of them had a full share in the motives which produced the present Constitution." In particular, he cited, as he had in *Vices*, "1. the multiplicity of the laws passed by the several States. 2. the mutability of their laws. 3. the injustice of them. 4. the impotence of them: observing that Mr. Paterson's plan contained no remedy for this dreadful class of evils, and could not therefore be received as an adequate provision for the exigencies of the Community" (1 Farrand 318–319).

Second, he cited the New Jersey Plan as being "particularly defective" in that it was to be ratified by the state legislatures rather than the people of the states. As a result, the New Jersey Plan "could not therefore render the acts of Congs. in pursuance of their powers even legally *paramount* to the Acts of the States" (1 Farrand 316–317). Again, Madison's reasoning can be traced back to *Vices*: Because state legislatures rather than the people of the states had ratified the Articles of Confederation, the authority of Congress under the Articles depended (in some states) merely on state legislation. Accordingly, the problem of subsequently enacted state laws remained: Since the national government under the New Jersey plan was based on ratification by state legislatures, arguably a state could override a federal directive by enacting its own subsequent law.

In the end, the critics prevailed. The Committee of the Whole rejected the New Jersey Plan by a vote of 7 to 3, with Maryland divided (1 Farrand 313).

The Convention would next take up the congressional negative on July 17. In the interim, it spent much time on the highly contentious issue of state representation: whether states would be represented in Congress by an equal number of representatives per state or in proportion to their population. Luther Martin of Maryland (who left the Convention early and later opposed ratification) spoke, according to Madison's notes, "at great length and with great eagerness" in favor of equal representation. In so doing, he asserted that "the States, particularly the smaller, would never allow a negative to be exercised over their laws" (1 Farrand 437–438). Meanwhile, Madison explained that "[t]he negative (on the State laws) proposed, will make [Congress] an essential branch of the State Legislatures & of course will require that it should be exercised by a body established on like principles with the other branches of those Legislatures" (1 Farrand 447). The references to the negative at this point were in support of arguments about state representation in Congress. The Convention would directly consider the congressional negative itself in just a few weeks.

Shortly before the Convention again took up the negative, Edmund Randolph privately communicated to James Madison a possible compromise plan that might serve as "an accomodating proposition to the small States."[56] Resolution 3 expressly recognized the right of states to "mak[e] all laws not contrary to the articles of Union; subject to the supremacy of the General Government in those instances only in which that supremacy shall be expressly declared by the articles of the Union." While the plan maintained the congressional negative, it gave the states an appeal to the federal courts from any exercise of the negative. If the courts "adjudged [the negative] to be contrary to the power granted by the articles of the Union," the negative "shall be void." Finally, the plan permitted individuals "injured or oppressed by the partiality or injustice" of any state law to sue in federal court. The federal court could invalidate the law "if found contrary to the principles of equity and justice." Randolph's compromise plan was never considered by the Convention. But the fact that Randolph suggested such a plan foreshadowed the direction the Convention soon would take: downplaying (in the case of the Convention, eliminating altogether) the congressional negative and relying instead on the courts to enforce the supremacy of federal law.

On July 17, the Convention considered the congressional negative again, and this time rejected it outright. The key change in circumstances was the July 16 vote (5 to 4, with Massachusetts divided) to give states equal representation in the Senate (2 Farrand 15–16). The vote, which bolstered the power of small states relative to large states, gave rise to new opposition to the negative.[57] Some large states, which previously favored the negative, had second thoughts. For example, Gouverneur Morris of Pennsylvania (a state that previously had voted in favor of expanding the negative (1 Farrand 168)) "was more and more opposed" even to a narrower negative, arguing that "[t]he proposal of it would disgust all the States." According to Morris, the negative was "likely to be terrible to the States, and not necessary": If the courts did not invalidate the law, it could be repealed by federal statute (2 Farrand 27–28). Likewise, Roger Sherman of Connecticut found the negative "unnecessary" because the courts would invalidate state laws contrary to the Constitution. Luther Martin, who shortly thereafter would introduce the Supremacy Clause, asserted that a congressional power to negative state laws was "improper & inadmissible," questioning whether "all the laws of the States [must] be sent up to the Genl. Legislature before they shall be permitted to operate?" (2 Farrand 27).

Madison gave a strident defense of the negative, describing it again as "essential to the efficacy & security of the Genl. Govt." The negative was needed to prevent harmful state laws from taking effect. Otherwise, state legislatures "can pass laws which will accomplish their injurious objects before they can be repealed by the Genl. Legislre. or be set aside by the National Tribunals" (2 Farrand 27). State courts were not a suitable substitute, according to Madison, because the state courts were not independent of the state legislatures (citing Georgia and Rhode Island as examples). He recognized the practical limitations of the negative, but argued that they could be taken care of by permitting emergency state measures to take effect temporarily pending congressional review.

Madison's defense failed to persuade the Convention, which rejected the veto by a vote of 7 to 3. Scholars differ over the reason for the rejection. The relative power of the large states and the small states already has been alluded to as a contributing factor.[58] In addition, some highlight the practical concerns about the workability of the negative: "How could the national legislature possibly oversee the entire corpus of state lawmaking in an expanding union? Were state acts not to take effect until they had passed congressional muster? Might it not be necessary to appoint national proconsuls to evaluate pending laws within the originating states, or require the national legislature to sit continuously simply to review the continuing flow of state legislation?"[59] Professor Larry Kramer argues that the negative failed because the other delegates did not share Madison's views on the "supervisory" function of the negative: "to take advantage of the national government's size to protect private rights from factious state legislatures."[60] Instead, they concluded that other means could better serve the "defensive" function of the negative: "to protect the federal government from encroachments by the states on federal prerogatives." Whatever the reason or reasons, the negative was gone from the Constitution for good (although there would be one more attempt to revive it).

Luther Martin then proposed as an alternative a variation of the Supremacy Clause from the earlier New Jersey Plan:

> Resolved that the legislative acts of the United States made by virtue and in pursuance of the articles of Union and all Treaties made and ratified under the authority of the United

States shall be the supreme law of the respective States as far as those acts or Treaties shall relate to the said States, or their Citizens and Inhabitants—and that the Judiciaries of the several States shall be bound thereby in their decisions, any thing in the respective laws of the individual States to the contrary notwithstanding. (2 Farrand 22)

The delegates unanimously approved adoption of the Supremacy Clause. There is no record of any discussion before the vote.

Martin, who was a strong defender of states' rights and a leading opponent of ratification of the Constitution, later was quite defensive about having introduced the Supremacy Clause. In response to "The Landholder," who criticized Martin's opposition to ratification,[61] Martin explained that at the time he introduced the Supremacy Clause, the Constitution did not yet provide for federal trial courts. According to Martin, because it was his "wish and hope" that state courts would be the front-line adjudicatory body, "the propriety and the necessity that treaties duly made and ratified, and the laws of the general government should be *binding* on the state judiciaries, which were to decide upon them, must be evident to every capacity."[62] Martin argued, however, that under his version of the Supremacy Clause federal law was not "meant to be superior to our [i.e., a state's] *constitution* and bill of rights"; that change was made only later. After the change, in Martin's view the Supremacy Clause became "*worse* than *useless*; for being so altered as to render the treaties and laws made under the general government superior to our constitution, if the system is adopted, it will amount to a total and unconditional surrender to that government, by the citizens of this state, of every right and privilege secured to them by our constitution."

Although the Supremacy Clause was now part of the Constitution, its evolution was not complete. The next section traces the changes the clause would undergo.

Evolution of the Supremacy Clause

On July 26, the Convention adjourned to permit the Committee of Detail to work up a draft of the Constitution. The earliest complete draft is one prepared by Committee member Edmund Randolph (and edited by John Rutledge). That draft initially included the following Supremacy Clause, which apparently was crossed out by Rutledge: "All laws of a particular state, repugnant hereto, shall be void, and in the decision thereon, which shall be vested in the supreme judiciary, all incidents without which the general principles cannot be satisfied shall be considered, as involved in the general principle" (2 Farrand 144). Unlike the Supremacy Clause approved by the Convention as a whole, the clause in the Randolph-Rutledge draft provided for the supremacy of the Constitution, rather than merely the supremacy of federal statutes and treaties. It also gave the authority to invalidate state laws to the "supreme judiciary" rather than making federal law binding on state courts.

A subsequent draft of the Committee's work, written by James Wilson and again edited by Rutledge, more closely tracked the language approved by the Convention (2 Farrand 169). Its language is identical (except for minor differences in capitalization) to that in the Committee's August 6 report to the Convention as a whole. The final report provided as follows:

> The Acts of the Legislature of the United States made in pursuance of this Constitution, and all treaties made under the authority of the United States shall be the supreme law of the several States, and of their citizens and inhabitants; and the judges in the several States shall be bound thereby in their decisions; anything in the Constitutions or laws of the several States to the contrary notwithstanding. (2 Farrand 183)

The Supremacy Clause in the Committee of Detail draft departed from the clause previously approved by the Convention in several respects. First, it expressly provided that federal statutes and treaties were supreme not only to state laws but also to state constitutions, although it remained silent on the supremacy of the federal Constitution itself. Second, the clause as revised now addressed the "judges in the several States" rather than the "Judiciaries of the several States," which, according to Professor Julius Goebel, made the obligation to follow federal law "personal" to judges rather than directed to the institution of the judiciary as a whole.[63] Some have suggested that it extended the application of the Clause to federal judges as well as state judges.[64]

The Convention as a whole then considered the report of the Committee of Detail. It took up the Supremacy Clause on August 23, and unanimously approved an amendment proposed by John Rutledge to replace the first phrase in the Supremacy Clause ("The Acts of the Legislature of the United States made in pursuance of this Constitution") with the following language: "This Constitution & the laws of the U.S. made in pursuance thereof" (2 Farrand 389). Thus, at last not only federal statutes and treaties, but also the federal Constitution itself was given supreme status to state laws and constitutions. As Professor Rakove stated: "Quietly and uncontroversially, a clause which was originally offered as a weak alternative to the negative on state laws had been transformed into a potentially powerful basis for national supremacy."[65]

Later on that same day, Pinckney and Madison made one final effort—unsuccessful as it turned out—to revive the congressional negative (2 Farrand 390–391). They proposed that Congress have the power "[t]o negative all laws passed by the several States interfering in the opinion of the Legislature with the General interests and harmony of the Union; provided that two thirds of the members of each House assent to the same." Pinckney argued that the negative previously had been agreed to in principle, and asserted that "[t]he objection drawn from the predominance of the large States had been removed by the equality established in the Senate." Madison, of course, concurred, asserting that the changes made to the negative this time around were improvements over the original proposal. Similarly, James Wilson of Pennsylvania argued that the negative was "the key-stone wanted to complete the wide arch of Government we are raising." In his view, after-the-fact review by the courts was too late: "It will be better to prevent the passage of an improper law, than to declare it void when passed."

But the opponents of the negative carried the day. John Rutledge of South Carolina argued that the negative would bind the states "hand & foot" and "alone would damn and ought to damn the Constitution." Hugh Williamson of North Carolina took the position that the negative was "unnecessary" and that further consideration—given that the negative already had been rejected—"was a waste of time." George Mason of Virginia raised a variety of practical objections: whether Congress would review all state laws and whether Congress would be in session continuously so as always to be available.

In the end, the Convention refused even to submit the negative to a committee for further consideration, by a vote of 6 to 5. The Convention would not consider the congressional negative again.

The Supremacy Clause was not quite in final form, however. On August 25, two days after rejecting the congressional negative for the final time, the Convention unanimously approved adding the words "or which shall be made" after the phrase "all treaties made" in the Clause. In Madison's words, the change "was meant to obviate all doubt concerning the force of treaties preexisting, by making the words 'all treaties made' to refer to them, as the words inserted would refer to future treaties" (2 Farrand 417).

The final changes to the Supremacy Clause came from the Committee of Style, consisting of Alexander Hamilton, William Johnson, Rufus King, Madison, and Gouverneur Morris (2 Farrand 547). The Committee's charge was to "revise the style of and arrange the articles agreed to by the House." The Committee issued its report on September 12. It placed the Supremacy Clause in Article VI, immediately before a provision requiring all judges (and others) to take an oath supporting the Constitution. The Committee inserted the phrase "the supreme law of the land" in place of "the supreme law of the several States, and of their citizens and inhabitants" (2 Farrand 603). It deleted the phrase "in their decisions" following "bound thereby," and replaced both usages of "the several states" with singular versions—once "every state" and once "any state." The Supremacy Clause thus reached its final form. (For a summary of the textual evolution of the Supremacy Clause, see Figure 2 in the Appendix to Part I.)

In the closing debates on the draft Constitution, several delegates supported additional protections for individual liberties, such as a bill of rights, for the new Constitution. The discussion is important because it foreshadows one of the principal objections to the Constitution—and in particular the Supremacy Clause—during its consideration by the states. On September 12, Elbridge Gerry and Hugh Williamson argued for a clause protecting the right to jury trial. George Mason agreed, adding that he "wished the plan had been prefaced with a Bill of Rights": "It would give great quiet to the people" (2 Farrand 587). Gerry moved that a committee be appointed to prepare a Bill of Rights; Mason seconded the motion. In opposition, Roger Sherman asserted that "[t]he State Declarations of Rights are not repealed by this Constitution; and being in force are sufficient" (2 Farrand 588). Mason responded, relying on the Supremacy Clause, that "[t]he Laws of the U.S. are to be paramount to State Bills of Rights." The Convention as a whole unanimously rejected Gerry's motion.

Two days later, a similar discussion took place with respect to the freedom of the press. Gerry and Charles Pinckney sought a provision declaring that "the liberty of the Press should be inviolably observed" (2 Farrand 617). Sherman responded that such a provision was not needed because "[t]he power of Congress does not extend to the Press" (2 Farrand 618). Again, the Convention rejected the proposal, this time by a vote of 7 to 4.

On September 15, Edmund Randolph proposed permitting state ratifying conventions to submit amendments to the Constitution, to be considered at a subsequent constitutional convention. Randolph warned that otherwise he could not sign the Constitution (2 Farrand 631–632). George Mason concurred. Elbridge Gerry likewise opposed the Constitution, listing a variety of objections. The Convention unanimously rejected Randolph's proposal, and approved the Constitution. The final version of the Supremacy Clause as reported by the Committee of Style, and approved by Convention, reads:

> This Constitution, and the Laws of the United States which shall be made in Pursuance thereof; and all Treaties made, or which shall be made, under the Authority of the United States, shall be the supreme Law of the Land; and the Judges in every State shall be bound thereby, any Thing in the Constitution or Laws of any State to the Contrary notwithstanding. (2 Farrand 663)

The Convention, having completed its business, adjourned on September 17.

Of the delegates remaining at the end, only three—Edmund Randolph, Elbridge Gerry, and George Mason—declined to sign the Constitution as approved by the Convention (2 Farrand 648–649). Several others left before the Convention was finished: Abraham Yates and Robert Lansing left on July 10, and Luther Martin on September 10.[66] Each of the nonsigners had a variety of reasons for objecting to the Constitution. Because of their status as participants in the Convention, their views played an important role in the debate over ratification.

Others disagreed with some aspects of the proposed Constitution, but nonetheless supported the final product as better than what went before. James Madison, whose preferred negative of state laws was rejected during the Convention, was one of these. Indeed, Madison's private view, expressed in a letter to Thomas Jefferson shortly before the close of the Convention, was that "the *plan should* it *be adopted* will neither effectually *answer* its *national object* nor prevent the local *mischiefs* which every where *excite disgusts* agst the *state governments*."[67] Benjamin Franklin was another, as he stated on the closing day of the Convention: "The opinions I have had of its errors, I sacrifice to the public good—I have never whispered a syllable of them abroad—Within these walls they were born, and here they shall die" (2 Farrand 643).

RATIFICATION BY THE STATES

Congress began discussing the proposed Constitution on September 26, 1787. While the debates in Congress focused on the form of transmittal to the states, Richard Henry Lee of Virginia urged Congress to consider possible amendments to the draft, including a bill of rights.[68] After several days of debate, Congress sent the proposed Constitution to the state legislatures—without recommendation or amendment—to be submitted to conventions in each of the states for consideration.[69]

The debate then moved to the states. Nine states needed to ratify the Constitution before it would take effect. The Supremacy Clause was prominent in the state debates on ratification, in newspapers and pamphlets as well as in the state ratifying conventions themselves. According to Alexander Hamilton in Federalist No. 33, the Supremacy Clause (along with the Necessary and Proper Clause) were "the sources of much virulent invective and petulant declamation against the proposed constitution."[70] In the view of Hamilton and other Federalists, those provisions were "held up to the people, in all the exaggerated colours of misrepresentation, as the pernicious engines by which their local governments were to be destroyed and their liberties exterminated—as the hideous monster whose devouring jaws would spare neither sex nor age, nor high nor low, nor sacred nor profane." Not surprisingly, the Anti-Federalists, who opposed ratification, disagreed with Hamilton's caricature of their views.

Anti-Federalist Criticisms of the Supremacy Clause

The Anti-Federalists' fundamental criticism of the Supremacy Clause was that it made the national government too powerful and thus was too great an infringement on state sovereignty. To some extent this argument overlapped with criticisms of the scope of congressional power, particularly the Necessary and Proper Clause (hence Hamilton's reference to both as prompting "virulent" attacks). For obvious reasons, this section focuses on the Anti-Federalist arguments concerning the Supremacy Clause.

The Anti-Federalists emphasized three main themes in attacking the Supremacy Clause. First, and most extreme, the Anti-Federalists argued that the Constitution would destroy the states altogether, resulting in a fully centralized national government. More troubling for the Federalists was the Anti-Federalists' second argument, that the Supremacy Clause would override state constitutional protections for individual rights contained in state bills of rights. Thus, the Anti-Federalists contended, a bill of rights should be appended to the Constitution. Although this criticism did not ultimately preclude ratification, it did bear fruit in the form of the first ten amendments to the Constitution. Third, the Anti-Federalists focused on the fact that the Supremacy Clause made federal treaties supreme to state constitutions and laws. Of particular concern was the lack of involvement by the House of Representatives in the treaty ratification process, and thus that the President, with the concurrence only of the Senate, could override state law by treaty.

The most dramatic criticism was that the new Constitution would abolish the states altogether. Edmund Randolph, one of the nonsigners at the Convention, expressed this fear in arguing for a second convention to consider amendments to the Constitution. Among the aspects "in which the constitution is most repugnant to my wishes," according to Randolph, was its failure "to prevent the one from being swallowed up by the other, under the cover of general words, and implication."[71] A good (albeit relatively mild) statement of this criticism is from the Federal Farmer, "considered to be one of the ablest Anti-Federalist pieces,"[72] who asserted that ratification of the Constitution would be the people's "last and supreme act": Whenever the Constitution or any federal law "shall be incompatible with the ancient customs, rights, the laws or the constitutions heretofore established in the United States, it will entirely abolish them and do them away."[73]

Other Anti-Federalists were more direct in their criticisms, blaming the Supremacy Clause for the consolidation of government that they viewed as inevitable under the Constitution. The Federal Republican, for example, wrote that the Supremacy Clause "proves clearly that the whole country is to be comprised into one large system of lordly government."[74] Agrippa argued that, under the new Constitution, "[i]t is therefore a complete consolidation of all the states into one, however diverse the parts of it may be."[75] Some writers, such as the Impartial Examiner, relied on scientific imagery to make the point:

> [T]he idea of two sovereignties existing within the same community is a perfect solecism. If they be supposed equal, their operation must be commensurate, and like two mechanical powers of equal *momenta* counteracting each other;—here the force of the one will be destroyed by the force of the other: and so there will be no efficiency in either. If one be greater than the other, they will be similar to two unequal bodies in motion with a given degree of velocity, and impinging each other from oppositive points;—[T]he motion of the lesser in this case will necessarily be destroyed by that of the greater: and so there will be efficiency only in the greater.[76]

As a result, "[i]f this constitution should be adopted, here the sovereignty of America is ascertained and fixed in the federal body at the same time that it abolishes the present independent sovereignty of each state."

Similar sentiments were regularly expressed in the debates in the state ratifying conventions. Robert Whitehill asserted in the Pennsylvania Convention that "Article 6, clauses 2 and 3 are concluding clauses that the state governments will be abolished."[77] Likewise, at the Virginia Convention, George Mason claimed that the Constitution "will destroy the State Governments, whatever may have been the intention."[78] Mr. Bloodworth argued at the North Carolina ratifying convention that "[i]t appears to me to sweep off all the constitutions of the states. It is a total repeal of every act and constitution of the states. The judges are sworn to uphold it. It will produce an abolition of the state governments. Its sovereignty absolutely annihilates them."[79] According to Amos Singletary in the Massachusetts Convention: Federal laws "are the Supreme Law of the Land and can destroy all the laws of the different states. If any man had advanced such a thing as this Constitution ten years ago he would have been called a tory."[80]

The power to tax was commonly used to illustrate the inevitability of the states' downfall. An Old Whig contended that because of the Supremacy Clause, "no individual state can collect a penny, unless by the permission of Congress .... Congress, being the supreme legislatures, may annul or repeal the laws of the individual states, whenever they please. Not a single source of revenue will remain to any state, which Congress may not stop at their sovereign will and pleasure."[81] Brutus wrote on several occasions that Congress could interfere with the states' ability to raise revenues. "Without money [the state governments] cannot be supported," Brutus asserted, "and they must dwindle away, . . . their powers absorbed in that of the general government."[82] Patrick Henry, a vocal opponent of ratification in the Virginia Convention, argued that the supremacy of the federal taxing power gave Congress "an unlimited, unbounded command over the soul of this Commonwealth."[83] After Congress satisfied its appetite for funds, Henry asked, "[W]hat can be left for the States?" His answer: "Not a sufficiency even to defray the expenses of their internal administration. They must therefore glide imperceptibly and gradually out of existence. This, Sir, must naturally terminate in a consolidation."

The less dramatic (and ultimately more successful) criticism of the Supremacy Clause by the Anti-Federalists was that it overrode the protections of the state bills of rights; hence, the new Constitution needed its own bill of rights. Thus, Elbridge Gerry, another of the nonsigners of the Constitution, cited as one of his "principal objections to the plan . . . that the system is without the security of a bill of rights."[84] According to Patrick Henry in the Virginia Convention, "That paper [i.e., the Constitution] is defective without such a Declaration of Rights.—It is unbounded without such restrictions."[85] The American Herald gave this warning: "If you adopt the proposed plan, you will subject yourselves to a government, where you will be *totally* unprotected by a BILL OF RIGHTS, (without which no system of government ought to be instituted) . . . ."[86]

George Mason, also a nonsigner, expressly attributed the need for a Bill of Rights to the Supremacy Clause. He complained in his "Objections to the

Constitution" that "[t]here is no Declaration of Rights; and the Laws of the general Government being paramount to the Laws & Constitutions of the several States, the Declaration of Rights in the separate States are no Security."[87] Mason reiterated his views in the Virginia Ratifying Convention, arguing that "if the laws and Constitution of the General Government, as expressly said, be paramount to those of any State, are not those rights with which we were afraid to trust our own citizens annulled and given up to the General Government? . . . If a check be necessary in our own State Government, it is much more so in a Government where our representatives are to be at the distance of 1000 miles from us without any responsibility."[88]

The Supremacy Clause was at the heart of the problem, because it made the federal Constitution—which did not contain a bill of rights—as well as federal statutes and treaties supreme over state constitutions, including state bills of rights. As John Smilie stated in the Philadelphia Convention: "This sweeping clause levels all the bills of rights of the several states . . . ."[89] Centinel was of the same view, asking "what security does the *Constitutions* of the several States afford for the *liberty of the press and other invaluable personal rights*, not provided for by the new plan?—Does not this sweeping clause subject every thing to the controul of Congress?"[90] The possible consequences were set out in detail in the report of the Dissent of the Minority of the Pennsylvania Convention:

> The first consideration that this review suggests, is the omission of a BILL OF RIGHTS ascertaining and fundamentally establishing those unalienable and personal rights of men, without the full, free, and secure enjoyment of which there can be no liberty, and over which it is not necessary for a good government to have the controul. The principal of which are the rights of conscience, personal liberty by the clear and unequivocal establishment of the writ of *habeas corpus*, jury trial in criminal and civil cases, by an impartial jury of the vicinage or county; with the common law proceedings, for the safety of the accused in criminal prosecutions and the liberty of the press, that scourge of tyrants; and the grand bulwark of every other liberty and, privilege; the stipulations heretofore made in favor of them in the state constitutions, are entirely superceded by this constitution.[91]

A solution suggested by some Anti-Federalists was to alter the Supremacy Clause to preserve state bills of rights. Former governor William Paca sought to introduce the following amendment to the Constitution in the Maryland Convention: "No Law of Congress, or Treaties, shall be effectual to repeal or abrogate the Constitutions, or Bill of Rights, of the States, or any of them, or any Part of the said Constitutions or Bills of Rights."[92] Instead, of course, Congress approved and the states ratified the Bill of Rights to the federal Constitution, in the form of the first ten amendments.

The other principal Anti-Federalist objection to the Supremacy Clause was its interaction with the treaty power (i.e., that it made treaties the supreme law of the land). One concern was that the President together with the Senate—but without the House of Representatives—could make treaties. As George Mason argued: "By declaring all Treaties supreme Laws of the Land, the Executive & the Senate have, in many Cases, an exclusive Power of Legislation; which might have been avoided, by proper Distinctions with Respect to Treaties, and requiring the Assent of the House of Representatives, where it cou'd be done with Safety."[93] Likewise, Elbridge Gerry cited "that treaties of the highest importance may be formed by the President with the advice of two thirds of a *quorum* of the Senate."[94] As the Federal Farmer explained:

> By the article before recited, treaties also made under the authority of the United States, shall be the supreme law: It is not said that these treaties shall be made in pursuance of the constitution—nor are there any constitutional bounds set to those who shall make them: The president and two thirds of the senate will be empowered to make treaties indefinitely, and when these treaties shall be made, they will also abolish all laws and state constitutions incompatible with them. The power in the president and senate is absolute, and the judges will be bound to allow full force to whatever rule, article or thing the president and senate shall establish by treaty, whether it be practicable to set any bounds to those who make treaties, I am not able to say: If not, it proves that this power ought to be more safely lodged.[95]

Others objected to the broad scope of the treaty power, which the Supremacy Clause made supreme. According to William Findley at the Pennsylvania Convention: "The power of making treaties ought to be confined. They are declared the supreme laws of the land, therefore they may be of such a nature as to repeal or infringe the very Constitution."[96] The Dissent of the Minority of the Pennsylvania Convention likewise emphasized the broad reach of the treaty power: "[T]hey form treaties with foreign nations, that may controul and abrogate the constitutions and laws of the several states. Indeed, there is no power, privilege or liberty of the state governments, or of the people, but what may be affected by virtue of this power."[97] Cato, writing to the people of New York, made clear that the supremacy of treaties was more than just theoretically important: "By treaties you may defalcate part of the empire; engagements may be made to raise an army, and you may be transported to Europe, to fight the wars of ambitious princes; money may be contracted for, and you must pay it; and a thousand other obligations may be entered into; all which will become the supreme law of the land, and you are bound by it."[98] According to an Old Whig: "If Great Britain, for instance, were willing to enter into a treaty with us, upon terms which would be inconsistent with the liberties of the people and destructive of the very being of a Republic, the consent of our president for the time being, and of two thirds of the senators present, even though the senators present should be but a very small part of the senate, will give such a treaty the validity of a law."[99]

Anti-Federalists suggested several amendments to the Supremacy Clause to constrain the treaty power. Robert Whitehill in the Pennsylvania Convention proposed the most far-reaching:

13. That no treaties which shall be directly opposed to the existing laws of the United States in Congress assembled shall be valid until such laws shall be repealed or made conformable to such treaty, neither shall any treaties be valid which are contradictory to the Constitution of the United States, or the constitutions of the individual states.[100]

Patrick Henry argued in the Virginia Convention: "One amendment which has been wished for in this respect, is, that no treaty should be made without the consent of a considerable majority of both Houses."[101] A final narrower amendment was suggested by the Society of Western Gentlemen in Virginia: to limit the Supremacy Clause to treaties made after ratification of the new Constitution, thereby excluding previously made treaties, such as the Treaty of Peace.[102] That amendment provides some support for Henry Knox's assertion that the "real objection[ ]" to the Supremacy Clause in Virginia was with "Treaties being the supreme law of the land thereby compelling the payment of the british debts."[103]

The Federalist Response

The Federalists responded to each of these criticisms, with varying degrees of persuasiveness. Fears that the Constitution would abolish the states, the Federalists argued, were overblown. A Native of Virginia in his "Observations upon the Proposed Plan of Federal Government" asserted that the Constitution would abridge state authority by "no more than . . . necessary to make a strong federal government. Sufficient still remains with the State Legislatures to preserve the quiet, liberty, and welfare, of their citizens."[104] Thomas McKean was more blunt in his remarks in the Pennsylvania Convention: "Those that first said [the Supremacy Clause] gave to Congress the power of superseding the state governments cannot persist in it; for no person can, with tolerable face, read the clause over and infer that such may be the consequence."[105]

Supporters of the Constitution sought to assuage those concerned about the loss of state sovereignty by highlighting the need for a strong central government. Hamilton explained in Federalist No. 33 that supremacy was inherent in the nature of a constitution. As such, the Supremacy Clause was "only declaratory of a truth, which would have resulted by necessary and unavoidable implication from the very act of constituting a Federal Government, and vesting it with certain specified powers."[106] Otherwise, "what would [the laws of the Union] amount to, if they were not to be supreme? It is evident they would amount to nothing. . . . A LAW by the very meaning of the term includes supremacy. . . . It otherwise would be a mere treaty, dependent on the good faith of the parties, and not a government . . . ." Without the supremacy of federal law, in other words, things would be no better than under the Articles of Confederation. A Freeholder emphasized the point: Were federal laws not supreme, "they might as well not make laws at all, and Congress must remain the same helpless body it is now, and the states be forever jarring with, and rivalling one another without commerce, or credit; the means of defence at home, or of procuring it abroad."[107]

Hamilton addressed the specific concern of the Anti-Federalists about federal control over state taxes in two ways. First, in Federalist No. 31 he sought to focus the debate on "the composition and structure of the government, not to the nature or extent of its powers."[108] State governments had "complete sovereignty" under their constitutions, yet the Anti-Federalists did not seem concerned about state abuses. If anything, "a disposition in the State governments to encroach upon the rights of the Union, is quite as probable, as a disposition in the Union to encroach upon the rights of the State Governments." In such a conflict, the state government is likely to prevail over the federal government because "strength is always on the side of the people" and "the State governments will commonly possess most influence over them." Thus, "there is greater probability of encroachments by the members upon the Federal Head, than by the Federal Head upon the members."

Second, in Federalist No. 33 Hamilton argued that the federal government did not have the authority under the Constitution to restrict the state power to tax. According to Hamilton, "a law for abrogating or preventing the collection of a tax laid by the authority of a State (unless upon imports and exports) would not be the supreme law of the land, but an usurpation of power not granted by the constitution."[109] As a result, "the individual States would, under the proposed constitution, retain an independent and uncontroulable authority to raise revenue to any extent of which they may stand in need by every kind of taxation except duties on imports and exports."

The Federalists took a variety of approaches in responding to calls for a bill of rights. Initially, Madison harshly critiqued the view that the Constitution should have preserved the state constitutions, including state bills of rights.[110] A constitution formed under such a principle would have been "evidently and radically defective," Madison wrote in Federalist No. 44. Even in states that recognized the supremacy of federal law under the Constitution, such a proposal would have undercut federal power, which would have been subservient to state law. To the extent some states did not recognize the supremacy of the Articles, the new Constitution would have been no better. The result would be nonuniformity: "[A]s the Constitutions of the States differ much from each other, it might happen that a treaty or national law of great and equal importance to the States, would interfere with some and not with other Constitutions, and would consequently be valid in some of the States at the same time that it would have no effect in the others." In short, "the world would have seen for the first time, a system of government founded on an inversion of the fundamental principles of all government; it would have seen the authority of the whole society every where subordinate to the authority of the parts; it would have seen a monster in which the head was under the direction of the members."

Nor was a bill of rights necessary in the federal Constitution. That the Constitution delegated only limited powers to the federal government, the Federalists argued, provided sufficient protection for individual liberties. In the case of state governments, James Wilson explained in a speech in Philadelphia on October 6, 1787, "[E]very [power] which is not reserved is given." In the case of the federal government, however, every power not expressly delegated is reserved to the states and people.

> This distinction being recognized, will furnish an answer to those who think omission of a bill of rights, a defect in the proposed constitution: for it would have been superfluous and absurd to have stipulated with a federal body of our own creation, that we should enjoy those privileges, of which we are not divested either by the intention or the act, that has brought that body into existence.[111]

Wilson used the freedom of the press as an illustration. Because the Constitution did not give Congress the power "to regulate literary publications, . . . the proposed system possesses no influence whatever upon the press." Indeed, not only was it unnecessary to protect the freedom of the press in the Constitution, it would have been counterproductive: "that very declaration might have been construed to imply that some degree of power was given, since we undertook to define its extent." Marcus dressed up the argument in more colorful imagery in responding to the plea for a bill of rights in George Mason's *Objections to the Constitution*: "[A]fter expressly defining the powers that are to be exercised, to say that they shall exercise no other powers (either by a general or particular enumeration) would seem to me both nugatory and ridiculous. As well might a Judge when he condemns a man to be hanged, give strong injunctions to the Sheriff that he should not be beheaded."[112]

The Federalists relied on the text of the Supremacy Clause to reinforce this argument. Under the Clause, only federal statutes enacted "in Pursuance" of the Constitution are the supreme law of the land. Cassius VI laid out the importance of this language, which later would be cited as textual authority for the power of judicial review of federal law:

> This is the article, my countrymen, which knaves and blockheads have so often dressed up in false colours . . . . But in the name of common sense I would ask, of what use would be a bill of rights, in the present case?—It can only be to resort to when it is supposed that Congress have infringed the unalienable rights of the people:—but would it not be much easier to resort to the federal constitution, to see if *therein* power is given to Congress to make the law in question. If such power is *not* given, the *law* is in fact a *nullity*, and the

people will not be bound thereby. For let it be remembered, that *such laws*, and *such only*, as are *founded on this constitution*, are to be the supreme law of the land . . . .[113]

The Anti-Federalists were not persuaded by this textual argument, however. According to A Countryman from Dutchess County, "*pursuance* is a vague term, and, I presume, generally implies little more than in 'in consequence, etc.' "[114] Thus, it hardly presents any sort of constraint on congressional powers. Likewise, the Dissent of the Minority of the Pennsylvania Convention expressed skepticism: "In our opinion, 'pursuant to the constitution,' will be co-extensive with the *will* and *pleasure* of Congress, which, indeed, will be the only limitation of their powers."[115]

Finally, the Federalists recited a laundry list of arguments to counter the Anti-Federalists' concerns about the supremacy of treaties. First, and most important, the supremacy of treaties was essential to American national security. Other countries must be able to rely on agreements made by the federal government. John Jay explained in Federalist No. 64, that "a treaty is only another name for a bargain; and that it would be impossible to find a nation who would make any bargain with us, which should be binding on them *absolutely*, but on us only so long and so far as we may think proper to be bound by it."[116] Likewise, the federal government must be able to carry out its treaty obligations without state interference. "[I]f Congress cannot enforce the observance of her treaties," A Freeholder argued, "no nation will treat with her, and . . . the situation of America if ever involved in a war would then be truly awful."[117] In short, according to James Madison, to permit state law to override a treaty "would bring on the Union the just charge of national perfidy, and involve us in war."[118]

Second, other countries recognized treaties as the supreme law of the land. Thomas McKean stated in the Pennsylvania Convention: "I believe there is no nation in the world in which [treaties] are not considered as the supreme law of the land, and, consequently, obligatory upon all judges and magistrates. They are a common concern, and obedience to them ought to be a common duty."[119] Madison, too, made this point.[120] The thrust of the argument was to reinforce the need for the United States to take the same approach, because its treaty partners would expect it to do so.

Third, even under the Articles of Confederation, Congress and the states already had recognized that treaties were supreme. Marcus III cited the resolutions adopted by Congress in response to John Jay's report on violations of the Treaty of Peace: "Did not Congress very lately unanimously resolve in adopting the very sensible letter of Mr. Jay, that a treaty when once made pursuant to the sovereign authority, *ex vi termini* became immediately the law of the land?"[121] James Madison pointed to the state laws enacted in response to the congressional resolutions: "Many of the States have recognized the treaties of Congress to be the supreme law of the land. Acts have passed within a year, declaring this to be the case.— I have seen many of them."[122]

Fourth, treaties were subject to the same constitutional constraints as statutes. George Nicholas explained in the Virginia Convention that "[t]hey can make no treaty which shall be repugnant to the spirit of the Constitution, or inconsistent with the delegated powers. The treaties they make must be under the authority of the United States, to be within their province."[123] Nicholas seemed to conflate treaties with statutes, however, because he continued that "[i]t is sufficiently secured, because it only declares, that in *pursuance* of the powers given they shall be the supreme law of the land." But as the Anti-Federalists noted, the Supremacy Clause uses "in pursuance of" only in referring to the laws of the United States, not federal treaties.

Fifth, even though the Constitution did not give the House of Representatives a vote on treaty ratification, it may nonetheless have a role in the process. James Wilson suggested in the Pennsylvania Convention that "though the House of Representatives possess no active part in making treaties, yet their legislative authority will be found to have strong restraining influence upon both President and Senate."[124] He looked to England, where the king would give notice to the Parliament when some law must be enacted or repealed "before the treaty can operate." Wilson asked: "[W]ill not the same thing take place here?"

* * * * *

In the end, all thirteen states ratified the Constitution.[125] Delaware was first on December 7, 1787. New Hampshire was the ninth state to ratify, on June 21, 1788, at which point the Constitution took effect in the ratifying states. Among the most hotly contested states were Massachusetts (which ratified by a vote of 187–168), New York (by a vote of 30–27), and Virginia (by a vote of 89–79). North Carolina and Rhode Island ratified only after Congress had approved the Bill of Rights and submitted it to the states for ratification.

From Ratification to the Present

FOUNDATIONAL CASES

The allocation of power between the states and the federal government continued to be the source of conflict following ratification of the Constitution. The country's first political parties were divided over the question, with the Federalist Party of John Adams and Alexander Hamilton favoring a strong national government while the Republican Party (also known as the Democratic-Republican Party) of Thomas Jefferson and James Madison advocated greater authority in the states. In a series of foundational cases, the Supreme Court (led beginning in 1801 by Chief Justice John Marshall, a Federalist) interpreted the Supremacy Clause in favor of a strong national government, albeit not unreservedly so. The cases are worth discussing because of their importance and because of the role of the Supremacy Clause in the Court's analysis. In addition, they provide the foundation for the doctrinal role of the Supremacy Clause today.

Ware v. Hylton (1796) is the first case in which the Supreme Court invalidated a state law as contrary to federal law, in that case the Treaty of Peace ending the Revolutionary War. It provides the backdrop for the analysis of treaties under the Supremacy Clause. Marbury v. Madison (1803) is widely credited with establishing the doctrine of judicial review over federal statutes and is central to considering the relationship between the Supremacy Clause and the courts. In McCulloch v. Maryland (1819), the Supreme Court held a federal instrumentality (the Bank of the United States) immune from state taxation. The case thus provides the starting point for discussing the doctrine of Supremacy Clause immunity (also known as federal immunity or intergovernmental immunity). Finally, in Gibbons v. Ogden (1824), the Court held that a New York law authorizing a steamboat monopoly conflicted with federal law and thus was invalid, applying the doctrine of federal preemption. The following discussion presents the cases chronologically and, of course, emphasizes the role of the Supremacy Clause in the decisions.[126]

Ware v. Hylton (1796)

The earliest of the cases (and the only one for which Marshall was not Chief Justice) was Ware v. Hylton, in which the Supreme Court for the first time invalidated a state law as contrary to a federal treaty. The treaty at issue was the Treaty of Peace with Great Britain, and the state law was one cited by the British in their complaints about American failures to abide by the treaty. The decision in *Ware* thus was the culmination of efforts dating back to the Confederation era to establish the supremacy of treaties over state law, including Hamilton's argument in Rutgers v. Waddington and Jay's recommendations in his report to Congress.

The case started as Jones v. Hylton. Jones was a British subject who sought to recover on a bond against Daniel Hylton & Co. Hylton's defense to the claim was that it already had paid, albeit paid to the state of Virginia rather than to Jones. A 1777 Virginia statute permitted debtors to pay to the state treasury any debt they owed to a British subject. The law deemed the payment to the state to satisfy the debt. Jones' response was that the Virginia statute was contrary to the Treaty of Peace and thus invalid, so that Hylton's payment to the state was no defense.

The Virginia statute was one of those cited by the British in their 1786 letter complaining of American breaches of the Treaty of Peace. Indeed, the payment by Hylton into the Virginia treasury may have been included in the list of such payments attached to the British letter.[127] Article IV of the Treaty of Peace provided that "creditors on either side, shall meet with no lawful impediment to the recovery of the full value in sterling money, of all bona fide debts heretofore contracted." John Jay in his report to Congress had little trouble in concluding that the Virginia law and others like it violated Article IV: "British creditors have no sort of concern with any payments (made on account of the debts due to them) other than such as they have either accepted, directed or approved; for in relation to the creditor, all such payments are as if they had never been made, and he is justifiable in proceeding against his debtor accordingly."[128]

The circuit court, however, ruled in favor of Hylton (with then Chief Justice Jay in dissent). Supreme Court Justice Iredell, sitting as a Circuit Justice, wrote an opinion that he published in connection with the report of the case in the Supreme Court. Iredell stated his view that prior to the ratification of the Constitution, Article IV "could not at that time be carried into effect in any other manner, than by a repeal of the statutes of the different States, constituting the impediments to their recovery, and the passing of such other acts as might be necessary to give the recovery entire efficacy, in execution of the treaty." That was the reason Congress in 1787 recommended the states repeal all laws inconsistent with the Treaty of Peace. The Constitution, however, "affords the first instance of any government" making treaties "the supreme law of the land." As a result, according to Iredell, treaties now were binding even without state laws implementing the treaty's provisions. He argued:

> Under this constitution therefore, so far as a treaty constitutionally is binding, upon principles of moral obligation, it is also by the vigour of its own authority to be executed in fact. It would not otherwise be the supreme law in the new sense provided for, and it was so before in a moral sense.

Thus, "when this constitution was ratified, the case as to the treaty in question stood upon the same footing as if every act constituting an impediment to a creditor's recovery had been expressly repealed, and any further act passed, which the public obligation had before required." Under the language of the treaty, Iredell concluded, Ware was still able to recover the debt—but from the state rather than from Hylton.

Jones appealed to the United States Supreme Court. While the appeal was pending Jones died, and the administrator of his estate, John Tyndal Ware, was substituted as a party. Hence the name of the case became Ware v. Hylton. Interestingly, Hylton's counsel in the case was John Marshall, later to become the most famous Chief Justice of the Supreme Court. Ware v. Hylton was the only case Marshall ever argued before the Court.[129]

The Supreme Court reversed, holding that the Virginia law violated Article IV of the Treaty of Peace. Each Justice published his own opinion seriatim (i.e., individually, with no opinion for the Court as a whole). Justice Iredell did not participate because he had heard the case in circuit court. Most of the Justices' discussions focused on interpreting the language of the treaty to show that it in fact invalidated the Virginia law and either assumed or asserted that the Treaty was the supreme law of the land. For example, Justice Paterson simply concluded that "[i]f the legislature had authority to make the act, the congress could, by treaty, repeal the act, and annul every thing done under it." Similarly, Justice Cushing stated that "here is a treaty, the supreme law, which overrules all State laws upon the subject, to all intents and purposes; and that makes the difference."

Justice Chase's opinion, however, addressed the supremacy issue at length. First, Chase argued that even under the Articles of Confederation treaties "were superior to the laws of the States": "They were so declared by Congress on the 13th of April, 1787; were so admitted by the legislatures and executives of most of the states; and were so decided by the judiciary of the general government, and by the judiciaries of some of the state governments." Second, regardless, the Supremacy Clause of the Constitution removed any doubt about the matter. The Constitution was established by the people of the United States, who had established the state constitutions as well. Accordingly, "they had the power to change or abolish the state constitutions, or to make them yield to the general government, and to treaties made by their authority." He continued:

> A treaty cannot be the supreme law of the land, that is, of all the United States, if any act of a state legislature can stand in its way. If the constitution of a State (which is the

fundamental law of the State, and paramount to its legislature) must give way to a treaty, and fall before it, can it be questioned whether the less power, an act of the state legislature must not be prostrate? . . . If a law of a State, contrary to a treaty, is not void, but voidable only by a repeal, or nullification by a state legislature, this certain consequence follows, that the will of a small part of the United States may control or defeat the will of the whole.

Chase identified four key points in his analysis of the supremacy of federal treaties over state statutes. First, he emphasized that the Supremacy Clause is "retrospective" (i.e., that it makes treaties entered into under the Articles of Confederation as well as those under the Constitution the supreme law of the land). The key language in the Clause is: "Treaties made, or which shall be made, under the Authority of the United States." "Treaties made" refers to those already made under the Articles; Treaties "which shall be made" are ones that will be made under the Constitution. Second, Chase reiterated that the laws of the states are "prostrated" before the treaty. Third, as a result, Article IV of the Treaty of Peace "has superior power to the legislature of any State." And, fourth, the Supremacy Clause requires state judges to declare "null and void" state laws contrary to the supreme federal law. According to Chase, "[n]ational or federal judges are bound by duty and oath to the same conduct." At bottom, Chase concluded that Article IV of the Treaty of Peace permitted Ware to recover from Hylton despite Virginia law.

Ware v. Hylton is important in the history of the Supremacy Clause for setting the doctrinal stage for cases dealing with the supremacy of treaties. It also was practically important at the time both domestically and internationally. But most fundamentally, the decision is important because, as stated by Professor David Currie, "in *Ware* the Court for the first time struck down a state law under the supremacy clause, establishing for all time its power of judicial review of state laws."[130]

Marbury v. Madison (1803)

Much already has been written about Marbury v. Madison, particularly in recognition of the 200th anniversary of the decision.[131] Scholarly opinion on *Marbury* ranges from viewing the case as "a landmark, perhaps the most prominent, of American constitutional law,"[132] to a "suitable candidate[] for what Leon Trotsky so memorably labeled the 'dustbin of history,'" a case that should be relegated to "well-deserved obscurity."[133] I will not try to reconcile those dramatically differing opinions here. Regardless of whether *Marbury* deserves its exalted status, it has such a status, and so is worth discussing. But because Chief Justice Marshall's opinion relies only briefly on the Supremacy Clause, the discussion of the case will be short.

William Marbury was one of forty-two justices of the peace named for the District of Columbia shortly before the outgoing Federalist administration left office. Lame duck President John Adams signed into law the act authorizing the appointments on Friday, February 27, 1801, and forwarded the nominations to the Senate on Monday, March 2. The next day (the day before Republican President Thomas Jefferson took office), the Senate confirmed the nominations. By March 4, when the new administration took power, all but a handful of the commissions had been delivered by Adams' Secretary of State, who was none other than John Marshall (who had been confirmed as Chief Justice but continued to serve as Secretary of State). Jefferson directed his Secretary of State, James Madison, not to deliver the remaining commissions, which included Marbury's.

Marbury filed an action in the United States Supreme Court, seeking a writ of mandamus directing Madison to deliver the commission. In its opinion, after much discussion about whether Marbury was entitled to the commission and whether mandamus was available against the Secretary of State (which even at the time was criticized as unnecessary to the decision[134]), the Court held that it lacked jurisdiction to issue the requested order: The provision of the Judiciary Act authorizing the Court to issue such a writ of mandamus was unconstitutional.[135] Although the Court might have avoided the constitutional issue by construing the Judiciary Act differently (Professor Lucas A. Powe says that Chief Justice Marshall "absolutely butcher[ed] the construction" of the Act[136]), Marshall found a conflict between the statute and the Constitution. He asked rhetorically: "If an act of the legislature, repugnant to the constitution is void, does it, notwithstanding its invalidity, bind the courts, and oblige them to give it effect?" The answer, of course, is no. Indeed, "[i]t is emphatically the province and duty of the judicial department to say what the law is." According to Marshall, the "very essence of judicial duty" is to decide whether the Constitution or the statute applies in such a case. Given that "the constitution is superior to any ordinary act of the legislature, the constitution, and not such ordinary act, must govern the case to which they both apply."

In upholding the Supreme Court's power to invalidate a federal statute as contrary to the Constitution, Marshall relied only briefly on the Supremacy Clause. His discussion consisted of a grand total of two sentences at the end of the opinion, and reads almost like an afterthought:

> It is also not entirely unworthy of observation, that in declaring what shall be the *supreme* law of the land, the *constitution* itself is first mentioned; and not the laws of the United States generally, but those only which shall be made in *pursuance* of the constitution, have that rank.
>
> Thus, the particular phraseology of the constitution of the United States confirms and strengthens the principle, supposed to be essential to all written constitutions, that a law

repugnant to the constitution is void; and that *courts*, as well as other departments, are bound by that instrument.

And that is it. The strengths and weaknesses of Marshall's argument (as embellished by modern scholars) will be taken up in the next part.

The practical result of the opinion is that Marbury lost, with the Court denying his request for mandamus relief. But while doing so, the Court asserted the power of judicial review over federal statutes—that is, the power to invalidate federal laws as contrary to the Constitution. The Court previously had recognized the power of judicial review as to state laws in Ware v. Hylton, and had reviewed the validity of a federal law in Hylton v. United States (1796), although there it had expressly reserved the question whether it had the power to do so. "Seen in this light," according to Professor Charles Hobson, "the *Marbury* opinion has been acclaimed as a brilliant political coup, at once bold and cautious, a masterpiece of judicial statesmanship in which the court yielded the immediate point while gaining its more important long-range aims."[137] Whether an accurate characterization or not, it certainly is true that the power of judicial review, as exercised by the Court in *Marbury*, is central to the Supreme Court's role in our system of government—and that the *Marbury* Court justified the power, in part, as based on the Supremacy Clause.

McCulloch v. Maryland (1819)

At issue in *McCulloch* was the constitutionality of a Maryland tax on bank notes issued by the Second Bank of the United States. Congress passed legislation chartering the Second Bank in 1816, after the War of 1812 had revealed the need for a central bank. (The First Bank of the United States had been chartered in 1791, and in 1811 Congress declined to renew its charter.) President James Madison, who had been a strident opponent of the First Bank while a congressman, signed into law the legislation creating the Second Bank.

Upon its creation, the Second Bank functioned very much as the central bank of the United States (like the Federal Reserve does today). The Bank handled payments by the federal government of its obligations (without charge), and bank notes it issued were treated as legal tender for the payment of debts. On the other hand, private investors, rather than the government, were in control of the Bank, which was very much a for-profit business. The United States held only 20 percent of the capital stock of the bank, and appointed only five of twenty-five directors to its board of directors.[138] As Secretary of the Treasury William H. Crawford wrote to the President of the Bank, Langdon Cheves, in 1819: "[T]he first duty of the Board [of directors of the Bank] is to the stockholders; the second is to the nation." Cheves, however, asserted that the Bank should not "conduct its business with a view to the largest possible profit."[139]

Within two years of its chartering, the Second Bank was roundly despised, especially in the western and southern states. The Bank's policy of loose credit had been followed with a poorly timed tightening of credit, exacerbating the worst recession the country had yet suffered. Moreover, officials at several of the Bank's branch offices had engaged in extensive speculation on the bank's stock. A congressional investigation was started in 1818, and abuses were widely rumored. Indeed, McCulloch later lost his job (in May 1819) as a result, although eventually he was acquitted of criminal charges.[140]

As a result of the popular hostility toward the Bank (and perhaps also to protect state-chartered banks from a powerful competitor), a number of states enacted laws directed at the Bank. Maryland enacted a stamp tax on all notes issued by a bank chartered "without authority from the state." (The only such bank in Maryland was the Bank of the United States.) The statute required all bank notes issued by such a bank to be on "stamped paper," with the amount of the stamp tax ranging from ten cents to twenty dollars depending on the face amount of the note. The bank could avoid the note tax by paying $15,000 per year to the state. The Maryland statute involved in *McCulloch* was far from the most onerous. Other states imposed even larger taxes on the bank's operations, and some outlawed the bank altogether within their borders.[141] Plainly the Maryland tax was not merely a means for raising revenue, but was designed to discourage or exclude the Bank from operating in the state.

The case that reached the United States Supreme Court was a "test" case, in which both parties cooperated to seek a judicial resolution of the controversy. James McCulloch was the cashier at the Baltimore branch of the Bank of the United States; he issued bank notes that were not on the stamped paper required by Maryland law. The Maryland courts upheld application of the tax, and the dispute went to the United States Supreme Court. The case was argued by "perhaps the greatest collection of prominent advocates in the history" of the Supreme Court bar,[142] including Daniel Webster, William Pinkney, and the Attorney General of Maryland Luther Martin (who had introduced the Supremacy Clause at the Constitutional Convention and then left before the Constitution was finished). The argument lasted nine days, ending on March 3, 1819. Three days later, on March 6, 1819, the Court issued its opinion unanimously striking down the tax.

In the first portion of the opinion, for which *McCulloch* is most famous, Chief Justice Marshall held that Congress had the power to incorporate the Bank, engaging in his famous analysis of the Necessary and Proper Clause of the Constitution. Of interest here is the second part of the opinion, in which the Court held the Maryland tax invalid. The Bank's federal charter was silent on whether the Bank was subject to state taxes. If the charter had addressed the issue, this part of the case would have been easy. If the charter had prohibited state taxes being imposed on the Bank, the issue would have been one of preemption: Assuming Congress had the authority to prohibit the state tax, the federal law would preempt the state law, and the federal law would control. Here, however, there was no express prohibition of state taxes.

Marshall began by recognizing that, under the Constitution, both the federal government and the state governments had the power to impose taxes. Moreover, no provision in the Constitution expressly barred the states from taxing instrumentalities of the federal government. But that was not the end of the matter, according to the Court. Even without a specific prohibition, the nature of the Constitution necessarily precludes states from exercising any power "as is in its nature incompatible with, and repugnant to, the constitutional laws of the Union." As such, "[a] law, absolutely repugnant to another, as entirely repeals that other as if express terms of repeal were used."

The principle underlying the claim of immunity of the Bank from tax, according to Marshall, was the supremacy of federal law, "a principle which so entirely pervades the constitution, is so intermixed with the materials which compose it, so interwoven with its web, so blended with its texture, as to be incapable of being separated from it without rending it into shreds." Here, the Court's opinion echoes the argument in Federalist No. 33—that the Supremacy Clause was unnecessary because the supremacy of federal law would follow from the Constitution even without express language to that effect. Marshall continued: "It is the very essence of supremacy to remove all obstacles to its action within its own sphere, and so to modify every power vested in subordinate governments, as to exempt its own operations from their own influence." Such a power, even if not express, is "necessarily implied" in the Constitution.

Under the Court's analysis to this point, state statutes seeking to outlaw the Bank of the United States would be invalid. Such statutes plainly would be "repugnant" to the law chartering the Bank, and would interfere with the federal government's use of the Bank for its own purposes. But imposition of a state tax would not necessarily have the same result. Certainly, at some point a tax would be indistinguishable from an outright ban. Indeed, Marshall's famous "power to tax involves the power to destroy" (echoing Daniel Webster's argument to the Court) makes that clear. But not in every case. The attorneys for Maryland argued that the Constitution entrusts the states, not the courts, with deciding whether a particular tax on a federal activity is too high.

Marshall rejected that argument. He refused to engage in "the perplexing inquiry, so unfit for the judicial department," of when a state tax on the federal government is so high as to interfere with the government's functioning. Instead, taxing "the means employed by the government of the Union . . . is itself an abuse, because it is the usurpation of a power which the people of a single State cannot give." The key phrase is "single state." Marshall made the point that only Congress, in which all states are represented, should make decisions affecting the federal government. A single state, like Maryland, is looking out for the interests of its citizens, not the citizens of all the states. "When they tax the chartered institutions of the States, they tax their constituents . . . . But when a State taxes the operations of the government of the United States, it acts upon institutions created, not by their own constituents, but by people over whom they claim no control." "[T]he action of the whole on a part" is permissible, according to the Court, but "the action of a part on the whole" is not.

Moreover, permitting states to tax one instrumentality of the federal government would open the rest up to taxation as well: "They may tax the mail; they may tax the mint; they may tax patent rights; they may tax the papers of the custom-house; they may tax judicial process; they may tax all the means employed by the government, to an excess which would defeat all the ends of government. This was not intended by the American people. They did not design to make their government dependent on the States." As Marshall concluded: "The question is, in truth, a question of supremacy; and if the right of the States to tax the means employed by the general government be conceded, the declaration that the constitution, and the laws made in pursuance thereof, shall be the supreme law of the land, is empty and unmeaning declamation."

In sum, the Court held that "the States have no power, by taxation or otherwise, to retard, impede, burden, or in any manner control, the operations of the constitutional laws enacted by congress to carry into execution the powers vested in the general government. This is, we think, the unavoidable consequence of that supremacy which the constitution has declared." The Court concluded by suggesting an important limit to its holding. According to the Court, its decision "does not extend to a tax paid by the real property of the bank, in common with the other real property within the State, nor to a tax imposed on the interest which the citizens of Maryland may hold in this institution, in common with other property of the same description throughout the State." In other words, state taxes that did not single out the federal government, but that applied equally to others in the state, might be constitutional. However, in Weston v. City Council of Charleston (1829), the Court in an opinion by Chief Justice Marshall struck down a tax on holders of bonds issued by the federal government with no discussion of whether the tax was discriminatory.

Interestingly, Marshall did not address in *McCulloch* Maryland's argument (made in most detail by Joseph Hopkinson) that the Bank of the United States was essentially a private bank operating under a federal charter, and thus no different from any other private citizen in being subject to state tax. Hopkinson argued that the government's interest in the bank was simply as a shareholder, the same sort of interest it could have in any corporation. Nor did the government control the management of the bank. According to Hopkinson: "Strip it of its name, and we find [the Bank of the United States] to be a mere association of individuals, putting their money into a common stock, to be loaned for profit, and to divide the gains. The government is a partner in the firm, for gain also. . . . It is not, then a bank of the United States, if by that we mean an institution belonging to the government, directed by it, or in which it has a permanent, indissoluable interest."

Five years later in Osborn v. Bank of the United States (1824), the Court rejected that argument directly while otherwise reaffirming *McCulloch*.[143] *Osborn* involved the state of Ohio's seizure of $100,000 as payment of taxes imposed on the Bank of the United States. Most of the case dealt with jurisdictional matters. Near the end of the opinion, however, Marshall recognized that if the Bank of the United States were a "mere private corporation," it "would certainly be subject to the taxing power of the State, as any individual would be." But, he concluded, "[t]he Bank is not considered as a private corporation, whose principal object is individual trade and profit; but as a public corporation, created for public and national purposes." Regardless of whether Marshall was correct on the facts,[144] the distinction remains an important one today: The Supreme Court applies different immunity standards to instrumentalities of the federal government than it applies to private parties who deal with the federal government.

Gibbons v. Ogden (1824)

The final of the classic Supreme Court cases considered here is Gibbons v. Ogden, in which the Court invalidated a steamboat monopoly granted by the New York legislature. The state legislature originally granted the monopoly in 1787 to John Fitch, the inventor of the steamboat, and then transferred it to Robert Livingston in 1798 after Fitch's death. In 1807, a steamboat built by Livingston and Robert Fulton had a successful trial voyage on the Hudson River, and in 1808 the New York legislature extended their monopoly for thirty years.

After the state courts upheld the monopoly against legal challenge, the Livingston group began granting licenses to other ferry operators—for a hefty fee. Unsuccessful competitors followed the "if you can't beat 'em, join 'em" strategy. One such competitor was Aaron Ogden, whose own attempt to operate a ferry service was blocked by Livingston's monopoly rights. After his lobbying efforts to override the monopoly failed, in 1815 Ogden purchased rights from the Livingston group to operate a ferry from New York City to Elizabethtown Point, New Jersey.[145]

Thomas Gibbons was Ogden's partner in the ferry business. But Gibbons and Ogden had a falling out, and Gibbons started his own ferry line in competition with Ogden. (One of Gibbons' boats was piloted by Cornelius Vanderbilt, who later would become famous as a railroad tycoon.) Ogden filed suit in New York Chancery Court seeking an injunction against Gibbons' operation of a competing ferry. Gibbons responded by arguing that he was entitled to operate the ferry because he had a license under the Federal Coasting Act of 1793 for "carrying on the coasting trade." Chancellor James Kent rejected Gibbons' argument and enjoined him from continuing to compete against Ogden. Kent reasoned that the federal coasting license merely indicated that the steamboat was an American rather than foreign vessel, and thus subject to lower tariff and tonnage duties. Because Ogden's state law monopoly rights did not conflict with the federal act, the state law was valid.[146] The New York Court of Errors affirmed.

Gibbons then took the case to the United States Supreme Court. It was originally filed in 1820, but in 1821 the Supreme Court dismissed the case because the record did not show that the New York court had entered a final judgment. The case was finally set for argument in February 1824. Another all-star cast of lawyers argued the case: Daniel Webster and William Wirt for Gibbons; Thomas Oakley and Thomas Emmet for Ogden. (Ogden had originally retained William Pinkney to argue the case on his behalf, but Pinkney had died before the case was reset for argument.) The argument, which lasted for five days, was (in Wirt's words) a "combat worth witnessing."[147]

Chief Justice Marshall wrote the opinion for the Court, which he delivered "in a low, feeble voice."[148] (Two weeks earlier, Marshall had fallen at his Washington boarding house, suffering a concussion and dislocating his shoulder, which delayed his work on the opinion.) After finding that interstate navigation was within Congress' commerce power, Marshall moved on to consider the central issue in the case: whether the federal government had exclusive power to regulate interstate commerce (which would have precluded New York's steamboat monopoly even without any action by Congress) or whether state power and federal power were concurrent and so could coexist. Marshall wrote that "[t]here is great force in [the exclusive power] argument, and the Court is not satisfied that it has been refuted." But the Court did not decide the case on that basis.

Instead, the Court relied on Gibbons' license under the Federal Coasting Act, holding that the New York monopoly grant conflicted with the federal license and thus was invalid. As we would say today, the Federal Coasting Act preempted the New York law establishing the steamboat monopoly. The question, according to Marshall, was "whether the laws of New-York, as expounded by the highest tribunal of that State, have, in their application to this case, come into collision with an act of Congress, and deprived a citizen of a right to which that act entitles him." If there is such a collision, it does not matter whether the state is exercising a concurrent power to regulate interstate commerce or a power to regulate its own intrastate commerce. "In one case and the other," Marshall explained, "the acts of New-York must yield to the law of Congress." The Court rejected the suggestion that state law and federal law "affect the subject, and each other, like equal opposing powers." Under the Supremacy Clause, whenever state laws "interfere with, or are contrary to" a federal statute or treaty, "the act of Congress, or the treaty, is supreme and the law of the State, though enacted in the exercise of powers not controverted, must yield to it." Here, the Court concluded that the Federal Coasting Act "implies, unequivocally, an authority to licensed vessels to carry on the coasting trade"; it does not merely identify the ship as American. The New York law granting a steamboat monopoly "comes . . . in direct collision" with the federal act so construed, and thus is invalid.

"For the one and only time in his career on the Supreme Bench, Marshall had pronounced a 'popular' opinion."[149] The anti-monopoly holding of the Court, opening up steamboat lines to competition, was well received by the general public. As a legal matter, *Gibbons* was "a highly ambiguous and perhaps an ambivalent decision."[150] The Court avoided deciding whether the federal commerce power was concurrent or exclusive, relying instead on what Supreme Court Justice Felix Frankfurter later called "esoteric statutory construction" to invalidate the steamboat monopoly.[151] But the decision nonetheless is "nationalist" in outlook, affirming the power of the federal government to override state law, and laying the foundation for preemption doctrine, the most frequent use of the Supremacy Clause today.

SUPREMACY AND STATES' RIGHTS

The Supremacy Clause, while central to federal-state relations on a day-to-day basis, comes to the fore during critical times in the nation's history—times of intense conflict between states and the federal government. This section briefly surveys three such times in bringing the history of the Supremacy Clause up to the present.[152] It begins by discussing the nullification crisis of 1832, when South Carolina unilaterally sought to nullify a federal law, the so-called Tariff of Abominations. It then considers the states' rights theories underlying the secession of eleven Southern states leading to the Civil War. It concludes by examining the doctrine of interposition and southern resistance to the Supreme Court's decisions requiring the desegregation of the public schools.

During each of these conflicts, supporters of states' rights sought to justify the state's resistance to federal law by relying on variations of "compact theory": the theory that the federal government was formed by a compact, or agreement, among sovereign states, and that the federal government thus acts as an agent of the states using the powers they delegated to it. Nullification posits that each individual state has the power to declare a federal law unconstitutional (i.e., in excess of the powers delegated to the federal government) and to treat such a law as null and void within its borders. Secession is the (asserted) option of a state to withdraw from the union altogether following a material breach of the federal compact. Interposition is a more variable concept, sometimes synonymous with nullification, sometimes something less than nullification but more than mere protest.[153] This section discusses each of these doctrines as they relate to the Supremacy Clause.

Nullification and the "Tariff of Abominations"

In 1828, Congress enacted a protective tariff. Northern manufacturers benefitted from the tariff because the tariff made competing imports more expensive. Southern (predominantly agricultural) interests opposed the tariff, contending it was unfair (because they paid the increased prices) and unconstitutional (because the tariff was designed to do more than simply raise revenue). When Congress reenacted this "Tariff of Abominations" in 1832, South Carolina responded by "nullifying" the tariff.[154] The idea of nullification is that a single state can determine that a federal law is unconstitutional and refuse to enforce the law within its boundaries. As the South Carolina Ordinance of Nullification declared, the tariff "violated the true meaning and intent of the Constitution" and therefore was "null, void, and no law, nor binding upon this State, its officers or citizens."[155] The Ordinance further threatened that Congressional authorization of the use of force against South Carolina would be "inconsistent with the longer continuance of South Carolina in the Union." In other words, if the federal government sent in troops to enforce the tariff, South Carolina would secede.

John C. Calhoun, who while Vice President secretly drafted the South Carolina nullification ordinance, was the leading intellectual voice behind nullification.[156] Near the end of his life, Calhoun stated that "[i]f you should ask me the question [what] I would wish engraved on my tombstone, it is *Nullification*."[157] Calhoun derived the states' right of nullification from compact theory, which, as described above, viewed the Constitution as a compact or agreement among sovereign states. Under the compact, the federal government only has the power delegated to it by the states, and thus acts as an agent of the states. When the federal government as agent exceeds the scope of its delegated authority (i.e., violates the Constitution), a state can nullify the agent's unconstitutional act.[158]

As authority for nullification, Calhoun looked to the "Principles of '98"—the 1798 Kentucky and Virginia Resolutions, passed by those states' legislatures in response to the Alien and Sedition Acts. The Kentucky Resolutions, drafted by then–Vice President Thomas Jefferson, stated as follows:

> *Resolved,* that the several States composing the United States of America, are not united on the principle of unlimited submission to their general government; but that by compact under the style and title of a Constitution for the United States and of amendments thereto, they constituted a general government for special purposes, delegated to that government certain definite powers, reserving each State to itself, the residuary mass of right to their own self-government; and that whensoever the general government assumes undelegated powers, its acts are unauthoritative, void, and of no force: That to this compact each State acceded as a State, and is an integral party, its co-States forming, as to itself, the other party: That the government created by this compact was not made the exclusive or final judge of the extent of the powers delegated to itself; since that would have made its discretion, and

not the Constitution, the measure of its powers; but that as in all other cases of compact among parties having no common Judge, *each party has an equal right to Judge for itself, as well of infractions as of the mode and measure of redress.*[159]

The Virginia Resolutions, drafted by James Madison, provided "that in case of a deliberate, palpable and dangerous exercise of other powers not granted by the said compact, the states who are parties thereto have the right, and are in duty bound, to interpose for arresting the progress of the evil, and for maintaining within their respective limits, the authorities, rights and liberties appertaining to them."[160] The Resolutions then listed in detail the constitutional provisions violated by the Alien and Sedition Acts.

The remedy sought by the Resolutions, however, is not completely clear. The Kentucky Resolutions directed the state's U.S. senators and representatives "to use their best efforts to procure" a repeal of the Acts, and requested the governor to send the resolutions to other states, expressing confidence that the other states would take similar steps. The Virginia Resolutions similarly appealed to other states to join in taking "necessary and proper" steps to protect states' rights, whatever those steps might be. Kentucky and Virginia were to be disappointed: No other states joined them, and a number flatly repudiated their positions.[161] Follow-up resolutions by Kentucky reasserted that a "*nullification . . . of all unauthorized acts . . . is the rightful remedy*," but concluded that the state would "bow to the laws of the Union" after making a "solemn PROTEST."[162] A report to the Virginia General Assembly in 1800 by Madison reaffirmed the "truth" of the original resolutions and concluded by renewing its protest against the Acts.[163] Thus, Professor Robert B. McKay has written that the Kentucky and Virginia Resolutions argue for a states' right to "interpos[e] of its sovereignty against the allegedly unlawful federal action," but only for long enough to seek support from other states.[164] If other states do not join, "the interposing state or states would seem obligated to accede to the unwelcome act or decision."

The response to the South Carolina Nullification Ordinance was swift. On December 10, 1832, President Andrew Jackson issued a proclamation attacking nullification as unjustified.[165] According to Jackson, nullification was based on the "strange position" that the Constitution "permits a State to retain its place in the Union, and yet be bound by no other of its laws than those it may choose to consider as constitutional." The Supremacy Clause, a provision that "no federative government could exist without," rendered any attempt to justify nullification "superfluous." Jackson's conclusion was unequivocal: "I consider, then, the power to annul a law of the United States, assumed by one State, *incompatible with the existence of the Union, contradicted expressly by the letter of the Constitution, unauthorized by its spirit, inconsistent with every principle on which it was founded, and destructive of the great object for which it was formed.*"

James Madison was appalled that nullification supporters relied on the Kentucky and Virginia Resolutions to justify their actions. He denied that the resolutions provided any support for nullification.[166] An individual state cannot nullify a federal law, Madison argued: "A plainer contradiction in terms, or a more fatal inlet to anarchy, cannot be imagined." Instead, "[t]he final appeal in such cases must be to the authority of the whole, not to that of the parts separately and independently," which was the view that "dictated the clause declaring that the Constitution & laws of the U.S. should be the supreme law of the Land, anything in the constn or laws of any of the States to the contrary notwithstanding." Joseph Story's constitutional law treatise likewise contained an extensive critique of nullification, relying importantly on the Supremacy Clause to refute Calhoun's arguments. Story wrote: "If [the Constitution] is the supreme law, how can the people of any state, either by any form of its own constitution, or laws, or other proceedings, repeal, or abrogate, or suspend it?"[167]

The famous Hayne-Webster debates, between Senator Robert Y. Hayne of South Carolina and Senator Daniel Webster of Massachusetts, present the competing viewpoints in sharp relief. Although the ostensible topic of the debate was a resolution on federal lands, the orators took on broader issues of constitutional theory. According to Hayne, state sovereignty requires that states have the final say on the constitutionality of federal acts. Otherwise, if "the federal government is the exclusive judge of the extent as well as the limitations of its powers, it seems to me utterly subversive of the sovereignty and independence of the States."[168] Webster characterized Hayne as arguing "not only that this general government is the creature of the States, but that it is the creature of each of the States severally . . . . It is the servant of four-and-twenty masters, of different wills and different purposes, and yet bound to obey all."[169] This position was an "absurdity," according to Webster, arising "from a misconception as to the origin of this government and its true character":

> It is, Sir, the people's Constitution, the people's government, made for the people, made by the people, and answerable to the people. The people of the United States have declared that the Constitution shall be the supreme law. We must either admit the proposition, or dispute their authority. The States are, unquestionably, sovereign, so far as their sovereignty is not affected by this supreme law. But the State legislatures, as political bodies, however sovereign, are yet not sovereign over the people. So far as the people have given power to the general government, so far the grant is unquestionably good, and the government holds of the people, and not of the State governments. We are all agents of the same supreme power, the people.

Webster's closing words, which justified his nickname of "Defender of the Union," were: "Liberty *and* Union, now and forever, one and inseparable!"

The nullification crisis ended in compromise.[170] Congress passed the Force Act, which authorized President Jackson to use the military against South Carolina to enforce the tariff, while at the same time reducing the amount of the tariff. South Carolina passed an ordinance nullifying the Force Act, but rescinded its previous nullification of the tariff. Both sides were able to save face, and the states' rights challenge to federal supremacy dissipated—but only for the time being.

Secession and the Civil War

South Carolina's threat to secede during the nullification crisis of 1832 was safely diffused. But the issue of slavery was not one that could be resolved by compromise, and it would split the nation. Military action by the federal government—an option for enforcing federal law that the framers rejected—was in the end necessary to end slavery and reunite the union. A full discussion of the events leading up to the Civil War has been recounted by others[171] and is beyond the scope of this book. Instead, the focus here is on the role of the Supremacy Clause in those events.

South Carolina was the first state to secede from the union, on December 20, 1860. Eventually, eleven states in all seceded to form the Confederate States of America. The seceding states relied on two theories to justify secession.[172] One was a natural law right of revolution, as stated in the Declaration of Independence.[173] The other was compact theory. It is well established law that one party's (uncured) material breach of a contract discharges the other party's continued obligation to perform under the contract. Starting from the premise that the United States was created by a compact among the states, the Southern states argued that a material breach of that compact would justify them in treating the compact as terminated. The South Carolina Declaration of the Causes of Secession explains that "in every compact between two or more parties, the obligation is mutual; that the failure of one of the contracting parties to perform a material part of the agreement, entirely releases the obligation of the other; and that, where no arbiter is provided, each party is remitted to his own judgment to determine the fact of failure, with all its consequences."[174] The repeated failures of the northern states to abide by the Constitution's provisions on the return of escaped slaves (among others), according to South Carolina, constituted a material breach of the compact and justified the state in seceding from the union.

Interestingly, Professor William Freehling argues that compact theory became less important and the natural law right to revolution more important as the states of the Deep South, which were the first to secede, sought to persuade Upper South states to join them in seceding.[175] The Southern fear that asserting a right to revolution would trigger slave revolts receded as years passed after the last major revolts with no further unrest. Conversely, the arguments in support of finding a material breach weakened as national fugitive slave laws turned Calhoun's view of states' rights on its head. Southern states favored a strong national government to enforce federal laws requiring the return of runaway slaves. Northern states—most notably Wisconsin—sought to nullify federal fugitive slave laws.[176] Under these circumstances, in Freehling's words, the natural law right to revolution was the "ideal states' rights theory for 1860."

Regardless of the theory underlying secession, the secessionists agreed that the Supremacy Clause was not inconsistent with the right of states to secede. Professor J.G. Randall explains their reasoning:

> There is a distinction between "supreme law" and "paramount authority." Supreme law is exercised by the government, but paramount authority resides with the people. . . .
>
> The people, they said, may bestow supreme power where they will, and what they bestow they may recall. Thus the people of the States, possessing the right to bestow supreme governmental power as they should see fit, conferred such power upon a general government as their agent, limiting, to that extent, their State *governments*, but not limiting their own sovereignty. According to this interpretation, the "supreme law clause" involved no diminution, much less a final surrender, of that sovereignty which resides in the people of the States, and the Articles of Confederation were as truly the Supreme law of the land as the Constitution.[177]

Others have rationalized secession with the Supremacy Clause on the ground that the Constitution does not prohibit states from seceding, and what is not prohibited is permitted.[178]

It is no coincidence that the seceding Southern states called their new government the "*Confederate* States of America" (emphasis added). As President Jefferson Davis explained in his Message to the Confederate States Congress on April 29, 1861, the Southern states "proceeded to form a new compact amongst themselves by new articles of confederation,"[179] consciously "harkening back" to the Articles of Confederation, "a state-dominated league of national identity."[180] Such a conception was reflected in the preamble to the Confederate Constitution, which began "WE the People of the Confederate States, each State acting in its sovereign and independent character," and replaced "in Order to form a more perfect Union" with "in order to form a permanent federal government."[181] That said, many provisions of the Confederate Constitution were virtually identical to those in the United States Constitution, including a Supremacy Clause, which was the same except for replacing "United States" with "Confederate States."[182] Although court decisions applying the Confederate Supremacy Clause sound very much like U.S. Supreme Court decisions applying the Supremacy Clause in the U.S. Constitution,[183] there is one important difference: "[T]he C.S.A. Constitution and those laws in pursuance thereof were supreme, with the qualification that the state courts would function as the preeminent interpreter of both fundamental and statutory laws within their respective jurisdictions."[184]

President Abraham Lincoln set out the constitutional case against secession. In his First Inaugural address, Lincoln argued that the union was "perpetual."[185] The Constitution does not by its terms permit secession, and thus is to "endure forever—it being impossible to destroy it, except by some action not provided for in the instrument itself." Lincoln further took on compact theory on its own terms, arguing that one party has no right to rescind a contract; one party can breach it, but all contracting parties must agree (which obviously was not the case here) before it can be rescinded. Thereafter, in his Message to Congress in Special Session on July 4, 1861, he rejected the idea that states as sovereigns preexisted the union. Only Texas "ever was a sovereignty. And even Texas gave up the character on coming into the Union; by which act, she acknowledged the Constitution of the United States, and the laws and treaties of the United States made in pursuance of the Constitution, to be, for her, the supreme law of the land."[186]

Congress relied on the Supremacy Clause in challenging the Southern states' right to secede as well as in justifying the Civil War. New York Senator William H. Seward argued that "[t]he Constitution of the United States, and the laws made in pursuance thereof, are the supreme law of the land, paramount to all legislation of the States, whether made under their Constitution, or by even their organic conventions. The Union can be dissolved, not by secession, with or without armed force, but only by the voluntary consent of the people of the United States, collected in the manner prescribed by the Constitution of the United States."[187] The Resolutions on the Theory of Secession and Reconstruction, proposed in 1862 by Senator and radical abolitionist Charles Sumner (and which are best known for the argument that by seceding the Southern states effectively committed suicide) contended that secession was "inoperative and void" because "the Constitution, which is the supreme law of the land, cannot be displaced in its rightful operation within this territory, but must ever continue the supreme law thereof, notwithstanding of the doings of any pretended governments acting singly or in confederation, in order to put an end to its supremacy."[188] The Crittenden Resolutions on the Objects of the War, passed by the House of Representatives in 1861, explained that "this war is not waged upon our part in any spirit of oppression, nor for any purpose of conquest or subjugation, nor purpose of overthrowing or interfering with the rights or established institutions of those States, but to defend and maintain the supremacy of the Constitution and to preserve the Union, with all the dignity, equality, and rights of the several States unimpaired."[189] The Johnson Resolutions passed by the Senate were to the same effect, adding that the war was "to defend and maintain the supremacy of the Constitution and all laws made in pursuance thereof."

The military defeat of the South in the Civil War ended secession as a political strategy. Thereafter, in Texas v. White (1869), the Supreme Court rejected secession as a constitutional option, holding the Texas ordinance of secession "absolutely null." Upon statehood, Texas "entered into an indissoluble relation" with the other states, the Court explained. It was "something more than a compact; it was the incorporation of a new member into the political body. And it was final."[190] Today, Professor Cass Sunstein states, "no serious scholar or politician now argues that a right to secede exists under American constitutional law."[191]

Interposition and Civil Rights

Although the Civil War put secession to rest, compact theory manifested itself again almost one hundred years later in response to the Supreme Court's decision in Brown v. Board of Education (1954)[192] requiring desegregation of the public schools. The theory was "rediscovered" by William Old, the County Attorney of Chesterfield County, Virginia,[193] and then publicized by James J. Kilpatrick in a series of editorials in the Richmond *News Leader.*[194] Kilpatrick, today a nationally syndicated conservative columnist, argued that the states "'*are in duty bound*' to interpose against the evil" of desegregation.[195] This doctrine of "interposition," which Kilpatrick traced back to the Kentucky and Virginia Resolutions (recall that Madison's Virginia Resolutions declared that "states are in duty bound, to interpose for arresting the progress of the evil"), was, according to Kilpatrick, an "honorable, legal and constitutional means" of resisting desegregation. When later asked about the editorials in connection with the 150th anniversary of the Richmond paper, Kilpatrick stated that they were "an effort to elevate the debate above the blood in the streets. The hope was that it might in some obscure way have calmed the waves of passion. That was one of the motives, and the other was to keep the schools segregated until things settled down."[196]

In response to Kilpatrick's urging, a number of Southern states adopted "interposition resolutions."[197] The Virginia interposition resolutions, for example, recited that "the powers of the Federal Government result solely from the compact to which the States are parties," and that the states "have agreed voluntarily to delegate certain of their sovereign powers, but only those sovereign powers specifically enumerated, to a Federal Government thus constituted."[198] The resolutions continued by characterizing the Supreme Court's decision in *Brown* as an improper attempt to amend the Constitution, and as such "constitutes a deliberate, palpable, and dangerous attempt by the court itself to usurp the amendatory power that lies solely with not fewer than three-fourths of the States." They concluded that "whenever the Federal Government attempts the deliberate, palpable and dangerous exercise of powers not granted it, the States who are parties to the compact have the right, and are in duty bound, to interpose for arresting the progress of the evil." While asserting a right to "interposition," to the extent southern states sought to justify unilateral defiance of the Supreme Court, their actions were nullification dressed up under another name.[199]

As a legal matter, interposition and state interposition resolutions had little impact. Lewis F. Powell, a Virginia lawyer and later a Supreme Court Justice, wrote that interposition was "simply legal nonsense."[200] (Powell engaged Kilpatrick in a public debate on interposition, after which Kilpatrick reportedly said, "Good, God, did I get chewed up last night!"[201]) The NAACP largely ignored the doctrine in its legal challenges to segregation.[202] When courts did address the doctrine, they forcefully rejected it. The three-judge court in Bush v. Orleans Parish School Board (E.D. La. 1960) wrote: "The conclusion is clear that interposition is not a *constitutional* doctrine. If taken seriously, it is illegal defiance of constitutional authority. Otherwise, 'it amounted to no more than a protest, an escape valve through which the legislators blew off steam to relieve their tensions.' However solemn or spirited, interposition resolutions have no legal efficacy." In denying a motion for stay of the three-judge court's judgment, the United States Supreme Court stated that "[t]he main basis for challenging this ruling is that the State of Louisiana 'has interposed itself in the field of public education over which it has exclusive control.' This objection is without substance, as we held, upon full consideration, in *Cooper* v. *Aaron*" (Bush v. Orleans Parish School Board, 1960). More colorfully, Circuit Judge John Minor Wisdom, writing for another three-judge court, stated that "[a] hundred years ago in ordeal by battle this nation settled forever the issue of interposition. The reality of national sovereignty prevailed over metaphysical state sovereignty" (United States v. Manning, W.D. La., 1963). Elsewhere, Judge Wisdom stated bluntly that "the Supremacy Clause makes hash of the so-called Doctrine of Interposition."[203] As a result, the last vestiges of compact theory were pushed outside the mainstream; the theory "is not a viable one at this point in our history."[204]

The states' "massive resistance" to desegregation went beyond interposition resolutions, however, to legislative interference and outright defiance of court orders. In Little Rock, Arkansas, Governor Orval Faubus called out the Arkansas National Guard to keep black students out of Little Rock Central High School.[205] Eventually, a court order and federal troops were necessary to enable the students to attend. The school district thereafter sought a court order permitting it to delay implementation of its (modest) desegregation plan because of public hostility caused by the actions of the Governor and other public officials. The Supreme Court rejected the request in Cooper v. Aaron (1958), holding that opposition to desegregation stirred up by state officials was no excuse for delay.

The Supreme Court then went on to address whether Arkansas officials were bound by its ruling in *Brown* even though they were not parties to that case—in the Court's words, whether there is a "duty on state officials to obey federal court orders resting on this Court's considered interpretation of the United States Constitution." The Court answered with a definitive yes. It quoted the Supremacy Clause and Chief Justice Marshall in Marbury v. Madison ("It is emphatically the province and duty of the judicial department to say what the law is"), and then described *Marbury* as "declar[ing] the basic principle that the federal judiciary is supreme in the exposition of the law of the Constitution." "[T]hat principle," according to the Court, "has ever since been respected by this Court and the Country as a permanent and indispensable feature of our constitutional system." Accordingly, the Court's interpretation of the Fourteenth Amendment in *Brown* "is the supreme law of the land, and Art. VI of the Constitution makes it of binding effect on the States 'any Thing in the Constitution or Laws of any State to the Contrary notwithstanding.'" Any state legislator, executive officer, or judge who refuses to follow the Court's decisions violates his or her oath to uphold the United States Constitution. In such a case, "'it is manifest that the fiat of a state Governor [or other state official], and not the Constitution of the United States, would be the supreme law of the land; that the restrictions of the Federal Constitution upon the exercise of state power would be but impotent phrases'" (quoting Sterling v. Constantin, 1932).

Under the doctrine of judicial supremacy as stated in *Cooper*, the Supremacy Clause includes as the "supreme Law of the Land" not only the Constitution and federal statutes and treaties, but also Supreme Court interpretations of the Constitution and federal statutes and treaties. As Professor Lucas A. Powe, Jr. explains, "*Cooper* was different [from Marbury v. Madison], for it claimed not only the right to interpret the Constitution but also the right to be final, that is, to bind not only the parties but everyone else."[206] That principle was asserted to overcome state resistance to desegregation; its current status is discussed in Part II.

ENDNOTES

1. Sir James Whitelocke, *The Rights of the People Concerning Impositions* (London: 1658) 9, quoted in 3 John Phillip Reid, *Constitutional History of the American Revolution: The Authority to Legislate* (Madison: University of Wisconsin Press, 1991) 63–64.

2. Alexander Hamilton, "The Farmer Refuted" (Feb. 23, 1775), in 1 Harold C. Syrett, ed., *The Papers of Alexander Hamilton* (New York: Columbia University Press, 1961) 81, 98, quoted in Gordon S. Wood, *The Creation of the American Republic 1776–1787* (Chapel Hill: University of North Carolina Press, 1969) 345.

3. 3 Reid, *Constitutional History of the American Revolution* 75.

4. Wood, *The Creation of the American Republic* 348.

5. 6 Geo. III, c. 12, § 1 (Eng. 1766).

6. Alden Bradford, ed., *Speeches of the Governors of Massachusetts from 1765 to 1775* (Boston: Russell and Gardner, 1818) 336, 340, quoted in Wood, *The Creation of the American Republic* 344.

7. 3 Reid, *Constitutional History of the American Revolution* 76.

8. Martin S. Flaherty, "More Apparent Than Real: The Revolutionary Commitment to Constitutional Federalism," 45 *U. Kan. L. Rev.* (1997) 993, 994; see William Hartwell Bennett, *American Theories of Federalism* (University, Ala.: University of Alabama Press, 1964) 15–37; Jack P. Greene, *Peripheries and Center: Constitutional Development in the Extended Polities of the British Empire and the United States, 1607–1788* (Athens: University of Georgia Press, 1986).

9. 3 Reid, *Constitutional History of the American Republic* 83 (quoting Henry Goodricke, *Observations on Dr. Price's Theory and Principles of Civil Liberty and Government* (York, England: 1776) 43–44).

10. Flaherty, 45 *U. Kan. L. Rev.* 999–1000.

11. The king was the link that held Great Britain and the colonies together. See, e.g., Hamilton, "The Farmer Refuted," in 1 *Papers of Alexander Hamilton* 98–99:

> It is in vain to assert, that two or more distinct legislatures cannot exist in the same state. If, by the same state, be meant the same individual community, it is true. Thus, for instance there cannot be two supreme legislatures in Great-Britain, or two in New-York. But, if, by the same state, be understood a number of individual societies, or bodies politic, united under one common head, then, I maintain, that there may be one distinct compleat legislature in each: Thus there may be one in Great-Britain, another in Ireland, and another in New-York, and still these several parts may form but one state. In order to this, there must indeed be some connecting, pervading principle; but this is found in the person and prerogative of the King. He it is that conjoins all these individual societies, into one great body politic. He it is, that is to preserve their mutual connexion and dependence, and make them all co-operate to one common end the general good.

12. Wood, *The Creation of the American Republic* 352–353.

13. Wood, *The Creation of the American Republic* 353 (quoting "'An American' to the Earl of Carlisle and Others" (July 16, 1778), in 4 Harry Alonzo Cushing, ed., *The Writings of Samuel Adams* (New York: G.P. Putnam's Sons, 1908) 37).

14. 5 *Journals of the Continental Congress 1774–1789* (Washington, D.C.: United States Government Printing Office, 1904) 546, 546–552. (A somewhat revised draft is reprinted alongside the Dickinson draft at 5 *Journals of the Continental Congress* 674, 674–689.)

15. Merrill Jensen, *The Articles of Confederation: An Interpretation of the Social-Constitutional History of the American Revolution 1774–1781* (Madison: University of Wisconsin Press, 1940) 130.

16. Jensen, *The Articles of Confederation* 170–175.

17. Letter from Thomas Burke to Richard Caswell (Apr. 29, 1777), in 2 Edmund C. Burnett, ed., *Letters of Members of the Continental Congress* (Washington, D.C.: Carnegie Institution, 1923) 345, 346.

18. Letter from Burke to Caswell (Apr. 29, 1777), in 2 *Letters of Members of the Continental Congress* 346.

19. Articles of Confederation, art. II (Mar. 1, 1781).

20. Edward S. Corwin, "The Progress of Constitutional Theory Between the Declaration of Independence and the Meeting of the Philadelphia Convention," 30 *Am. Hist. Rev.* (1925) 511, 527.

21. 9 *Journals of the Continental Congress* 833, 911.

22. Caleb Nelson, "Preemption," 86 *Va. L. Rev.* (2000) 225, 251; see also Peter Weston, "The Place of Foreign Treaties in the Courts of the United States: A Reply to Louis Henkin," 101 *Harv. L. Rev.* (1987) 511, 514 (arguing that Article XIII might be interpreted as establishing "a relationship in which federal claims are superior to state law and yet are nonjusticiable in the face of *subsequently adopted* state law to the contrary").

23. James Madison, "Vices of the Political System of the United States," in 9 Robert A. Rutland, ed., *The Papers of James Madison* (Chicago: University of Chicago Press, 1975) 348, 351–352.

24. James Madison, "Proposed Amendment of Articles of Confederation," in 3 *Papers of James Madison* 17, 17–18.

25. 2 Irving Brant, *James Madison: The Nationalist 1780–1787* (Indianapolis: Bobbs-Merrill Co., 1948) 109–120.

26. Definitive Treaty of Peace Between the United States of America and his Britannic Majesty, 8 Stat. 80 (Sept. 3, 1783); Provisional Articles Between the United States of America and his Britannic Majesty, 8 Stat. 54 (Nov. 30, 1782).

27. John Adams, "A Memorial" (Nov. 30, 1785), in 4 *Secret Journals of the Acts and Proceedings of Congress* (Boston: Thomas B. Wait, 1821) 186, 187.

28. Letter from British Secretary of State Carmarthen to John Adams (Feb. 28, 1786), in 4 *Secret Journals* 187, 187–202.

29. John Jay, "Report to Congress from the Secretary for Foreign Affairs" (Oct. 13, 1786), in 4 *Secret Journals* 185, 204.

30. Edward S. Corwin, *Court Over Constitution* (Princeton: Princeton University Press, 1938) 27 n.26; see also Edward S. Corwin, *National Supremacy: Treaty Power vs. State Power* (New York: Henry Holt & Co., 1913) 29. For the report of the case, as well as copies of many of the pleadings, see 1 Julius Goebel Jr., ed., *The Law Practice of Alexander Hamilton* (New York: Columbia University Press, 1964) 282–419.

31. 1 *Law Practice of Alexander Hamilton* 377–383.

32. 1 *Law Practice of Alexander Hamilton* 310.

33. 32 *Journals of the Continental Congress* 124, 124–125.

34. 32 *Journals of the Continental Congress* 177, 177–184.

35. James Madison, "Notes on Debates" (Mar. 21, 1787), in 9 *Papers of James Madison* 326, 327.

36. For a report on how the states responded, see Letter from Thomas Jefferson to George Hammond (May 29, 1792), in 23 Charles T. Cullen, ed., *The Papers of Thomas Jefferson* (Princeton: Princeton University Press, 1990) 551, 578–579.

37. Alexander Hamilton, "Remarks on Act Repealing Laws Inconsistent with Treaty of Peace," New York Assembly (Apr. 17, 1787), in 4 *Papers of Alexander Hamilton* 150, 152.

38. Resolution of Congress (Feb. 21, 1787), in 13 John P. Kaminski & Gaspare J. Saladino, eds., *The Documentary History of the Ratification of the Constitution* (Madison: State Historical Society of Wisconsin, 1981) 45.

39. Madison, "Vices," in 9 *Papers of James Madison* 348–358.

40. Letter from James Madison to N.P. Trist (Dec. 1831), in 3 Max Farrand, ed., *The Records of the Federal Convention of 1787*, rev. ed. (New Haven: Yale University Press, 1937) 516.

41. Jack N. Rakove, *Original Meanings: Politics and Ideas in the Making of the Constitution* (New York: Alfred A. Knopf, 1996) 171–172.

42. Charles Warren, *The Making of the Constitution* (Boston: Little, Brown, & Co., 1929) 112–113.

43. 1 Farrand 18.

44. Letter from James Madison to Thomas Jefferson (Mar. 19, 1787), in 9 *Papers of James Madison* 317–322; Letter from James Madison to Edmund Randolph (Apr. 8, 1787), in 9 *Papers of James Madison* 368–371; Letter from James Madison to George Washington (Apr. 16, 1787), in 9 *Papers of James Madison* 382–387.

45. Letter from Madison to Washington (Apr. 16, 1787), in 9 *Papers of James Madison* 383–384.

46. Letter from Madison to Jefferson (Oct. 24, 1787), in 10 *Papers of James Madison* 209.

47. Letter from Madison to Randolph (Apr. 8, 1787), in 9 *Papers of James Madison* 370.

48. Letter from Madison to Washington (Apr. 16, 1787), in 9 *Papers of James Madison* 383.

49. 6 Geo. III, c. 12, § 1 (Eng. 1766).

50. Jack N. Rakove, "The Great Compromise: Ideas, Interests, and the Politics of Constitution Making," 44 *Wm. & Mary Q.* (1987) 424, 432.

51. Letter from Thomas Jefferson to James Madison (June 20, 1787), in 10 *Papers of James Madison* 63, 64.

52. James S. Liebman & William F. Ryan, "'Some Effectual Power': The Quantity and Quality of Decisionmaking Required of Article III Courts," 98 *Colum. L. Rev.* (1998) 696, 720 n.117.

53. Charles F. Hobson, "The Negative on State Laws: James Madison, the Constitution, and the Crisis of Republican Government," 36 *Wm. & Mary Q.* (1979) 215, 226 n.24.

54. Viet D. Dinh, "Reassessing the Law of Preemption," 88 *Geo. L.J.* (2000) 2085, 2088–2090.

55. Liebman & Ryan, 98 *Colum. L. Rev.* 726.

56. Edmund Randolph, "Suggestion for Conciliating the Small States" (July 10, 1787), in 3 Farrand 55.

57. Liebman & Ryan, 98 *Colum. L. Rev.* 729.

58. Professor Robert H. Birkby finds no evidence that replacing the congressional negative with the Supremacy Clause was a "conscious compromise" between the large states and small states, instead concluding that "the development of the Supremacy Clause is just one more illustration of the American politics of accommodation." Robert H. Birkby, "Politics of Accommodation: The Origin of the Supremacy Clause," 19 *Western Pol. Q.* (1966) 123, 134.

59. Jack N. Rakove, "The Origins of Judicial Review: A Plea for New Contexts," 49 *Stan. L. Rev.* (1997) 1031, 1046–1047.

60. Larry D. Kramer, "Madison's Audience," 112 *Harv. L. Rev.* (1999) 611, 649–651.

61. The Landholder No. X, Maryland Journal (Feb. 29, 1788), in 16 *Documentary History* 265.

62. Luther Martin: Address No. II, Maryland Journal (March 21, 1788), in 16 *Documentary History* 452, 452–453.

63. 1 Julius Goebel, Jr., *History of the Supreme Court of the United States: Antecedents and Beginnings to 1801* (New York: MacMillan Publishing Co., 1971) 236.

64. William P. Murphy, *The Triumph of Nationalism* (Chicago: Quadrangle Books, 1967) 220 ("Under the Committee version, the federal judges sitting in the states would also be empowered to enforce national supremacy instead of leaving it to the state judges").

65. Rakove, *Original Meanings* 174.

66. 2 Herbert J. Storing, "Introduction," *The Complete Anti-Federalist* (Chicago: University of Chicago Press, 1981) 3.

67. Letter from James Madison to Thomas Jefferson (Sept. 6, 1787), in 10 *Papers of James Madison* 163, 163–164. For a detailed discussion by Madison of his views on the new Constitution, see Letter from Madison to Jefferson (Oct. 24, 1787), in 10 *Papers of James Madison* 205–220.

68. Richard Henry Lee, "Proposed Amendments" (Sept. 27, 1787), in 1 *Documentary History* 337.

69. 33 *Journals of the Continental Congress* 549.

70. The Federalist No. 33 (Hamilton) (Jan. 2, 1788), in 15 *Documentary History* 216, 220.

71. Edmund Randolph, "A Letter of His Excellency Edmund Randolph, Esquire, on the Federal Constitution" (Oct. 10, 1787), in 15 *Documentary History* 117, 133–134.

72. 2 *Complete Anti-Federalist* 214.

73. Federal Farmer IV, "Letters to the Republican" (Oct. 12, 1787), in 14 *Documentary History* 42, 43.

74. A Federal Republican, "A Review of the Constitution" (Nov. 28, 1787), in 14 *Documentary History* 255, 269

75. Agrippa X, Massachusetts Gazette (Jan. 1, 1788), in 5 *Documentary History* 576.

76. The Impartial Examiner I, Virginia Independent Chronicles, (Feb. 20, 1787), in 8 *Documentary History* 387, 392.

77. Robert Whitehill, Debates of the Pennsylvania Convention (Dec. 8, 1787), in 2 *Documentary History* 526.

78. George Mason, Debates of the Virginia Convention (June 19, 1788), in 10 *Documentary History* 1402.

79. Mr. Bloodworth, Debate of the North Carolina Convention (July 29–30, 1788), in 4 Jonathan Elliot, ed., *The Debates in the Several State Conventions on the Adoption of the Federal Constitution* (Washington: 1836) 179.

80. Amos Singletary, Debates of the Massachusetts Convention (Jan. 29, 1788), in 6 *Documentary History* 1365.

81. An Old Whig VI, Philadelphia Independent Gazette (Nov. 24, 1787), in 14 *Documentary History* 215, 216.

82. Brutus I, New York Journal (Oct. 18, 1787), in 13 *Documentary History* 411, 415.

83. Patrick Henry, Debates of the Virginia Convention (June 7, 1788), in 9 *Documentary History* 1045–1046.

84. Elbridge Gerry, "Objections to Signing the National Constitution" (Nov. 3, 1787), in 13 *Documentary History* 546, 548.

85. Patrick Henry, Debates of the Virginia Convention (June 19, 1788), in 10 *Documentary History* 1394.

86. American Herald (Jan. 14, 1788), in 5 *Documentary History* 709, 710–711.

87. George Mason, "Objections to the Constitution" (Oct. 7, 1787), in 8 *Documentary History* 40, 43.

88. George Mason, Debates of the Virginia Convention (June 11, 1788), in 9 *Documentary History* 1158.

89. John Smilie, Debates of the Pennsylvania Convention (Nov. 28, 1787), in 2 *Documentary History* 386.

90. Centinel II, Philadelphia Freeman's Journal (Oct. 24, 1787), in 13 *Documentary History* 457, 460.

91. "Dissent of the Minority of the Pennsylvania Convention," Pennsylvania Packet (Dec. 18, 1787), in 15 *Documentary History* 7, 25.

92. "Amendments Proposed by William Paca in the Maryland Convention" (Apr. 29, 1788), in 17 *Documentary History* 240, 241.

93. George Mason, "Objections to the Constitution" (Oct. 7, 1787), in 8 *Documentary History* 40, 44–45.

94. Elbridge Gerry, "Objections to Signing the National Constitution" (Nov. 3, 1787), in 13 *Documentary History* 546–550.

95. Federal Farmer IV, "Letters to the Republican" (Oct. 12, 1787), in 14 *Documentary History* 42, 43.

96. William Findley, Debates of the Pennsylvania Convention (Dec. 7, 1787), in 2 *Documentary History* 523.

97. "Dissent of the Minority of the Pennsylvania Convention," in 15 *Documentary History* 29.

98. Cato VI, New York Journal (Dec. 13, 1787), in 14 *Documentary History* 428, 431–432.

99. An Old Whig III, Philadelphia Independent Gazetteer (Oct. 20, 1787), in 13 *Documentary History* 425, 426.

100. Robert Whitehill, Debates of the Pennsylvania Convention (Dec. 12, 1787), in 2 *Documentary History* 598.

101. Patrick Henry, Debates of the Virginia Convention (June 25, 1788), in 10 *Documentary History* 1536.

102. "The Society of Western Gentlemen Revise the Constitution," Virginia Independent Chronicle (Apr. 30 & May 7, 1788), in 9 *Documentary History* 769, 779.

103. Letter from Henry Knox to John Sullivan (Apr. 9, 1788), in 17 *Documentary History* 40, 41.

104. A Native of Virginia, "Observations upon the Proposed Plan of Federal Government" (Apr. 2, 1788), in 9 *Documentary History* 655, 692.

105. Thomas McKean, Debates of the Pennsylvania Convention (Dec. 10, 1787), in 2 *Documentary History* 539.

106. The Federalist No. 33 (Hamilton), in 15 *Documentary History* 220, 222.

107. A Freeholder, Virginia Independent Chronicle (Apr. 9, 1788), in 9 *Documentary History* 719, 725.

108. The Federalist No. 31 (Hamilton) (Jan. 1, 1788), in 15 *Documentary History* 211, 214.

109. The Federalist No. 33 (Hamilton), in 15 *Documentary History* 222–223.

110. The Federalist No. 44 (Madison) (Jan. 25, 1788), in 15 *Documentary History* 469, 473–474.

111. James Wilson, "Speech at a Public Meeting in Philadelphia" (Oct. 6, 1787), in 13 *Documentary History* 337, 339–340.

112. Marcus I, Norfolk & Portsmouth Journal (Feb. 20, 1788), in 16 *Documentary History* 161, 163–164; see also Thomas McKean, Debates of the Pennsylvania Convention (Dec. 10, 1787), in 2 *Documentary History* 546–547 ("What occasion for a bill of rights when only delegated powers are given? One possessed of 1000 acres, conveys 250. Is it necessary to reserve the 750?").

113. Cassius VI, Massachusetts Gazette (Dec. 25, 1787), in 5 *Documentary History* 511, 513.

114. A Countryman from Dutchess County IV (Dec. 15, 1787), in 6 *Complete Anti-Federalist* 57, 59.

115. "Dissent of the Minority of the Pennsylvania Convention," in 15 *Documentary History* 23.

116. The Federalist No. 64 (Jay) (Mar. 5, 1788), in 16 *Documentary History* 309, 313.

117. A Freeholder, Virginia Independent Chronicle (Apr. 9, 1788), in 9 *Documentary History* 719, 725.

118. James Madison, Debates of the Virginia Convention (June 19, 1788), in 10 *Documentary History* 1396.

119. Thomas McKean, Debates of the Pennsylvania Convention (Nov. 28, 1787), in 2 *Documentary History* 416.

120. James Madison, Debates of the Virginia Convention (June 18, 1788), in 10 *Documentary History* 1382 ("If [treaties] are to have *any* efficacy, they must be the law of the land: They are so in every country.").

121. Marcus III, Norfolk & Portsmouth Journal (Mar. 5, 1788), in 16 *Documentary History* 322.

122. James Madison, Debates of the Virginia Convention (June 19, 1788), in 10 *Documentary History* 1395.

123. George Nicholas, Debates of the Virginia Convention (June 19, 1788), in 10 *Documentary History* 1389.

124. James Wilson, Debates of the Pennsylvania Convention (Dec. 11, 1787), in 2 *Documentary History* 562.

125. For an overview of ratification by the states, see Michael Allen Gillespie & Michael Lienesch, "Introduction," in *Ratifying the Constitution* (Lawrence: University Press of Kansas, 1989) 1–26 and the essays therein on the ratification debates in each of the states. See also Patrick T. Conley & John P. Kaminski, *The Constitution and the States: The Role of the Original Thirteen in the Framing and Adoption of the Federal Constitution* (Madison: Madison House, 1988).

126. For the sources relied on in preparing these case histories, see the bibliographical essay at the end of this volume.

127. 4 *Secret Journals* 202.

128. 4 *Secret Journals* 242.

129. William C. Stinchcombe, "Ware v. Hylton Editorial Note," 3 *The Papers of John Marshall* (Chapel Hill: University of North Carolina Press, 1979) 4, 5.

130. David P. Currie, *The Constitution in the Supreme Court: The First Hundred Years 1789–1888* (Chicago: University of Chicago Press, 1985) 41.

131. For two recent collections of writings on *Marbury*, see Mark A. Graber & Michael Perhac, eds., *Marbury Versus Madison: Documents and Commentary* (Washington, D.C.: CQ Press, 2002) (collection of essays on *Marbury*) and "Judicial Review: Blessing or Curse? Or Both? A Symposium in Commemoration of the Bicentennial of *Marbury v. Madison*," 38 *Wake Forest L. Rev.* (2003) 313–838. Further citations to the voluminous writings on *Marbury* can be found in the these two sources.

132. Charles F. Hobson, "Marbury v. Madison Editorial Note," 6 *Papers of John Marshall* 160; see also Jethro K. Lieberman, *Milestones! 200 Years of American Law: Milestones in Our Legal History* (St. Paul: West Publishing Co., 1976) vii (reporting results of 1974 American Bar Association poll in which *Marbury* was the leading vote-getter as a "milestone" Supreme Court decision).

133. Sanford Levinson, "Why I Do Not Teach *Marbury* (Except to Eastern Europeans) and Why You Shouldn't Either," 38 *Wake Forest L. Rev.* (2003) 553, 574; see also Michael J. Klarman, "How Great Were the 'Great' Marshall Court Decisions?," 87 *Va. L. Rev.* (2001) 1111, 1113 ("*Marbury*, it turns out, is a great deal less important than is commonly supposed") and Rakove, 49 *Stan. L. Rev.* 1039 ("If we did not already know that *Marbury* was so momentous a case, we would be hard pressed to explain why it is so celebrated.").

134. Currie, *The Constitution in the Supreme Court* 66 n.14. Another question, of course, is whether Marshall even should have participated in deciding the case, since it was his failure as Secretary of State to deliver the commissions that gave rise to the dispute in the first place.

135. For a detailed analysis of the opinion, see William W. Van Alstyne, "A Critical Guide to Marbury v. Madison," 1969 *Duke L.J.* 1.

136. L.A. Powe, Jr., "The Politics of American Judicial Review: Reflections on the Marshall, Warren, and Rehnquist Courts," 38 *Wake Forest L. Rev.* (2003) 697, 698.

137. Hobson, 6 *Papers of John Marshall* 163. For a pair of articles that analyze the decision from the perspective of political science and game theory, see Robert Lowry Clinton, "Game Theory, Legal History, and the Origins of Judicial Review: A Revisionist Analysis of *Marbury v. Madison*," 38 *Am. J. Pol. Sci.* (1994) 285–302 and Lee Epstein and Jack Knight, "The Strategic John Marshall (and Thomas Jefferson)," in Graber & Perhac, eds., *Marbury Versus Madison: Documents and Commentary* 41–59.

138. An Act to Incorporate the Subscribers to the Bank of the United States, 3 Stat. 266 (1816).

139. Quoted in Walter Buckingham Smith, *Economic Aspects of the Second Bank of the United States* (Cambridge: Harvard University Press, 1953) 58.

140. Ralph C.H. Catterall, *The Second Bank of the United States* (Chicago: University of Chicago Press, 1903) 78–79.

141. 1 Charles Warren, *The Supreme Court in United States History* (Boston: Little, Brown & Co., 1926) 505–506.

142. *Supreme Court Historical Society 1990 Yearbook* (remarks of retired Chief Justice Warren E. Burger, on the Bicentennial of the Supreme Court, Jan. 16, 1990), at <www .supremecourthistory.org/04_library/subs_volumes/04_c12_e.html>.

143. For a detailed history of *Osborn*, see Patricia L. Franz, "Ohio v. The Bank: An Historical Examination of *Osborn v. The Bank of the United States*," 23 *J. Sup. Ct. Hist.* (1999) 112.

144. For an argument that the Bank of the United States was not sufficiently public to be entitled to immunity from state tax, see Harold J. Plous & Gordon E. Baker, "*McCulloch v. Maryland*: Right Principles, Wrong Case," 9 *Stan. L. Rev.* (1957) 710.

145. For more background on the case, see Maurice G. Baxter, *The Steamboat Monopoly: Gibbons v. Ogden, 1824* (New York: Alfred A. Knopf, 1972) 3–36.

146. Kent had previously granted an injunction enforcing the Livingston Group's monopoly rights in a different case. See Livingston v. Van Ingen (N.Y. 1812). For more on Kent's role in these cases, see Thomas P. Campbell, Jr., "Chancellor Kent, Chief Justice Marshall and the Steamboat Cases," 25 *Syracuse L. Rev.* (1974) 497.

147. Letter from William Wirt to Judge Carr (Feb. 1, 1824), in 2 John P. Kennedy, *Memoirs of the Life of William Wirt* (Philadelphia: Blanchard and Lea, 1856) 143, 144,

quoted in Charles F. Hobson, "Gibbons v. Ogden Editorial Note," 10 *Papers of John Marshall* 7, 10.

148. 3–4 G. Edward White, *The Marshall Court and Cultural Change, 1815–35* (New York: Macmillan Publishing Co., 1988) 573 n.340.

149. 4 Albert J. Beveridge, *The Life of John Marshall* (Boston: Houghton Mifflin Co., 1919) 445.

150. 3–4 White, *The Marshall Court and Cultural Change* 580.

151. Felix Frankfurter, *The Commerce Clause Under Marshall, Taney and Waite* (Chapel Hill: University of North Carolina Press, 1937) 20.

152. For a more comprehensive survey, see Robert B. McKay, "'With All Deliberate Speed': A Study of School Desegregation," 31 *N.Y.U. L. Rev.* (1956) 991, 1017–1039.

153. McKay, 31 *N.Y.U. L. Rev.* 1038.

154. See, for example, Richard E. Ellis, *The Union at Risk: Jacksonian Democracy, States' Rights, and the Nullification Crisis* (New York: Oxford University Press, 1987) and William W. Freehling, *Prelude to Civil War: The Nullification Controversy in South Carolina, 1816–1836* (New York: Harper & Row, 1965).

155. South Carolina Ordinance of Nullification, 1 S.C. Stat. 329 (Nov. 24, 1832), in 1 Henry Steele Commager & Milton Cantor, eds., *Documents of American History,* 10th ed. (Englewood Cliffs, N.J.: Prentice Hall, 1988) 261, 261–262.

156. For a selection of Calhoun's writings, see Clyde N. Wilson, ed., *The Essential Calhoun* (New Brunswick: Transaction Publishers, 2000).

157. Margaret L. Coit, *John C. Calhoun* (Boston: Houghton Mifflin Co., 1950) 421.

158. See John Niven, *John C. Calhoun and the Price of Union* (Baton Rouge: Louisiana State University Press, 1988) 188; Freehling, *Prelude to Civil War* 159–173.

159. Kentucky Resolutions (Nov. 16, 1798), in 1 *Documents of American History* 178, 178–179.

160. Virginia Resolutions (Dec. 21, 1798), in 17 *Papers of James Madison* 188, 189.

161. See Kevin Raeder Gutzman, "From Interposition to Nullification: Peripheries and Center in the Thought of James Madison," 36 *Essays in History* (1994) 89, 103–104.

162. Kentucky Resolutions of 1799 (Feb. 22, 1799), in 1 *Documents of American History* 183, 184.

163. James Madison, "The Report of 1800," in 17 *Papers of James Madison* 307, 350.

164. McKay, 31 *N.Y.U. L. Rev.* 1038.

165. Andrew Jackson, "Proclamation" (Dec. 10, 1832), in 2 James D. Richardson, ed., *A Compilation of the Messages and Papers of the Presidents, 1789–1902* (Washington, D.C.: Bureau of National Literature and Art, 1903) 640.

166. James Madison, "Notes on Nullification," in 9 Gaillard Hunt, ed., *The Writings of James Madison* (New York: G.P. Putnam's Sons, 1910) 573, 575, 607.

167. 1 Joseph Story, *Commentaries on the Constitution of the United States*, 2d ed. (Boston: Charles C. Little & James Brown, 1851) 237.

168. Register of Debates, 21st Cong., 1st Sess. 58 (Jan. 25, 1830), quoted in 3–4 White, *The Marshall Court and Cultural Change* 492.

169. Daniel Webster, "Second Reply to Hayne" (Jan. 26–27, 1830), in 1 Charles M. Wiltse, ed., *The Papers of Daniel Webster: Speeches and Formal Writings, 1800–1833* (Hanover, N.H.: University Press of New England, 1986) 285, 330 & 348.

170. Ellis, *The Union at Risk* 170–177.

171. See, for example, 1 William W. Freehling, *The Road to Disunion: Secessionists at Bay 1776–1854* (New York: Oxford University Press, 1990); Harry V. Jaffa, *A New Birth of Freedom: Abraham Lincoln and the Coming of the Civil War* (Lanham, MD: Rowman & Littlefield Publishers, 2000). For a constitutional history of the period, see Bernard Schwartz, *From Confederation to Nation: The American Constitution, 1835–1877* (Baltimore: Johns Hopkins University Press, 1973).

172. Robert J. Kaczorowski, "Revolutionary Constitutionalism in the Era of the Civil War and Reconstruction," 61 *N.Y.U. L. Rev.* (1986) 863, 873.

173. Declaration of Independence, para. 2 ("whenever any Form of Government becomes destructive of these Ends, it is the Right of the People to alter or to abolish it, and to institute new Government").

174. South Carolina Declaration of Causes of Secession (Dec. 24, 1860), in 1 *Documents of American History* 372, 373.

175. William W. Freehling, "The Slaveholders' (Amazing) Theory of Secession and the Renewal of U.S. Constitutional History" (Feb. 20, 2003) (Weil Centennial Lecture, University of Texas School of Law, Austin, TX), at <www.utexas.edu/law/depts/media/Reels/Louisiana/louisiana1.ram>.

176. See, for example, Robert J. Kaczorowski, "The Tragic Irony of American Federalism: National Sovereignty Versus State Sovereignty in Slavery and in Freedom," 45 *U. Kan. L. Rev.* (1997) 1015, 1039. The Supreme Court rejected Wisconsin's attempt at nullification in Ableman v. Booth (1859).

177. J.G. Randall, *Constitutional Problems Under Lincoln*, rev. ed. (Urbana: University of Illinois Press, 1951) 14.

178. H. Newcomb Morse, "The Foundations and Meaning of Secession," 15 *Stetson L. Rev.* (1986) 419, 425 n.35.

179. Jefferson Davis, "Message to Congress" (April 29, 1861), in 1 James D. Richardson, ed., *The Messages and Papers of Jefferson Davis and the Confederacy* (New York: Chelsea House, 1966) 63, 69.

180. William P. Kreml, *The Constitutional Divide: The Private and Public Sectors in American Law* (Columbia, S.C.: University of South Carolina Press, 1997) 72.

181. Constitution of the Confederate States of America, preamble, reprinted in Marshall L. De Rosa, *The Confederate Constitution of 1861: An Inquiry into American Constitutionalism* (Columbia: University of Missouri Press, 1991) 135.

182. Confederate Constitution, art. VI(3) ("This Constitution, and the laws of the Confederate States made in pursuance thereof, and all treaties made, or which shall be made, under the authority of the Confederate States, shall be the supreme law of the land; and the Judges in every State shall be bound thereby, anything in the Constitution or laws of any State to the contrary notwithstanding.").

183. See Cobb v. Stallings (Ga. 1864) ("As between these conflicting laws, (if they be in conflict,) the law of the Confederate States is Supreme, and the law of Georgia must yield. So says the Constitution, and we cannot say otherwise"); State ex rel. Dawson (Ala. 1864) (Phelan, J.) ("The constitution of the Confederate States, and laws made in pursuance thereof, are the supreme law of the land; and if the laws of the State, and those of the Confederate States aforesaid, come in conflict, the former, as the paramount law, must prevail"); and Simmons v. Miller (Miss.1864) ("[T]he power of a State, in such cases, is

subordinate to that of the Confederate States Government; and, whenever it is exercised by the latter, it excludes the power of the State over the subject-matter; and if it has been exercised by the State before its exercise by the Confederate States, it ceases to the State, and the power of the Confederate States becomes paramount over the subject. This results necessarily from the constitution, and the laws made by the Confederate States in pursuance of it, being the supreme law.")

184. DeRosa, *The Confederate Constitution of 1861*, at 113–114.

185. Abraham Lincoln, "First Inaugural Address" (Final Text) (Mar. 4, 1861), reprinted in 4 Roy P. Basler ed., *Collected Works of Abraham Lincoln* (New Brunswick, N.J.: Rutgers University Press, 1953) 262, 264–265.

186. Abraham Lincoln, "Message to Congress in Special Session" (July 4, 1861), reprinted in 4 *Collected Works of Abraham Lincoln* 432–441.

187. Cong. Globe, 36th Cong., 2d sess. (Jan. 12, 1861) 341.

188. Sumner's Resolutions on the Theory of Secession and Reconstruction (Feb. 11, 1862), in 1 *Documents of American History* 406, 406.

189. The Crittenden-Johnson Resolutions on the Objects of the War (July 1861), in 1 *Documents of American History* 395, 395–396.

190. Currie, *The Constitution in the Supreme Court, 1789–1888*, at 312 (stating that the Court's reasoning in Texas v. White "hardly seems an adequate treatment of an issue on which reasonable people had differed to the point of civil war").

191. Cass R. Sunstein, "Constitutionalism and Secession," 58 *U. Chi. L. Rev.* (1991) 633, 633. But see Morse, 15 *Stetson L. Rev.* 436 ("The Southern States, in all likelihood, were exercising a perfectly legitimate right in seceding from the Union"). For a more nuanced view, see Sanford Levinson, "Freedom: Politics: They Whisper: Reflections on Flags, Monuments, State Holidays, and the Construction of Social Meaning in a Multicultural Society," 70 *Chi.-Kent L. Rev.* (1995) 1079, 1117 ("My own view . . . emphasizes at once the plausibility of secession as a constitutional argument and the betrayal of any claim to support for secession in the actual case because of the reality of chattel slavery").

Professor Akhil Reed Amar has written extensively on sovereignty and secession. See Akhil Reed Amar, "The Consent of the Governed: Constitutional Amendment Outside Article V," 94 *Colum. L. Rev.* (1994) 457, 507 (rejecting state's unilateral right to secede, and finding Supremacy Clause "logically inconsistent with the sovereignty of the people of each state"); Akhil Reed Amar, "Some New World Lessons for the Old World," 58 *U. Chi. L. Rev.* (1991) 483, 502 ("Only a national majority, not a majority of a single state or region, can lawfully dissolve the American Union"); and Akhil Reed Amar, "Of Sovereignty and Federalism," 96 *Yale L.J.* (1987) 1425, 1462 (arguing that ratification of the Constitution "prospectively abolished [the pre-existing sovereign right of any non-ratifying state to secede from its sister states] for each state People who joined the Union, thereby melting themselves into the larger common sovereignty of the People of America").

192. See also Brown v. Board of Education (1955) (*Brown II*) (requiring desegregation to proceed "with all deliberate speed").

193. McKay, 31 *N.Y.U. L. Rev.* 1017.

194. See also James Jackson Kilpatrick, *The Sovereign States: Notes of a Citizen of Virginia* (Chicago: Henry Regnery Co., 1957) 305 ("The States have submitted too long to Federal usurpations. At their grave peril, they can submit no longer. Through every device of interposition they can bring to bear—political, legislative, judicial—once more they

must invoke their sovereign powers to insist that Federal encroachments be restrained."). For further discussion, see Joseph J. Thorndike, "'The Sometimes Sordid Level of Race and Segregation': James J. Kilpatrick and the Virginia Campaign against *Brown*," in Matthew D. Lassiter & Andrew B. Lewis, *The Moderates' Dilemma: Massive Resistance to School Desegregation in Virginia* (Charlottesville: University Press of Virginia, 1998) 51–71.

195. Quoted in Lucas A. Powe, Jr., *The Warren Court and American Politics* (Cambridge: Harvard University Press, 2000) 59–60.

196. Bill McKelway, "Editorial Pages Often Inspire Heated Emotion," *Richmond Times-Dispatch* (Oct. 15, 2000), at <www.timesdispatch.com/150th/sqstar4.shtml>.

197. See Davison M. Douglas, "The Rhetoric of Moderation: Desegregating the South During the Decade After *Brown*," 89 *Nw. U. L. Rev.* (1994) 92, 93, & n.5 (listing interposition resolutions).

198. S.J. Res. 3, 1956 Va. Acts 1213; see *The Doctrine of Interposition: Its History and Application*, Va. Sen. Doc. 21 (1957).

199. McKay, 31 *N.Y.U. L. Rev.* 1038 ("to the extent they claim such unqualified right of disobedience, they should properly be described as modern examples of the sterner doctrine of nullification").

200. Mark V. Tushnet, *Making Civil Rights Law: Thurgood Marshall and the Supreme Court, 1936–1961* (New York: Oxford University Press, 1994) 240.

201. John C. Jeffries, Jr., *Justice Lewis F. Powell, Jr.* (New York: Charles Scribner's Sons, 1994) 146–148.

202. Tushnet, *Making Civil Rights Law* 241.

203. United States v. Barnett (5th Cir. 1965) (en banc) (Wisdom, J., dissenting). Wisdom was dissenting from the court of appeals' decision terminating criminal contempt proceedings against Mississippi Governor Ross Barnett, for his actions in trying to keep James Meredith out of the University of Mississippi. The majority found changed circumstances (in the form of substantial compliance with prior court orders) justified ending the proceedings. Its decision was by no means an endorsement of interposition.

204. H. Jefferson Powell, *A Community Built on Words: The Constitution in History and Politics* (Chicago: University of Chicago Press, 2002) 218–219 n.48.

205. Powe, *The Warren Court and American Politics* 157–162.

206. Powe, *The Warren Court and American Politics* 160.

Appendix to Part I

May 1787	**29**	Virginia Plan proposed containing congressional negative of state laws
	31	Negative unanimously extended to state laws contrary to treaties
		Committee of the Whole approves congressional negative
June 1787	**8**	Committee of the Whole rejects broader congressional negative
	13	Committee of the Whole reports Virginia Plan including congressional negative to Convention
	15	New Jersey Plan proposed containing early version of Supremacy Clause
	19	Committee of the Whole rejects New Jersey Plan
July 1787	**17**	Convention rejects congressional negative
		Luther Martin introduces revised version of the Supremacy Clause; Convention approves unanimously
Aug. 1787	**6**	Committee of Detail reports draft Constitution including revised Supremacy Clause to Convention
	23	Convention approves amendment to Supremacy Clause making Constitution supreme law
		Pinckney and Madison effort to revive congressional negative rejected
	25	Convention approves amendment clarifying treaty language in Supremacy Clause
Sept. 1787	**12**	Committee of Style reports final changes to Supremacy Clause text
	15	Convention gives final approval to Constitution

Figure 1. Supremacy Clause Timeline

June 15, 1787: As introduced by William Paterson as Resolution 6 of the New Jersey Plan

Resd. that all Acts of the U. States in Congs. made by virtue & in pursuance of the powers hereby & by the articles of confederation vested in them, and all Treaties made & ratified under the authority of the U. States shall be the supreme law of the respective States so far forth as those Acts or Treaties shall relate to the said States or their Citizens, and that the Judiciary of the several States shall be bound thereby in their decisions, any thing in the respective laws of the Individual States to the contrary notwithstanding. (1 Farrand 245)

July 17, 1787: As introduced by Luther Martin and approved by the Convention

Resolved that the legislative acts of the United States made by virtue and in pursuance of the articles of Union and all Treaties made and ratified under the authority of the United States shall be the supreme law of the respective States as far as those acts or Treaties shall relate to the said States, or their Citizens and Inhabitants—and that the Judiciaries of the several States shall be bound thereby in their decisions, any thing in the respective laws of the individual States to the contrary notwithstanding. (2 Farrand 22)

August 6, 1787: As reported by the Committee of Detail

The Acts of the Legislature of the United States made in pursuance of this Constitution, and all treaties made under the authority of the United States shall be the supreme law of the several States, and of their citizens and inhabitants; and the judges in the several States shall be bound thereby in their decisions; anything in the Constitutions or laws of the several States to the contrary notwithstanding. (2 Farrand 183)

August 23, 1787: As amended by the Convention (with amendment indicated in bold)

This Constitution & the laws of the U.S. made in pursuance thereof, and all treaties made under the authority of the United States shall be the supreme law of the several States, and of their citizens and inhabitants; and the judges in the several States shall be bound thereby in their decisions; anything in the Constitutions or laws of the several States to the contrary notwithstanding. (2 Farrand 389)

Figure 2. Evolution of the Supremacy Clause *(continues)*

August 25, 1787: As amended by the Convention (with amendment indicated in bold)

This Constitution & the laws of the U.S. made in pursuance thereof, and all treaties made **or which shall be made** under the authority of the United States shall be the supreme law of the several States, and of their citizens and inhabitants; and the judges in the several States shall be bound thereby in their decisions; anything in the Constitutions or laws of the several States to the contrary notwithstanding. (2 Farrand 417)

September 15, 1787: Final version as approved by the Convention

This Constitution, and the Laws of the United States which shall be made in Pursuance thereof; and all Treaties made, or which shall be made, under the Authority of the United States, shall be the supreme Law of the Land; and the Judges in every State shall be bound thereby, any Thing in the Constitution or Laws of any State to the Contrary notwithstanding. (2 Farrand 663)

Figure 2. Evolution of the Supremacy Clause

PART II

Analysis

The Supremacy Clause and the Courts

INTRODUCTION

On the evening of July 31, 2001, after the Alabama State Judicial Building was closed for the day, Chief Justice Roy S. Moore of the Alabama Supreme Court had installed in the rotunda of the building a two-and-a half ton granite monument to the Ten Commandments.[1] On the top of the cube-shaped monument were two stone tablets engraved with the text of the Ten Commandments (from the King James Bible), depicted so as to "call to mind an open Bible resting on a lectern."[2] On the sides of the monument were quotations from nonreligious sources. One quotation on each side was larger than the others. Those were from the Declaration of Independence ("Laws of nature and of nature's God"), the national motto ("In God We Trust"), the Judiciary Act of 1789 ("So help me God"), and the Pledge of Allegiance ("One nation under God, indivisible, with liberty and justice for all"). The monument was paid for wholly with private funds, not taxpayer dollars.

The next day, at the unveiling ceremony for the monument, Moore explained that he sought "to restore the moral foundation of law" by "recogniz[ing] the source of that morality": "that God upon whom this nation and our laws were founded." The quotations around the base of the monument, according to Moore, provided "every ounce of support for the acknowledgment of the sovereignty of that God and those absolute standards upon which our laws are based." "[N]o documents surround[] the Ten Commandments," Moore said, "because they stand alone as an acknowledgment of that God that's contained in our pledge, contained in our motto, and contained in our oath." Coral Ridge Ministries, an evangelical Christian media group, filmed both the installation and the unveiling of the monument, and sold the video to raise funds for its own uses and to pay for Moore's legal defense in the lawsuit that soon followed.

This was not the first time Moore had been involved in a controversy over displaying the Ten Commandments in a public building. While a state trial judge, Moore posted in his courtroom a wooden plaque listing the Ten Commandments and began court sessions by having a minister lead a Christian prayer. Lawsuits challenging those practices were dismissed on procedural grounds without resolving whether the practices were lawful (Alabama Freethought Ass'n v. Moore, N.D. Ala. 1995; State ex rel. James v. ACLU, Ala. 1998). Moore then ran for Chief Justice of the Alabama Supreme Court as the "Ten Commandments Judge." As described by the federal district court, "[V]irtually everything put out by the campaign referenced the Ten Commandments."

Three Alabama attorneys filed suit against Moore challenging the placement of the monument in the judicial building. The district court found that Moore's actions constituted an unconstitutional establishment of religion and gave him 30 days in which to remove the monument (Glassroth v. Moore, M.D. Ala. 2002). When Moore failed to do so, the district court entered an order enjoining him from failing to remove the monument from the building's public spaces, which the court then stayed pending appeal. (The order permitted Moore to move the monument to his office, which the district court suggested would be lawful.)

A press account of the district court hearing that culminated in entry of the injunction describes a polite but pointed confrontation between Moore and the district judge.[3] During the hearing, Moore contended that the Supremacy Clause required state judges to follow the U.S. Constitution, but not the rulings of federal judges: "I'm bound to the Constitution, not this federal court," Moore argued. The district judge rejected the view, asserting that under Moore's interpretation, a federal district judge might not have to follow U.S. Supreme Court decisions. He asked Moore's lawyers: "What if the Supreme Court of the United States makes a decision I disagree with? . . . Can I just ignore the decision of the United States Supreme Court based on Article VI?" The district judge also reminded Moore of prior cases in which federal judges needed to order Alabama state officials (such as former Alabama Governor George Wallace) to abide by desegregation rulings: "Are you saying that none of those orders was valid under Article VI?" But when plaintiffs' counsel argued that Moore was undermining the rule of law in the United States, the district judge instead was willing to "assume he'll comply with the law."

The Eleventh Circuit affirmed the district court's judgment on appeal (Glassroth v. Moore, 11th Cir. 2003). The court of appeals held that the placement of the monument violated the Establishment Clause, analyzing the issue at length. At the end of the opinion, the court turned to Moore's alternative argument that as chief judicial officer of the State of Alabama, he took an oath to uphold the federal and state constitutions "as he best understands them, not as understood by others." According to Moore, "courts are bound by the Constitution, not by another court's interpretation of that instrument," and thus he is not "answerable to a higher judicial authority in the performance of his duties as administrative head of the state judicial system." In other words, the federal courts cannot tell him what to do in this case; he is entitled to follow his own interpretation of the federal and state constitutions.

The court characterized Moore's argument as "target[ing] a core principle of the rule of law in this country," and described his position as championing a regime in which "each high government official can decide whether the Constitution requires or permits a federal court order and can act accordingly." Rejecting the argument, the court stated that it found "nothing in law or logic to support his theory" and (as had the district court) likened Moore's position to that of southern governors resisting federal court desegregation orders. "Any notion of high government officials being above the law did not save those governors from having to obey federal court orders," the court stated, "and it will not save this chief justice from having to comply with the court order in this case." Among other authorities, the court of appeals cited the Supremacy Clause and the Supreme Court's decisions in Cooper v. Aaron (1958) and Sterling v. Constantin (1932), quoting *Sterling* for the proposition that "if a state Governor could nullify a federal court order 'that the fiat of a state Governor, and not the Constitution of the United States, would be the supreme law of the land; that the restrictions of the Federal Constitution upon the exercise of state power would be but impotent phrases.'" The court concluded:

> The rule of law does require that every person obey judicial orders when all available means of appealing them have been exhausted. The chief justice of a state supreme court, of all people, should be expected to abide by that principle. We do expect that if he is unable to have the district court's order overturned through the usual appellate processes, when the time comes Chief Justice Moore will obey that order. If necessary, the court order will be enforced. The rule of law will prevail.

The district court's stay expired when the Eleventh Circuit affirmed its judgment, and Moore failed timely to seek a further stay from the Eleventh Circuit. As a result, the district court issued its judgment and threatened substantial fines if Moore did not remove the monument by August 20, 2003 (Glassroth v. Moore, M.D. Ala. 2003). Moore flatly refused to comply with the district court's order. Moore stated: "I have no intention of removing the monument of the Ten Commandments and the moral foundation of law. To do so would, in effect, result in the disestablishment of our systems of justice in this state. This I cannot and will not do."[4] Moore then sought emergency relief from the U.S. Supreme Court, arguing that he should be permitted to "establish justice by acknowledging the guidance and favor of Almighty God, placed upon him by his oath of office and the Constitution of Alabama."[5] The Court denied his request.

Even after the district court's deadline passed, Moore remained adamant that the monument would stay. He was supported by five hundred protesters from around the country, who gathered outside the Judicial Building. Twenty-two were arrested after they refused to leave the area around the monument itself.[6] But on August 21, the day after the deadline, Moore's colleagues on the Alabama Supreme Court unanimously overruled him and ordered the building manager "to take all steps necessary to comply with the injunction as soon as practicable."[7] After quoting the Supremacy Clause, they explained that "[t]he justices of this Court are bound by solemn oath to follow the law, whether they agree with it or not." On August 22, the Judicial Inquiry Commission of the State of Alabama brought a complaint against Moore, alleging that he violated judicial ethics rules by willfully failing to comply with a court order.[8] Moore was suspended pending resolution of the complaint (and ultimately removed from office). Finally, on August 27, the monument was taken off public display and moved to a nonpublic area of the building.[9]

The question whether the display of the Ten Commandments in a state court building violates the Establishment Clause of the United States Constitution is an interesting one, but not the subject here. Instead, the important question for present purposes is who makes that determination (and, more specifically, what the Supremacy Clause has to say about it). Could Chief Justice Moore justify his action as permitted by the Alabama Constitution? To what extent could Moore rely on his own interpretation of the Establishment Clause as a ground for disregarding a court order? This part considers possible answers to those questions in the course of a more general discussion of the relationship between the Supremacy Clause and the courts.

SUPREMACY AND JUDICIAL REVIEW

The extent to which the United States Constitution establishes the doctrine of judicial review—that is, permits courts to invalidate statutes as contrary to the Constitution—is a matter of longstanding and ongoing dispute. A full analysis of the issue is beyond the scope of this volume.[10] Instead, this section considers only one part of the debate: What does the Supremacy Clause suggest about the availability of judicial review under the U.S. Constitution? As noted in Part I, the Supreme Court in Marbury v. Madison (1803) relied on the Supremacy Clause briefly in recognizing the power of the Supreme Court to hold a federal statute unconstitutional. This section expands on that discussion, first considering judicial review of state laws and then judicial review of federal laws.

Judicial Review of State Laws

The plain text of the Supremacy Clause addresses judicial review of state laws, albeit in a somewhat roundabout way. The so-called State Judges Clause is the final part of the Supremacy Clause, and provides that the "Judges in every State shall be bound [by the U.S. Constitution, federal statutes, and treaties], any Thing in the Constitution or Laws of any State to the Contrary notwithstanding." Commentators agree that this language gives state court judges the power to invalidate state statutes as contrary to federal law. As Professor Larry Kramer explains, this language "'bound' state judges to give federal law priority," "remov[ing] all doubts" about whether state judges had the power of judicial review over state law.[11] Thus, through the Supremacy Clause, "the [Constitutional] Convention impressed state judges into national service, obliging them not only to subordinate their own state law obligations to federal ones, but also actively to police state law and void any (even the most fundamental) if it was inconsistent with any (even the least important) federal law."[12]

The State Judges Clause does not, however, address whether *federal* judges have the power of judicial review over state laws that conflict with federal law. Although some have argued that the phrase "Judges in every State" includes federal court judges and not just state court judges,[13] that does not solve the problem: The Justices of the U.S. Supreme Court are not located in a state but in the District of Columbia, and still would not be covered by the clause.[14] Moreover, such a reading is unlikely given that the clause goes on to reference state laws and state constitutions. Indeed, one might argue that the negative implication of the State Judges Clause is that federal judges lack the power of judicial review. By expressly providing that state judges have the power (and duty) to invalidate state laws that conflict with federal law, arguably the Framers implied that federal courts have no such power.

Yet even critics of judicial review with respect to federal laws generally agree that federal courts as well as state courts have the power to hold state laws unconstitutional.[15] The basis for such a conclusion may be a matter of necessity. As Justice Oliver Wendell Holmes wrote: "I do not think the United States would come to an end if we lost our power to declare an Act of Congress void. I do think the Union would be imperiled if we could not make that declaration as to the laws of the several States."[16] Apparently, the source of that power is not the text of the Supremacy Clause.[17] Nonetheless, it is important to understand why the Framers found it necessary specifically to address state court judges and not federal judges in the State Judges Clause.

The answer, according to Professor Henry Hart, is that the State Judges Clause deals with "the special problem, peculiar to the state judges, of conflict between the commands of their own government and those of a different government."[18] Under governing choice-of-law principles, judges had discretion whether to apply the law of a foreign country. Foreign law applied only if recognized under principles of comity, not of its own force. State court judges who viewed federal law as foreign law might have declined to follow the federal law provisions. The Supremacy Clause overcame this potential problem by making federal law binding on state court judges. Federal law is not foreign law; it is the "supreme Law of the Land" that state judges are bound to follow. For the same reason, there was no need for the State Judges Clause to include federal judges, because "[u]nlike the state courts, federal courts could not possibly have deemed federal law to be the law of a foreign sovereign."[19]

Therefore, to the extent Chief Justice Moore of the Alabama Supreme Court argued that placing the Ten Commandments in a state judicial building is proper under or required by the Alabama Constitution, his argument is flatly contrary to the Supremacy Clause, and a federal court has the power so to hold.[20] But Moore's argument went further: He also took the position that he is not bound by a federal court's interpretation of the U.S. Constitution. As a judicial officer of the State of Alabama, he takes an oath to apply faithfully the Constitution and laws of the United States. Moore's view is that, as such, he must follow his own interpretation, and not a federal court's interpretation, of the U.S. Constitution.

Certainly government officials in addition to federal judges are bound to follow the United States Constitution in carrying out their duties.[21] Moreover, even the Supreme Court recognizes that some cases present issues that are more appropriately decided by other branches of the federal government, and thus are "non-justiciable."[22] But Moore's argument that he can disregard the order of a federal court in a case in which he is a party has been roundly and rightly criticized.[23] The rule of law in this country depends on individuals abiding by court orders directed at them, whether they agree with the orders or not.[24] As Chief Justice Marshall wrote in *Marbury*, "[t]he government of the United States has been emphatically termed a government of laws, and not of men."

Moreover, in Cooper v. Aaron (1958), the Supreme Court went further and asserted that its decisions are the supreme law of the land and that the Court has the final say in interpreting the Constitution (what has been called the doctrine of "judicial supremacy," as distinct from the narrower doctrine of judicial review). According to the *Cooper* Court, Marbury v. Madison "declared the basic principle that the federal judiciary is supreme in the exposition of the law of the Constitution," and thus, the Supreme Court's interpretation of the Constitution "is the supreme law of the land, and Art. VI of the Constitution makes it of binding effect on the States 'any Thing in the Constitution or Laws of any State to the Contrary notwithstanding.'" *Cooper*, of course, was the Court's response to defiance of its desegregation rulings, and might be understood "as asserting only the supremacy of *federal* officers' interpretation of the law over *state* officers' interpretations," instead of judicial supremacy over the other branches of the federal government.[25] But, regardless, under *Cooper*, Chief Justice Moore's defiance of a federal court order—which both the district court and the court of appeals compared to the defiance by southern governors of federal court desegregation orders—is indefensible.

Judicial Review of Federal Laws

To what extent does the Supremacy Clause support judicial review of federal law, rather than state law? The power of judicial review of federal law has, of course, been settled since *Marbury*, but it remains subject to debate in academic circles (and occasionally the political arena). A number of commentators have echoed Chief Justice Marshall's argument in *Marbury* that the language in the Supremacy Clause establishes (or at least supports) judicial review of federal law.[26] Professor Bradford Clark, for example, contends that the Supremacy Clause "designates as 'the supreme Law of the Land' only those 'Laws of the United States . . . made in Pursuance' of the Constitution. If a federal statute satisfies this condition, courts must apply the statute notwithstanding contrary state law." But "[i]f the federal statute fails this condition," Professor Clark argues, "it does not qualify as 'the supreme Law of the Land' and courts remain free to apply state law. Thus, in order to apply the Supremacy Clause, courts must necessarily consider and resolve challenges to the constitutionality of federal statutes."[27]

Other commentators, however, reject the contention.[28] Some argue that to be made "in Pursuance" of the Constitution, a law merely must be enacted pursuant to proper constitutional procedures, such as being passed by both houses of Congress and signed by the President.[29] On this view, once a court determines that the proper procedures have been complied with, the federal statute becomes part of the "supreme Law of the Land" and must be enforced by the courts. Others contrast the language providing that treaties "made, or which shall be made, under the Authority of the United States" also are supreme law. The qualifying language with respect to treaties, Professor David Currie contends, addresses *when* the treaties were made; arguably the "in Pursuance" of language should be construed the same way.[30] Still others cite back to the State Judges Clause and note the absence of any express provision authorizing judicial review of federal laws (as opposed to state laws).[31] Arguably, the authorization in the State Judges Clause of judicial review of state law gives rise to a negative inference that courts have no such authority with respect to federal law.

Finally, a handful of commentators offers a more fundamental objection: They argue that while the Supremacy Clause makes the Constitution the supreme law, the Framers' understanding of the Constitution as "law" differed from ours. According to Professor Larry Kramer: "Their Constitution was *not* ordinary law, *not* peculiarly the stuff of courts and judges. It was . . . a special form of popular law, law made by the people to bind their governors, and so subject to rules and considerations that made it qualitatively different from (and not just superior to) statutory or common law."[32] As a "political-legal" document,[33] the Constitution (under this view) was binding on everyone, but could not be enforced in court—presenting obvious difficulties for the doctrine of judicial review.

The responses to these arguments are well summarized in a recent law review article by Professors Saikrishna Prakash and John Yoo in the *University of Chicago Law Review*.[34] First, as for the argument that "in Pursuance" of the Constitution means only following proper procedures in enacting a law, they contend that (1) the plain meaning of the phrase "calls to mind the entire Constitution rather than just the requirements of Article I, section 7"; (2) it would be "extremely odd" for unconstitutional federal statutes to nonetheless be the "supreme Law of the Land"; and (3) some degree of judicial review would follow even under the narrow interpretation as courts would have to review compliance with required procedures. Second, the argument based on the comparison to treaties is not persuasive (according to Professor Clark) because of the drafting history of the Supremacy Clause (described in Part I), which shows that the Framers understood the "in Pursuance [of]" language to impose substantive, not merely temporal, restrictions on when federal statutes constitute supreme law.[35] Third, drawing a negative inference from the State Judges Clause is unjustified because even those skeptical of judicial review concede that federal judges have the power of judicial review over state laws—although the text of the State Judges Clause does not support that power, either. Finally, the view that the Constitution is only a "political-legal" document not enforceable by the courts likewise proves too much—because that view would undercut the basis for judicial review of state law as well. It also is in tension with the language of the Supremacy Clause, which lists the Constitution, federal statutes, and treaties together as the supreme law, without suggesting that only statutes and treaties, but not the Constitution itself, are judicially enforceable. Prakash and Yoo thus conclude that, with only a handful of exceptions, "the entire Constitution is a judicially cognizable document to be interpreted and applied by courts in cases where they have jurisdiction."

Of course, whatever questions there may be about judicial review of federal law, those questions are magnified when it comes to judicial supremacy—"the notion that judges have the last word when it comes to constitutional interpretation and that their decisions determine the meaning of the Constitution for everyone."[36] As applied to questions of federal law, the issue is the extent to which Congress and the executive branch can substitute their own interpretations of the Constitution for the Supreme Court's interpretations. In some circumstances, such as legislators deciding whether to pass legislation or the President deciding whether to veto a bill, federal officials clearly have an unreviewable power to follow their own interpretations of the Constitution.[37] And some commentators continue to assert that each branch of the federal government can adopt its own, independent interpretations of the Constitution over a much broader range of issues.[38] Nonetheless, according to Professor Kramer, "[i]t seems fair to say that, as a descriptive matter, judges, lawyers, politicians, and the general public today accept the principle of judicial supremacy—indeed, they assume it as a matter of course."[39]

DUTY OF STATE COURTS TO ENFORCE FEDERAL LAW

A further implication of the Supremacy Clause, reinforced by Article III of the Constitution, is that state courts cannot wholly decline to consider federal law claims, at least when state courts will consider analogous state law claims. In other words, state courts have a duty—albeit of uncertain scope—to enforce federal law.

In Howlett v. Rose (1990), the Supreme Court set out the basic principles that govern this duty of state courts, which it described as "[t]hree corollaries" to the supremacy of federal law set out in the Supremacy Clause:

- First, "[a] state may not deny a federal right, when the parties and controversy are properly before it, in the absence of a 'valid excuse.'"
- Second, "[a]n excuse that is inconsistent with or violates federal law is not a valid excuse: The Supremacy Clause forbids state courts to dissociate themselves from federal law because of disagreement with its content or a refusal to recognize the superior authority of its source."
- Third, "[w]hen a state court refuses jurisdiction because of a neutral state rule regarding the administration of the courts, we must act with utmost caution before deciding that it is obligated to entertain the claim."

This section considers these basic principles. It first describes Testa v. Katt (1947), the leading case holding that state courts have a duty to enforce federal law. It then discusses what might constitute a valid excuse for a state court's refusal to hear a federal claim, as well as the applicability of state court procedures to cases involving federal claims. Finally, it compares the Supremacy Clause's "commandeering" of state court judges to enforce federal law with the Supreme Court's "anti-commandeering rule" for other state officials.

Testa v. Katt

The leading case recognizing the duty of state courts to enforce federal law is Testa v. Katt (1947). Testa bought a car from Katt, who ran a car dealership in Rhode Island, for $1100. The car was subject to federal price controls, which fixed a maximum price for the car of $890. Testa sued Katt in state court in Rhode Island under § 205 of the federal Emergency Price Control Act seeking treble damages (three times the overcharge) plus attorneys' fees. Testa prevailed in the Rhode Island trial court, but the state supreme court reversed. It concluded that the Emergency Price Control Act was a "penal" statute, and that a state did not need to enforce the penal laws of a foreign sovereign, here the federal government. Thus, Testa could not bring an action under § 205 in Rhode Island state court.

The United States Supreme Court unanimously reversed. Even assuming that § 205 was a penal statute, the entire premise of the state supreme court's decision was misguided, according to the Court. The Rhode Island court wrongly assumed that it could treat federal statutes the same way it treated statutes of foreign sovereigns or even other states. "Such a broad assumption flies in the face of the fact that the States of the Union constitute a nation" and "disregards the purpose and effect" of the Supremacy Clause. The Supremacy Clause makes federal law the "supreme Law of the Land," with the result that states cannot disregard the policy behind the federal statute in favor of their own state policy.

The Court relied heavily on its prior decisions in Claflin v. Houseman (1876) and Mondou v. New York, New Haven & Hartford R.R. (1912). The issue in *Claflin* was slightly, but importantly, different from the issue in *Testa*. There, the question was whether state courts had concurrent jurisdiction with federal courts to hear a claim under the Bankruptcy Act—not whether states had to hear the federal claim, but whether they *could*. The *Claflin* Court's analysis was helpful to the *Testa* Court, however, because it rejected the concept central to the state court's opinion—that the United States was like a foreign sovereign to the state. Instead, the *Claflin* Court explained (relying on the Supremacy Clause) that "[t]he laws of the United States are laws in the several States, and just as much binding on the citizens and courts thereof as the State laws are. The United States is not a foreign sovereignty as regards the several States, but is a concurrent, and, within its jurisdiction, paramount sovereignty." As a result, the Court in *Claflin* held that the state courts had concurrent jurisdiction and could hear the Bankruptcy Act claim.

In *Mondou*, the Court went further and held that a state court had a duty to hear a federal claim otherwise within its jurisdiction. The issue in *Mondou* was whether a plaintiff could bring a claim under the Federal Employers' Liability Act ("FELA")[40] "as of right, in the courts of the States when their jurisdiction, as fixed by local laws, is adequate to the occasion." The Court concluded that state courts had concurrent jurisdiction over FELA claims and then held that the state courts had a duty to hear the claims. In so holding, it strongly asserted the supremacy of federal law (in language quoted in full by the Court in *Testa*):

> The suggestion that the act of Congress is not in harmony with the policy of the State, and therefore that the courts of the State are free to decline jurisdiction, is quite inadmissible, because it presupposes what in legal contemplation does not exist. When Congress, in the exertion of the power confided to it by the Constitution, adopted that act, it spoke for all the people and all the States, and thereby established a policy for all. That policy is as much the policy of Connecticut as if the act had emanated from its own legislature, and should be respected accordingly in the courts of the State.

Mondou differed from *Testa* only in that the state court in *Mondou* had not relied on the "penal" nature of the federal law as the basis for dismissing the plaintiff's cause of action. Indeed, the *Testa* Court could have narrowly followed *Mondou* by holding that the state court had wrongly characterized the federal statute as a penal one.[41] Instead, the Court ruled more broadly that the purportedly penal nature of the statute was irrelevant and that the state court had a duty to hear the federal claim. In other words (as described by the Supreme Court in Printz v. United States (1997)), "*Testa* stands for the proposition that state courts cannot refuse to apply federal law—a conclusion mandated by the terms of the Supremacy Clause."[42]

Limits to the State Duty

Although the duty of state courts to enforce federal law is now well accepted, the limits of that duty (if any) have yet to be determined. In *Testa*, the Supreme Court rejected the argument that the Rhode Island policy against enforcement of penal statutes was a "valid excuse" for refusing to hear the federal claim. Thus, state public policy objections to provisions of federal law do not provide an acceptable basis for a state court to refuse to exercise jurisdiction. In other words, "[a]n excuse that is inconsistent with or violates federal law is not a valid excuse" (Howlett v. Rose, 1990). So what is a "valid excuse"?

At a minimum, to be valid the excuse must not discriminate against federal claims. In *Testa* itself, the parties had conceded that Rhode Island courts would have enforced a Rhode Island law similar to the federal law at issue. Thus, the state supreme court decision treated federal law claims differently from how it treated state law claims. Accordingly, the holding of *Testa* on its facts is limited to a requirement that state courts treat federal claims no differently from how they treat analogous state claims—that is, that state courts not discriminate against federal claims.

Other cases (before and after *Testa*) likewise have emphasized the impermissibility of state rules that discriminate against federal claims. In McKnett v. St. Louis & San Francisco Railway Co. (1934), Alabama courts refused to hear a FELA claim based on an out-of-state injury, even though they would have heard an analogous state law claim based on intrastate conduct. The Supreme Court reversed, holding that "[a] state may not discriminate against rights arising under federal laws." Similarly, in Howlett v. Rose (1990), the Court held that a state court could not refuse to adjudicate a federal civil rights claim when it would have heard a similar, although not identical, state law claim. The fact that state law did not provide for an identical cause of action to the federal civil rights claim was not a valid excuse; it simply reflected a state public policy objection to federal law of the sort rejected in *Testa*. The state court's discrimination against federal claims, the Court concluded, "flatly violates the Supremacy Clause." The Court added, addressing a situation not before it, that "[t]he requirement that a state court of competent jurisdiction treat federal law as the law of the land does not necessarily include within it a requirement that the State create a court competent to hear the case in which the federal claim is presented." The Supreme Court has not yet had to address that issue, which is perhaps just as well.[43]

When the nondiscrimination requirement is satisfied, the Court has recognized that a state procedural rule can provide a valid excuse in several other cases arising under FELA. In Missouri ex rel. Southern Railway Co. v. Mayfield (1950), the Supreme Court held that a state court could rely on the doctrine of *forum non conveniens* (which permits dismissal of a claim in favor of a more convenient forum) to dismiss a FELA claim. In Herb v. Pitcairn (1945), the Court upheld the dismissal of a claim as barred by the statute of limitations, when the plaintiff had originally filed suit in a state court without jurisdiction over the case even though a state court of proper jurisdiction was available to him. Finally, the Court held in Douglas v. New York, New Haven & Hartford R.R. (1929) that a state statute excluding from state court certain lawsuits between nonresidents (a statutory variation of the doctrine of *forum non conveniens*) was a "valid excuse" for dismissal of a FELA claim.

State Court Procedures and Federal Law Claims

Testa v. Katt did not address the procedures state courts may (or must) use in deciding federal claims. In other cases, however, the Supreme Court has declared as a "general and unassailable proposition" that "States may establish the rules of procedure governing litigation in their own courts" (Felder v. Casey, 1988). States "have great latitude to establish the structure and jurisdiction of their own courts," such that "[t]he general rule, 'bottomed deeply in belief in the importance of state control of state judicial procedure, is that federal law takes the state courts as it finds them'" (Howlett v. Rose, 1990).[44] Accordingly, parties asserting federal claims in state court generally must follow state procedures.

Professor Anthony J. Bellia, Jr., has identified two exceptions to this general rule. First, "Congress may require state courts to enforce federal procedural rules that are 'part and parcel' of a federal right of action."[45] This exception was established in several more FELA cases. In Central Vermont Railway Co. v. White (1915), at issue was a state rule that required a plaintiff to prove that his or her negligence did not contribute to the injury. The Supreme Court construed FELA as imposing the burden of proof instead on the defendant to prove the plaintiff's contributory negligence. Although the Court acknowledged the "general principle that matters respecting the remedy . . . depend on the law of the place where the suit is brought," it concluded that this was not a matter of procedure for which the state rule governed. Instead, "proof of plaintiff's freedom from fault is a part of the very substance of his case," so that the state court was required to follow the federal burden-shifting rule.

Thereafter, in Dice v. Akron, Canton & Youngstown R.R. (1952), the Court held that the right to a jury trial under FELA overrode a state rule directing that questions of fraud were to be decided by the judge.[46] The jury trial right is "part and parcel" of the remedy provided under FELA, the Court concluded, and is "too substantial a part of the rights accorded by the Act" to be displaced by the state's allocation of decision making authority to a judge. The Court distinguished its prior decision in Minneapolis & St. Louis R.R. v. Bombolis (1916), in which it had upheld application of a state rule permitting nonunanimous jury verdicts in FELA cases.[47] It explained that "[t]he *Bombolis* case might be more in point had [the state] abolished trial by jury in all negligence cases, including those arising under the Federal Act," instead of "singl[ing] out one phase of the question of fraudulent releases for determination by a judge rather than a jury."

Second, "Congress may, by implication, require state courts to follow federal procedural rules when application of a state procedural rule would unnecessarily burden a federal right."[48] This exception comes from the Supreme Court's decision in Felder v. Casey (1988) and is an application of preemption doctrine (discussed later in Part II). A Wisconsin law required all plaintiffs suing a state or local government or official to give prompt notice of the claim to the potential defendant and then to wait 120 days before filing suit. In *Felder*, the Wisconsin state courts had held that the notice-of-claim statute applied to federal civil rights claims and dismissed a claim against Milwaukee police officers because the plaintiff had failed to comply.

The Supreme Court reversed. It began by reiterating that states control procedures in state courts, but added that "[f]ederal law takes state courts as it finds them only insofar as those courts employ rules that do not 'impose unnecessary burdens upon rights of recovery authorized by federal laws'" (quoting Brown v. Western Railway (1949)). "The question," according to the Court, "is essentially one of pre-emption": Does the Wisconsin notice-of-claim law stand as an obstacle to Congress' purposes in enacting the federal civil rights laws? The Court held the Wisconsin law preempted because it imposed "a substantive condition on the right to sue governmental officials and entities." Although the state law did not discriminate between federal and state claims, it applied only to state government defendants, the very group Congress sought to subject to liability. Thus, the Court, concluded, "the statute discriminates against the precise type of claim Congress created." Commentators have criticized the Supreme Court's discrimination holding in *Felder*, suggesting that *Felder* thus may be the only case in which the Court has rejected a state's nondiscriminatory excuse for refusing to hear a federal claim.[49]

In Johnson v. Fankell (1997), the Court refused to extend *Felder* to a state rule governing when a defendant could appeal from an order rejecting a qualified immunity defense. The plaintiff filed a federal civil rights suit against officials of the Idaho Liquor Dispensary alleging that they deprived her of property (her job) without due process of law. The defendants moved to dismiss the suit on the basis of qualified immunity, an established defense to such an action. The state trial court denied the motion, and the defendants appealed. The state supreme court dismissed the appeal as premature because there was no final judgment: The defendants had to wait until the case was over before they could appeal. The rule as applied by the state supreme court differed from the rule that would have applied in federal court: In federal court, an order denying a qualified immunity defense is appealable immediately. On rehearing, the state supreme court rejected the defendants' argument that they had a federal right to an immediate appeal.

The United States Supreme Court affirmed, concluding that the state rule was not preempted by the federal civil rights laws. The Court began by emphasizing the "heavy burden" the challengers faced in the case, because the usual presumption against preemption "is buttressed by the fact" that the lower court decision "rested squarely on a neutral state rule regarding the administration of state courts." Conversely, the federal interest was weak because qualified immunity is a defense for state officials and thus implicates state, not federal interests. According to the Court, the lower court decision was more about balancing competing state interests than a conflict between federal and state interests of the sort usually implicating the Supremacy Clause. As such, the state rule on appealability was not preempted. In so holding, the Court distinguished Felder v. Casey on the ground that the state procedural rule in this case was neutral (i.e., nondiscriminatory) because it did not "target civil rights claims against the State." Instead, it applied "without regard to the identity of the party seeking the appeal or the subject matter of the suit."

The Supremacy Clause and the Anti-Commandeering Rule

In several recent cases, the Supreme Court has developed what has become known as the "anti-commandeering rule": Congress cannot "'commandee[r] the legislative processes of the States by directly compelling them to enact and enforce a federal regulatory program'" (New York v. United States, 1992 (quoting Hodel v. Virginia Surface Mining & Reclamation Ass'n, 1981)).[50] How can this anti-commandeering rule be squared with Liebman and Ryan's statement, quoted above, that "the [Constitutional] Convention impressed state judges into national service?"[51] The distinction, according to the Court, is the language of the Supremacy Clause, which creates a "judicial exception" to the anti-commandeering rule.

The first anti-commandeering case was New York v. United States (1992), in which the Court struck down a provision of the Low-Level Radioactive Waste Policy Amendments Act of 1985.[52] The Act required a state either to provide for disposal of radioactive waste generated within the state or else to take title to and possession of the waste itself. The Court held the provision unconstitutional because it "would 'commandeer' state governments into the service of federal regulatory purposes." In so holding, the Court distinguished cases like *Testa*, which require state courts to enforce federal law, as "no more than an application of the Supremacy Clause." It explained that "[f]ederal statutes enforceable in state courts do, in a sense, direct state judges to enforce them, but this sort of federal 'direction' of state judges is mandated by the text of the Supremacy Clause." The power of federal courts to order state officials to comply with federal law likewise is distinguishable. Not only does Article III of the Constitution grant such "judicial Power" to the federal courts, the Court reasoned, but the Supremacy Clause makes federal law the supreme law: "the power of federal courts to enforce federal law thus presupposes some authority to order state officials to comply." Nothing in the Constitution, however, (and certainly nothing in the Supremacy Clause) permits Congress to make comparable directions to state legislatures.

Thereafter, in Printz v. United States (1997), the Supreme Court held unconstitutional a provision of the Brady Handgun Violence Prevention Act that required state law enforcement officers to conduct background checks on handgun purchasers. In requiring state and local officials to administer a federal law, the Act violated the anti-commandeering principle of New York v. United States. The Court again distinguished *Testa* as "stand[ing] for the proposition that state courts cannot refuse to enforce federal law—a conclusion mandated by the terms of the Supremacy Clause." *Testa* "says nothing about whether state executive officers must administer federal law."[53] Thus, in *New York* and in *Printz*, the Supreme Court indicated that the anti-commandeering rule does not apply to state courts because of the Supremacy Clause and, in particular, the State Judges Clause.[54]

In Alden v. Maine (1999), however, the Court muddied the waters of the judicial exception. The Court held in *Alden* that Congress does not have the power under Article I of the Constitution to override state sovereign immunity, and thus cannot "subject nonconsenting States to private suits for damages in state courts." In support of its holding, the Court used the language of commandeering: "A power to press a State's own courts into federal service to coerce the other branches of the State, furthermore, is the power first to turn the State against itself and ultimately to commandeer the entire political machinery of the State against its will and at the behest of individuals." Although the Court acknowledged that state courts have a duty to enforce federal law, citing *Testa*, it rejected the idea that state courts could have a greater duty than federal courts. The Eleventh Amendment would have precluded the federal courts from hearing the case;[55] state sovereign immunity precludes Congress from requiring the state courts to hear it as well. The Supremacy Clause is not to the contrary. According to the Court, "There can be no serious contention . . . that the Supremacy Clause imposes greater obligations on state-court judges than on the Judiciary of the United States itself." In the end, the impact of *Alden* on the judicial exception to the anti-commandeering rule is unclear: "Perhaps the Court was simply using the language of commandeering loosely in this context," or perhaps the anti-commandeering rule now precludes the federal government from authorizing private parties to seek damages from a state in state court.[56]

Federal Preemption of State Law

INTRODUCTION

Steven Gwin bought a termite protection plan from a Terminix outlet. The plan promised life-time protection against termites.[57] One of the terms of the plan was an arbitration clause, under which any dispute between the parties was to be resolved by an arbitrator (a private judge) rather than in court. Arbitration clauses are increasingly common in consumer contracts. Many businesses, from pest control services to credit card issuers to computer makers, now include arbitration clauses in their standard form contracts with consumers.[58]

When Gwin sold the house, he transferred the plan to the Dobsons, the buyers of the house. The Dobsons discovered termites, and had the house treated by Terminix. They were unhappy with the results of the treatment, however, so they sued Terminix (and Gwin) in Alabama state court. Terminix sought to have the court send the case to arbitration, as provided in the contract. But Alabama law makes an arbitration clause entered into before a dispute arises (a predispute arbitration clause) unenforceable. Relying on Alabama law, the Dobsons sought to avoid arbitration and keep their case in court. Unlike Alabama law, however, the Federal Arbitration Act ("FAA") makes predispute arbitration clauses within its scope "valid, irrevocable, and enforceable."[59] Terminix relied on the FAA to argue that the court should enforce the arbitration clause.

Did the Dobsons have to arbitrate their dispute with Terminix? Both the State of Alabama and the federal government were acting within their powers to regulate. The Supremacy Clause dictates that a court should resolve the conflict between the FAA and Alabama law in favor of the FAA, and hold the arbitration clause enforceable. A federal statute preempts conflicting state law. One legal commentator has likened the role of the Supremacy Clause here to a "traffic cop": The Supremacy Clause does not make the rules to be enforced, but instead controls which traffic (rule) gets priority.[60] Another way of thinking of preemption is in card-game terms: Federal law "trumps" conflicting state laws. However viewed, the result under the Supremacy Clause is clear—in the event of a conflict, federal law controls over state law. The Dobsons had to arbitrate.

Although a variety of sources of federal law (such as the United States Constitution) can override state law, preemption doctrine focuses primarily on conflicts between state law (state constitutions, statutes, regulations, and judge-made common law doctrines) and federal statutes (and sometimes federal administrative regulations). The difficult question addressed by preemption doctrine is not what happens when federal law and state law conflict, but rather how to determine *when* they conflict.

Commentators find the Supreme Court's approach to preemption confusing (or perhaps just confused), both in setting out an overall framework for analysis and in applying the framework in particular cases. The following are samples of the criticisms:

- "[T]he United States Supreme Court has failed to articulate a coherent standard for deciding preemption cases, and its haphazard approach fails to provide meaningful guidance to lower courts, legislators, and citizens."[61]
- "[T]he Supreme Court's numerous preemption cases follow no predictable jurisprudential or analytical pattern."[62]
- "The Supreme Court's preemption jurisprudence is famous for its incoherence."[63]
- "[P]reemption jurisprudence is in a state of disarray."[64]
- "Modern preemption jurisprudence is a muddle."[65]

Some of the seeming confusion no doubt is due to the difficulty of applying preemption principles to vastly different federal statutes. And some of the doctrinal uncertainty seems to have been resolved in the Court's more recent preemption cases. But it remains true that predicting the outcome of preemption cases using the Supreme Court's doctrinal framework can be extremely difficult.

This Part begins by examining the importance of preemption doctrine and describing its relationship to the Supremacy Clause. Next, it surveys basic preemption doctrine. The Supreme Court's preemption cases set out a categorical approach, establishing rules for express preemption, implied preemption due to conflict with a particular federal law ("conflict preemption"), and implied preemption of an entire field ("field preemption"). In fact, the lines between these categories are not as clear as the Court's approach would suggest. The Part then examines the extent to which federalism concerns affect preemption doctrine. The Supreme Court applies a presumption against preemption in subject areas traditionally occupied by the states, thus requiring greater specificity before it will find federal preemption of state law. Trends in Supreme Court decisions reveal a willingness by the Court to find state laws preempted that is surprising given the "federalism revival" in recent years. Several attempts have been made to reform preemption doctrine, by legislation and by presidential directive, so far to little effect. Finally, the Part concludes with an in-depth analysis of preemption doctrine as applied in one substantive area—preemption of state arbitration laws by the Federal Arbitration Act—which shows just how difficult preemption issues can be. The FAA also illustrates that even when adopting supreme federal law, Congress may rely on a substantive standard of equality: Only state laws that discriminate against arbitration agreements are preempted by the FAA.

IMPORTANCE OF PREEMPTION DOCTRINE

By most measures, preemption doctrine has become increasingly important in recent decades. In many areas federal law is now "more primary than interstitial," a significant change from the early part of the twentieth century.[66] The growing reach of the federal government results in more potential conflicts between state law and federal law, and a corresponding increase in the number of cases in which preemption doctrine comes into play.

Various quantitative measures confirm the growing importance of federal preemption. A 1992 study by the U.S. Advisory Commission on Intergovernmental Relations (the most recent available) documents a dramatic increase in the number of federal preemption statutes enacted over the last century.[67] The Commission defined a "federal preemption statute" as a federal statute that meets one of three conditions: (1) the statute by its terms preempts state law; (2) the statute has been interpreted by a court to preempt state law; or (3) the statute was described in committee reports or other legislative history as intended to preempt state law.[68] From 1900–1909, Congress enacted only 14 federal preemption statutes. By the 1960s, the number had increased to 47, and then skyrocketed to over 100 in the 1970s and 1980s. (See Table 1.) More than half of all federal preemption statutes have been enacted since 1969.[69] Preemption relief statutes, defined by the Commission as statutes that modify federal preemption statutes (either by reducing the extent of preemption or clarifying uncertainty in the statute) also have increased in number, albeit not so dramatically.

The most common subject dealt with by federal preemption statutes is interstate commerce. (See Table 2.) The 1960s and 1970s were the most active decades for health and safety statutes: The number of federal preemption statutes dealing with those issues exceeded the number of statutes dealing with commerce in both decades, the only times that has happened. Also showing a sizable increase beginning in the 1960s were federal preemption statutes dealing with civil rights issues, which were notably absent during the first half of the twentieth century.

Preemption doctrine also has become increasingly important in the courts (although tailing off in recent years in the Supreme Court). One commentator reports that the Supreme Court decided as many preemption cases during the

Table 1
Federal Preemption and Preemption Relief Statutes

	Federal Preemption Statutes	Preemption Relief Statutes
Before 1900	30	3
1900–1909	14	1
1910–1919	22	1
1920–1929	17	3
1930–1939	33	4
1940–1949	16	3
1950–1959	27	4
1960–1969	47	2
1970–1979	108	5
1980–1989	100	7
1990–1999*	125*	5*
Totals*	539*	39*

Source: U.S. Advisory Commission on Intergovernmental Relations.
*The figures for 1990–1999 are based on extrapolations from data for 1990 and 1991.

Table 2
Federal Preemption Statutes by Subject Matter

	Banking & Finance	Civil Rights	Commerce	Health & Safety	Natural Resources	Tax & Other
Before 1900	0	7	15	4	1	3
1900–1909	0	0	7	5	2	0
1910–1919	1	0	16	3	1	1
1920–1929	2	0	12	3	0	0
1930–1939	8	0	21	2	0	2
1940–1949	1	0	9	3	2	1
1950–1959	3	1	10	6	3	4
1960–1969	5	7	9	23	3	0
1970–1979	15	10	31	32	9	11
1980–1989	13	6	35	26	6	14
1990–1991	2	2	11	6	0	4
Totals	50	33	176	113	27	40

Source: U.S. Advisory Commission on Intergovernmental Relations.

twenty years from 1980–2000 as it did during the forty years from 1940–1980.[70] No doubt the total was inflated to some extent by the Court's high caseloads during the 1980s. But even when caseloads are considered, the 1980s were a busy time for preemption cases: Preemption cases made up 9 percent of the Court's docket during the 1985–1987 terms, as compared to only 2 percent during the 1962–1964 terms.[71]

Predictions that the rate would continue to increase have proven unfounded, however. During the hearings on the Federalism Accountability Act of 1999, then-Senator Fred Thompson of Tennessee recited the docket figures from the 1960s and 1980s and stated: "[W]e are going to get more recent figures, and I dare say it is higher than 9 percent now, all having to do with or largely having to do with reading Congress' mind."[72] In fact, the expected increase did not occur (due in part, no doubt, to changes in the Court's standards for granting review of cases). During the 1999–2001 terms, just over 3 percent of the Court's docket consisted of preemption cases, down from the 9 percent during the mid-1980s.[73] The number of preemption cases also has come down substantially, from thirty-nine cases in the mid-1980s (albeit on a much larger docket), to nine cases from the 1999–2001 terms. Indeed, other cases regularly overshadow preemption cases in the Supreme Court, not only in publicity but in numbers as well. During the 1999–2001 terms, for example, the Court decided twenty cases in which the First Amendment right to free speech was the principal issue.[74] What is even more striking is that this decline in preemption cases is happening at the same time the Supreme Court has been significantly expanding other federalism doctrines, particularly Eleventh Amendment immunity of states from suit in federal court.

Nevertheless, it may well be true in the lower courts that preemption is "the most frequently used doctrine of constitutional law in practice."[75] In 1992, Supreme Court Justice John Paul Stevens found over 2800 court cases dealing with preemption by ERISA (the Employee Retirement Income Security Act[76]), cases involving preemption by one statute out of the entire universe of federal statutes.[77] A recent study updated the number to 5400 opinions that discuss ERISA preemption.[78] At the very least it is beyond dispute that preemption cases are very significant in absolute numbers in the federal and state courts.

Finally, it no longer is the case that "as a topic, preemption has largely been ignored by constitutional law scholars."[79] As the rest of this Part will demonstrate, preemption doctrine has been widely discussed in the legal literature in recent years. Certainly most preemption scholarship considers the preemptive effect of particular federal laws, often as applied to particular types of state laws, rather than preemption generally. Moreover, preemption doctrine certainly is underrepresented in law reviews relative to other constitutional law topics. Nevertheless, scholars have in recent years produced a number of thought-provoking analyses of preemption doctrine that greatly influenced the analysis in this Part.

PREEMPTION AND THE SUPREMACY CLAUSE

The Supreme Court consistently relies on the Supremacy Clause as authority for holding that federal law preempts state law. Thus, in Fidelity Federal Savings & Loan Ass'n v. de la Cuesta (1982), the Court explained that "pre-emption doctrine . . . has its roots in the Supremacy Clause." Similarly, in Gade v. National Solid Wastes Management Ass'n (1992), the Court stated that "pre-emption doctrine is derived" from the Supremacy Clause. The conclusion seems obvious. The clause makes federal law the "supreme Law of the Land." The effect of preemption is that the conflicting state law is ineffective and the federal law controls. By holding a state law preempted, the court recognizes that federal law is supreme.

Professor Stephen Gardbaum has challenged the view that the Supremacy Clause is the source of federal preemption doctrine.[80] He argues that supremacy and preemption are different concepts, with preemption the greater of the two. Supremacy means that a federal law overrides state law if the two conflict. By contrast, according to Gardbaum, preemption means that states have no power to act in a particular area, regardless of any conflict between federal and state law. Because preemption is a greater power than supremacy, the Supremacy Clause cannot be the source of the power to preempt, Gardbaum argues, for "[a] greater power cannot (logically) derive from a lesser one."

As Professor Viet Dinh explains, however, Gardbaum uses "preemption" more broadly than does the Supreme Court.[81] A federal statute that preempts state law does not, even when the federal government preempts an entire field of state legislation, preclude states from enacting legislation. It merely invalidates the state law after it is enacted. For this latter proposition, the Supremacy Clause rightly is identified as the controlling authority.

Certainly Gardbaum is correct, however, that one must be careful to distinguish between the effect of the Supremacy Clause, which is to resolve conflicts between state and federal law, and the power to enact preemptive legislation. The former derives from the Supremacy Clause. The latter comes from other powers of Congress enumerated in the Constitution. The Supremacy Clause does not itself grant Congress the power to legislate. Thus, statements such as the one in Northwest Central Pipeline Corp. v. State Corporation Comm'n (1989)—that "Congress has the power under the Supremacy Clause of Article VI of the Constitution to preempt state law"—are misleading if not incorrect.

In this respect the Supremacy Clause differs from James Madison's favored congressional negative.[82] The negative—which was included in the Virginia Plan but ultimately rejected by the Constitutional Convention—would have provided a source of power for Congress to act independent of other congressional powers. Indeed, the negative as conceived by Madison would have permitted Congress to veto state legislation "*in all cases whatsoever*,"[83] a wide-ranging power indeed. Of course, the negative merely permitted reactive rather than proactive steps by

Congress: Congress could veto legislation enacted by states but not rely on the negative to pass its own laws. Nonetheless, the fact that the Constitutional Convention rejected the congressional negative and replaced it with the Supremacy Clause is evidence that the Supremacy Clause itself is not a source of congressional power to act.[84]

Far and away the most commonly used source of congressional power to enact preemptive statutes is the Commerce Clause—Congress' power to regulate interstate commerce. It is not the exclusive source, however. For example, Congress also has enacted preemptive legislation relying on its power over bankruptcy (e.g., Perez v. Campbell, 1971) and patents (e.g., Bonito Boats, Inc. v. Thunder Craft Boats, Inc., 1989). The source of congressional power differs, but the preemption analysis is the same.

Although administrative regulations are not listed in the Supremacy Clause as the "supreme Law of the Land" (not surprisingly since administrative agencies did not exist when the Constitution was drafted), it is well settled that federal regulations, like federal statutes, can preempt state law.[85] However, to preempt state law, a federal agency must be acting within the authority delegated to it by Congress. Otherwise it has no authority to act at all, much less to preempt state law (New York v. Federal Energy Regulatory Comm'n, 2002).

CATEGORIES OF PREEMPTION ANALYSIS

Whether a particular federal statute preempts state law ultimately depends on the statute itself. As the Supreme Court stated in Retail Clerks International Ass'n, Local 1625 v. Schermerhorn (1963)—and has repeated frequently since—"[t]he purpose of Congress is the ultimate touchstone" in preemption analysis.[86] In other words, in deciding whether a federal statute preempts a state law, the Supreme Court must determine whether Congress intended to preempt the state law at issue. Thus, most preemption cases contain a lengthy analysis of the federal statute itself. What does the language of the statute mean? What does its structure suggest? Does the history of enactment by Congress—committee hearings, reports, and floor debates—provide any insights into what the statute means? And so forth.

The Supreme Court takes what has been called a "categorical" approach to preemption questions.[87] The Court has set out several categories of cases in which it will find that federal law preempts state law. In English v. General Electric Co. (1990), the Supreme Court described the categories as follows:

> Our cases have established that state law is pre-empted under the Supremacy Clause in three circumstances. First, Congress can define explicitly the extent to which its enactments pre-empt state law. See *Shaw* v. *Delta Air Lines, Inc.*, 463 U.S. 85, 95–98 (1983).

> Pre-emption fundamentally is a question of congressional intent, and when Congress has made its intent known through explicit statutory language, the courts' task is an easy one.
>
> Second, in the absence of explicit statutory language, state law is pre-empted where it regulates conduct in a field that Congress intended the Federal Government to occupy exclusively. Such an intent may be inferred from a "scheme of federal regulation . . . so pervasive as to make reasonable the inference that Congress left no room for the States to supplement it," or where an Act of Congress "touch[es] a field in which the federal interest is so dominant that the federal system will be assumed to preclude enforcement of state laws on the same subject." *Rice* v. *Santa Fe Elevator Corp.*, 331 U.S. 218, 230 (1947). . . .
>
> Finally, state law is pre-empted to the extent that it actually conflicts with federal law. Thus, the Court has found pre-emption where it is impossible for a private party to comply with both state and federal requirements, see, *e.g.*, *Florida Lime Growers, Inc.* v. *Paul*, 373 U.S. 132, 142–43 (1963), or where state law "stands as an obstacle to the accomplishment and execution of the full purposes and objectives of Congress." *Hines* v. *Davidowitz*, 312 U.S. 52, 67 (1941).

Thus, the three categories of preemption identified by the Court in *English* are express preemption, field preemption, and conflict preemption. The Court added, however, that "[b]y referring to these three categories, we should not be taken to mean that they are rigidly distinct." In other words, the categories can overlap and blend into one another. As will be seen, applying this framework is not as straightforward as the Court's description might make it seem.

EXPRESS PREEMPTION

The first preemption category identified by the Supreme Court is express preemption (as distinguished from implied preemption). Express preemption occurs when Congress addresses in a federal statute the degree to which the statute preempts state law. By comparison, implied preemption is when a federal statute preempts state law without addressing preemption in the terms of the statute (i.e., it preempts state law only by implication). The distinction between express preemption and implied preemption tracks distinctions elsewhere in the law between express and implied contract terms, express and implied conditions, express and implied rights of action, and so forth.

The Court's listing of express preemption as a category distinct from field and conflict preemption (the other two categories listed in English v. General Electric Co. (1990)) is somewhat problematic, however, because it mixes apples with oranges.[88] The distinction between express preemption and implied preemption focuses on how clearly Congress indicated its intent to preempt state law: Did Congress state in the statute that it preempted state law, or does a court have to imply such an intent? By comparison, the distinction between field preemption and conflict preemption focuses on how broadly Congress intended the preemptive statute to reach: Does the statute preempt merely some state statutes (those that conflict with the federal law) and not others, or does it preempt all state attempts to regulate in a particular field? Express preemption is not so much a third category of preemption analysis as a point on a wholly separate continuum along which preemption issues can be classified. Stated otherwise, on this view there really are (at least) four categories of preemption analysis: A statute with an express preemption clause might preempt either conflicting state laws or an entire field, just as a statute may impliedly preempt either conflicting state laws or an entire field.

As noted above, the ultimate question in preemption analysis is what did Congress intend when enacting the statute: To what degree, if at all, did Congress intend to displace state law? Congress may expressly define the scope of preemption either by identifying some state laws as preempted (using an express preemption clause) or by preserving at least some state laws from preemption (using a preemption savings clause). Although the Supreme Court asserted in *English* that "when Congress has made its intent known through explicit statutory language, the courts' task is an easy one," things are, of course, not that simple. The courts still need to construe the express preemption clause (or preemption savings clause) as they would any other statutory provision. And those clauses, just like other statutory provisions, can give rise to tricky issues of statutory interpretation that make the courts' task anything but easy.

Express Preemption Clauses

Express preemption clauses are commonplace in federal statutes. A computer search of federal statutes enacted from 1990–2000 found forty-two with clauses that by their terms preempt state law. The search was for federal statutes containing some form of the word "preempt," and so almost certainly was underinclusive. Other federal statutes, while plainly preempting state law, do not include the word "preempt" or "preemption" and so would not have been discovered by the search.[89] Thus, the number of federal statutes with express preemption clauses is surely higher (perhaps much higher).

Some express preemption clauses are simple, although by no means straightforward. The Federal Debt Collection Procedures Act of 1990, for example, provides that "[t]his chapter shall preempt State law to the extent such law is inconsistent with a provision of this chapter."[90] Others are more complex, specifically setting out at least some of the state statutes preempted. The ICC Termination Act of 1995, for example, provides:

> No State or political subdivision thereof and no interstate agency or other political agency of 2 or more States shall enact or enforce any law, rule, regulation, standard or other provision having the force and effect of law relating to the provision of pickup and delivery of express packages, newspapers, or mail in a commercial zone if the shipment has had or will

have a prior or subsequent movement by bus in intrastate commerce and, if a city within the commercial zone, is served by a motor carrier of passengers providing regular-route transportation of passengers subject to jurisdiction under subchapter I of chapter 135.[91]

Still others reference the standards for implied conflict preemption (discussed in more detail below). An example is a 1994 federal statute regulating the transport of hazardous materials:

[A] requirement of a State, political subdivision of a State, or Indian tribe is preempted if—

(1) complying with the requirement of the State, political subdivision, or tribe and a requirement of this chapter or a regulation prescribed under this chapter is not possible; or

(2) the requirement of the State, political subdivision, or tribe, as applied or enforced, is an obstacle to accomplishing and carrying out this chapter or a regulation prescribed under this chapter.[92]

Subsection (a)(1) of the statute enacts the impossibility strand of implied conflict preemption (a state law is preempted when compliance with both the federal law and the state law is impossible), while subsection (a)(2) enacts the obstacle strand (a state law is preempted when it stands as an obstacle to Congress' purposes in enacting the federal law).

Although express preemption clauses may answer some questions about the scope of preemption resulting from the statute, they can create difficult interpretative questions of their own. Cipollone v. Liggett Group, Inc. (1992) is illustrative. *Cipollone* was a lawsuit against tobacco companies on behalf of a smoker who died of lung cancer. The plaintiff asserted common-law damage claims for breach of express warranty, failure to warn, fraudulent misrepresentation, and conspiracy to misrepresent, all based at least in part on the tobacco companies' alleged failure to warn in cigarette labeling and advertising of the health hazards of smoking. One of the tobacco companies' defenses to the action was that such claims were preempted by the Public Health Cigarette Smoking Act of 1969.[93] The Act required the now familiar label ("WARNING: THE SURGEON GENERAL HAS DETERMINED THAT CIGARETTE SMOKING IS DANGEROUS TO YOUR HEALTH") on cigarette packages. It also contained the following express preemption provision: "(b) No requirement or prohibition based on smoking and health shall be imposed under State law with respect to the advertising or promotion of any cigarettes the packages of which are labeled in conformity with the provisions of this Act."

The Supreme Court, in a split opinion, held that the express preemption clause in the Act preempted some of the plaintiff's claims, but not the claims for failure to warn (to the extent based on actions of the tobacco companies in testing or research rather than advertising), breach of express warranty, fraudulent misrepresentation (to the extent based on allegedly false statements in advertising), and conspiracy to misrepresent. The plurality (Justices Stevens, O'Connor, White, and Chief Justice Rehnquist) carefully parsed the language of the express preemption clause, reasoning that: (1) liability for failure to warn based on research and testing practices does not depend on a state "requirement or prohibition . . . with respect to . . . advertising or promotion"; (2) liability for breach of express warranty is based on the representations of the party making the express warranty, and thus is not a "requirement . . . imposed under State law"; and (3) liability for fraudulent misrepresentation and conspiracy to misrepresent due to allegedly false advertising is not "based on smoking and health" but rather a broader duty not to lie. Three Justices (Blackmun, Kennedy, and Souter) would have held that the Act did not preempt any of plaintiff's state common-law damage claims, while two Justices (Scalia and Thomas) would have held that all of the plaintiff's claims were preempted. The net result was that six Justices agreed that some claims were preempted and seven Justices agreed that the other claims were not, but no five Justices could agree on a rationale. Even with the express preemption provision, the Court certainly did not have an "easy" task.

Preemption Savings Clauses

Preemption savings clauses are the mirror image of express preemption clauses. Express preemption clauses define what state laws Congress intends the statute to preempt. Preemption savings clauses define what state laws Congress intends the statute *not* to preempt (or sometimes what state laws Congress intended to be excluded from an express preemption clause). In recently enacted statutes, preemption savings clauses appear to be more common than express preemption clauses. Twice as many of the statutes found in a computer search of federal statutes enacted from 1990–2000 include preemption savings clauses as include express preemption clauses (84 versus 42), although the listing of express preemption clauses likely understates the total.

Preemption savings clauses take a variety of forms. Most simply, a statute might state that "[n]othing in this section preempts any State law."[94] Others, such as that in the Telephone Consumer Protection Act of 1991, are more elaborate, listing in some detail permissible state regulations:

> [N]othing in this section or in the regulations prescribed under this section shall preempt any State law that imposes more restrictive intrastate requirements or regulations on, or which prohibits—
>
> (A) the use of telephone facsimile machines or other electronic devices to send unsolicited advertisements;
>
> (B) the use of automatic telephone dialing systems;
>
> (C) the use of artificial or prerecorded voice messages; or
>
> (D) the making of telephone solicitations.[95]

Some preemption savings clauses permit states to adopt more protective standards (i.e., more protective of individual rights, the environment, or the like) than the federal law but not less protective, thereby establishing that the federal law sets a floor but not a ceiling (an issue that commonly arises in implied preemption cases). For example, the Religious Land Use and Institutionalized Persons Act of 2000 provides that "[n]othing in this Act shall be construed to preempt State law . . . that is equally as protective of religious exercise as, or more protective of religious exercise than, this Act."[96] In addition to permitting states to adopt more protective laws, such a clause implies that the federal act preempts less protective state laws (which it presumably does anyway). On occasion, a preemption savings clause may require states to enact new legislation to avoid federal preemption.[97]

In interpreting preemption savings clauses, the Supreme Court "has repeatedly 'declined to give broad effect to saving clauses where doing so would upset the careful regulatory scheme established by federal law' " (Geier v. American Honda Motor Co., 2000 (quoting United States v. Locke, 2000)). The Court in *Geier* applied this principle in construing the preemption savings clause in the National Traffic and Motor Vehicle Safety Act of 1966[98] as not saving from preemption state common-law tort actions that otherwise conflicted with the Act. While the application of the principle in *Geier* has been questioned (as reflecting a distrust of products liability actions),[99] its underlying rationale makes sense, at least in extreme cases: Construing a preemption savings clause too broadly may permit conflicting state laws that would "defeat [the statute's] own objectives, or potentially, as the Court has put it before, to 'destroy itself' " (Geier v. American Honda Motor Co., 2000 (quoting American Telephone & Telegraph Co. v. Central Office Telephone, Inc., 1998)).

Like express preemption clauses, preemption savings clauses can pose difficult interpretative issues. One recently litigated issue is whether clauses that preserve "state" regulations also preserve city or county regulations. In Wisconsin Public Intervenor v. Mortier (1991), the Supreme Court held that the Federal Insecticide, Fungicide, and Rodenticide Act (FIFRA) did not preempt an ordinance adopted by a Wisconsin town to regulate pesticide use. The FIFRA preemption savings clause provided that a "State may regulate the sale or use of any federally registered pesticide or device in the State, but only if and to the extent the regulation does not permit any sale or use prohibited by this subchapter."[100] The definition of "State" in the Act did not mention political subdivisions of the state.[101] The Supreme Court concluded that the "[m]ere silence" of the statute on the power of local governments to regulate was insufficient to preempt local law. Indeed, local governments are component parts of states, and so the Court declined to infer that Congress intended the definition of "State" to exclude cities and counties.

In City of Columbus v. Ours Garage Wrecker Service, Inc. (2002), the Court considered a preemption savings clause that differed in one key respect from that in *Mortier*. The provision of the preemption savings clause in the Interstate

Commerce Act (as amended), like the provision in *Mortier*, applied only to "a State."[102] But unlike *Mortier*, another sub-part of the same preemption savings clause (and, indeed, several other provisions in the same section) applied to "a State or a political subdivision of a State."[103] Because Congress used different language in the two provisions, under usual rules of statutory interpretation one would infer that it intended them to be construed differently. But the Supreme Court ruled otherwise, holding that the statutory language was not sufficiently clear to overcome the usual authority of a state to act directly or through political subdivisions. An interesting question is what Congress should have done differently. It may be that the only way Congress could have excluded local governments from the preemption savings clause would have been to state flatly that the provision did not apply to local governments.

IMPLIED PREEMPTION

Statutes that do not contain an express preemption provision (and even those that do) may nonetheless preempt state law by implication. A federal statute impliedly preempts state laws that conflict with it: when either compliance with both state and federal law is impossible (impossibility preemption) or when the state law creates an obstacle to Congress' purposes (obstacle preemption). In addition, a federal statute impliedly preempts state laws when the federal law occupies the entire regulatory field and thus precludes any state regulation in the area (field preemption). But sometimes the Supreme Court's preemption categories blur together, making it difficult to distinguish express preemption from implied preemption or field preemption from conflict preemption. As an alternative to traditional implied preemption analysis, one commentator has advocated a "logical contradiction" test that would significantly reduce the scope of implied preemption (particularly obstacle preemption). Congressional intent remains the "ultimate touchstone," but determining congressional intent in implied preemption cases is even more difficult than in express preemption cases.

Implied Conflict Preemption—Impossibility

The most basic form of conflict preemption is impossibility: A state statute is preempted when it is impossible for a party to comply with both federal law and state law. A case commonly cited as authority for impossibility preemption is Florida Lime & Avocado Growers, Inc. v. Paul (1963). At issue in *Florida Lime* was an alleged conflict between a California law prohibiting the sale in California of avocados with an oil content of less than 8 percent, and a federal marketing order authorizing the sale of avocados based on size, weight, and picking date, without regard to oil content. In the course of holding that the California law was not preempted, the Court stated that a state law would be preempted if it was physically impossible to comply with both the federal law and the state law. It gave as an example a state law that prohibited the sale of avocados with less than 8% oil content and a federal law that prohibited the sale of avocados with more than 7% oil content. In the case itself, the Court accepted the trial court's determination that Florida avocado growers could have complied with both federal and state law by waiting a little longer before picking the avocados. Thus, the two laws did not necessarily conflict.

Impossibility preemption is a narrow form of preemption, although there is some uncertainty about its precise application. Certainly compliance with both federal law and state law would be impossible (and thus the state law preempted) when the federal law requires an action that the state law forbids (or vice versa). In Barnett Bank of Marion County, N.A. v. Nelson (1996), the Supreme Court used as an example a case in which a federal law requires banks to sell insurance and a state law forbids it. The less certain case is when the state law forbids an action authorized but not required by the federal law, which is what was involved in *Barnett Bank:* Federal law authorized banks to sell insurance while state law forbid banks to sell insurance. Compliance with both federal law and state law was not literally impossible because the bank could simply decline to sell insurance.[104]

Others adopt a broader view of impossibility preemption, listing as examples Southland Corp. v. Keating (1984) (in which the parties could comply with a federal law making predispute arbitration clauses enforceable and a state law invalidating arbitration agreements with respect to certain claims by not including an arbitration clause in their contract) and McDermott v. Wisconsin (1913) (in which the parties could comply with differing federal and state labeling laws by not selling the product).[105] Indeed, the example of impossibility preemption used by the Court in *Florida Lime* would not satisfy the narrower view of impossibility preemption: The business could simply choose not to sell avocados in the state.

At bottom, the difference matters little. Even if not preempted under the rubric of impossibility preemption, a state statute that forbids actions authorized by Congress would be preempted as an obstacle to Congress' purpose in permitting the action. That is what the Court held in *Barnett Bank*. Either way the state law is preempted.

Implied Conflict Preemption—Obstacle to Federal Purposes

The second type of conflict preemption is obstacle preemption: A state law is preempted when it "stands as an obstacle to the accomplishment and execution of the full purposes and objectives of Congress" (Hines v. Davidowitz, 1941). Obstacle preemption is broader than impossibility preemption, and less well defined. As the Supreme Court explained in *Hines*:

There is not—and from the very nature of the problem there cannot be—any rigid formula or rule which can be used as a universal pattern to determine the meaning and purpose of every act of Congress. This Court, in considering the validity of state laws in the light of treaties or federal laws touching the same subject, has made use of the following expressions: conflicting; contrary to; occupying the field; repugnance; difference; irreconciliability; inconsistency; violation; curtailment; and interference. But none of these expressions provides an infallible constitutional test or an exclusive constitutional yardstick. In the final analysis, there can be no one crystal clear distinctly marked formula. Our primary function is to determine whether, under the circumstances of this particular case, Pennsylvania's law stands as an obstacle to the accomplishment and execution of the full purposes and objectives of Congress.

Obstacle preemption certainly includes cases in which a state law forbids behavior authorized by federal law (Barnett Bank of Marion County, N.A. v. Nelson, 1996), if the case is not treated as a form of impossibility preemption. But it includes far more as well.

The difficulty, of course, is determining when exactly it is that state law conflicts with Congress' purposes in enacting a law. Professor Laurence Tribe has identified a number of general principles that seem to govern in the Supreme Court's obstacle preemption cases.[106] First, state law is likely to be preempted if the purpose of the law is to discourage behavior that the federal law is trying to encourage. Even if the state law does not prohibit what the federal law promotes, it can have a similar effect by penalizing or discouraging it. Second, state law may be preempted if it encourages behavior that will interfere with the purposes of the federal law. A state law can be an obstacle to federal purposes not only by what it discourages but also by what it encourages—if what it encourages interferes with federal goals. Third, state law may be preempted when it "undermines a congressional decision in favor of national uniformity of standard—a situation similar in practical effect to that of federal occupation of a field." If the federal purpose is uniformity of regulation, any state law regulating in the area will be preempted, even if the state law is more protective (rather than less protective) than the federal law. In such a case, the federal law is not merely a floor below which state regulation may not fall, but also a ceiling. (Both the *Gade* case and the *Geier* case discussed below are examples.) Fourth, the more specific the federal purpose—assuming the state law still conflicts with it—the more likely a court will find preemption. General and abstract federal purposes are unlikely to preempt state law.

Identifying Congress' purpose (or purposes) is central to obstacle preemption, but it also is a step that invites criticism. According to Professor Erwin Chemerinsky, a court that wants to invalidate a state law as preempted can do so by construing the federal purpose broadly; a court that wants to uphold a state law can do so by construing the federal purpose narrowly.[107] Several Supreme Court preemption cases are suggestive of this point.

In Pacific Gas & Electric Co. v. State Energy Resources Conservation and Development Comm'n (1983), a public utility challenged California's moratorium on nuclear power plant construction as preempted by federal law. One theory was obstacle preemption: that the California moratorium stood as an obstacle to the federal purpose of promoting the use of nuclear power as an energy source. The Supreme Court acknowledged that a principal purpose of the Atomic Energy Act was to promote nuclear energy. But Congress did not intend to promote nuclear energy without regard to its cost. Instead, the congressional purpose was to promote nuclear energy (as Professor Chemerinsky puts it) "only to the extent it was economically feasible."[108] By defining the federal purpose narrowly (and defining the purpose of the state law narrowly as well, as based on economic concerns, not safety concerns), the Court avoided finding the state law preempted.

The Court in Gade v. National Solid Wastes Management Ass'n (1992) (discussed further below) took the opposite tack, holding that a state licensing requirement for hazardous waste workers was preempted by the federal Occupational Safety and Health Act. If the only purpose of the federal law had been to promote occupational safety and health, the state law would have been consistent with it and presumably not preempted. But the Court found that Congress not only sought to promote occupational safety and health, but also to avoid "duplicative, and possibly counterproductive, regulation." Given that purpose, the state law plainly was preempted.

Similarly, in Geier v. American Honda Motor Co. (2000), the Court held preempted a state law damages claim alleging that Honda negligently failed to equip an automobile model with a driver's side airbag. The federal rule, an administrative regulation adopted by the Department of Transportation ("DOT") pursuant to congressional delegation, required car manufacturers to include passive restraints (such as airbags) in some percentage, but less than all, of their model lines. According to the Court, DOT's purpose was to further auto safety by requiring an array of safety devices in cars, and thus the state lawsuit "would have presented an obstacle to the variety and mix of devices that the federal regulation sought." If, instead, the regulatory purpose had been to establish a minimum (but not maximum) degree of airbag usage in cars, the plaintiffs likely would have prevailed. That was the dissent's view: that the federal standards established minimum, not maximum, standards.

The Court's determination of the relevant purpose is not, of course, wholly unbounded. In its cases, the Court looks to the language and structure of the federal statute (or rule), its legislative history, and other objective indications of purpose. Nonetheless, as these cases suggest, obstacle preemption analysis can seem very outcome oriented, with the Court sometimes appearing to decide on the outcome and then justifying it by defining the congressional purpose, rather than the other way around.

Professor Caleb Nelson has criticized the Court's obstacle preemption doctrine on other grounds: as inconsistent with the text of the Supremacy Clause and as historically unwarranted.[109] He relies in particular on the concluding phrase in the Supremacy Clause ("any Thing in the Constitution or Laws of any State to the Contrary notwithstanding"), which he identifies as a *non obstante* clause, linking the standard for implied preemption to the traditional rules for determining whether a later statute repeals an earlier one. Viewing preemption as repeal of the inconsistent state law, the question becomes: "Can state and federal law stand together, or do they establish contradictory rules?" Accordingly, Nelson argues for what he calls a "logical contradiction" test for implied preemption. Under this test, "preemption occurs if and only if state law contradicts a valid rule established by federal law, and the mere fact that the federal law serves certain purposes does not automatically mean that it contradicts everything that might get in the way of those purposes."

The logical contradiction test is broader than impossibility preemption (viewed narrowly) but substantially less expansive than obstacle preemption. To illustrate application of the logical contradiction test, Nelson uses the following example:

> Imagine, for instance, that a valid rule of federal law gives workers the right to join a labor union (subject to certain qualifications), while state law purports to prohibit all union membership. It is physically possible for workers to comply with both laws by refraining from joining a union. But the logical-contradiction test would still mean that the state law is preempted: A court that enforced the state-law prohibition would be ignoring the federal-law right.[110]

From this example, the logical contradiction test appears to cover cases such as *McDermott* and *Southland*—classified by some as involving impossibility preemption and by others as involving obstacle preemption—but perhaps go no further. While the dissenting Justices in Geier v. American Honda Motor Corp. (2000) described obstacle preemption doctrine as "perhaps inadequately considered," relying in part on Nelson's argument, the Court seems unlikely to constrict its implied preemption analysis to this degree.

Implied Field Preemption

The final implied preemption category is field preemption: the preemption of state law that results "[w]hen the Federal Government completely occupies a given field or an identifiable portion of it" (Pacific Gas & Electric Co. v. State Energy Resources Conservation & Development Comm'n, 1983). In other words, a state law is preempted when it regulates in a field Congress intended to be exclusively federal. Field preemption differs from obstacle preemption because the federal law preempts even state laws with the same purpose—even if both are seeking to promote worker safety, for example.[111] Although the Supreme Court lists field preemption as a separate category from conflict preemption, it has acknowledged that "field pre-emption may be understood as a species of conflict pre-emption: A state law that falls within a pre-empted field conflicts with Congress' intent (either express or plainly implied) to exclude state regulation" (English v. General Electric Co., 1990).

According to Professor Laurence Tribe, "[F]ederal occupation of a field will not be lightly inferred."[112] Nonetheless, the Supreme Court has identified two circumstances in which it finds that Congress has occupied a regulatory field. The first circumstance is pervasive federal regulation: when "[t]he scheme of federal regulation [is] so pervasive as to make reasonable the inference that Congress left no room for the States to supplement it" (Rice v. Santa Fe Elevator Corp., 1947). The more pervasive the federal regulation, the more likely Congress occupied the field. The less pervasive the federal regulation, the less likely Congress occupied the field; otherwise, a legal vacuum might result, with state law preempted but with no particular federal regulation on point.[113] Fields that the Court has found occupied by pervasive federal regulation include the interstate sale of natural gas (Schneidewind v. ANR Pipeline Co., 1988) and aircraft noise in navigable airspace (City of Burbank v. Lockheed Air Terminal, 1973).

The second circumstance is a dominant federal interest: when a federal statute "touch[es] a field in which the federal interest is so dominant that the federal system will be assumed to preclude enforcement of state laws on the same subject" (Rice v. Santa Fe Elevator Corp., 1947). Immigration can be such a field, and Hines v. Davidowitz (1941) is the classic case.[114] In *Hines*, Pennsylvania enacted a statute requiring all aliens in the state to register annually and carry an alien registration card. A year later, Congress enacted a federal alien registration statute, providing for one-time registration and not requiring aliens to carry registration cards. The Supreme Court held that the federal registration statute preempted the state statute because federal law occupied the field. The Court stressed the supreme federal power over foreign affairs, including immigration, explaining that how state governments deal with citizens of other countries can have an important impact on the relations between those countries and the United States as a whole. In addition, the Court emphasized that Congress had adopted a "broad and comprehensive plan" governing immigration and citizenship, by statutes and treaties. As part of that plan, Congress enacted the alien registration statute at issue here (narrowly tailoring its provisions to protect civil liberties, the Court added).

But not all state laws that have something to do with immigration are preempted. The Court has held preempted state laws forbidding aliens to obtain commercial fishing licenses (Takahashi v. Fish & Game Comm'n, 1948) and denying in-state college tuition to aliens who live in but have not immigrated to the United States (Toll v. Moreno, 1982). But it has upheld a state law prohibiting the employment of illegal aliens whose employment would harm lawful residents

(De Canas v. Bica, 1976). Although the Court in *De Canas* reiterated that the federal power over immigration is exclusive, it made clear that not every state law that deals with immigration is a regulation of immigration preempted by federal occupation of the field.

Thus, once a court determines that Congress has occupied a particular field, the question remains whether the state regulation falls within the occupied field. In Pacific Gas & Electric Co. v. State Energy Resources Conservation & Development Comm'n (1983), for example, the Supreme Court concluded that the federal government had occupied the field of nuclear safety. But because California's nuclear moratorium was motivated by economic reasons, it was still not preempted. Had the state prohibition been motivated by safety concerns, the Court indicated (but did not decide) that it would have been preempted. Thereafter, the Court in English v. General Electric Co. (1990) explained that a state law falls within the field of nuclear safety if it either has the purpose of regulating nuclear safety or if it has "some direct and substantial effect" on the safety of nuclear power plants. On the facts, the Court held that a state law claim for intentional infliction of emotional distress, based on alleged retaliation against a whistle-blowing employee at a nuclear power plant, was not preempted. The purpose of the state law claim was to protect employees from abuse by employers, not regulate nuclear safety, and any effect of the law on nuclear safety was "neither direct nor substantial enough" to be preempted.

In recent years, the Court has been less likely to find field preemption than in the past.[115] As Justice Thomas wrote dissenting in Camps Newfound/Owatonna, Inc. v. Town of Harrison (1997): "[O]ur recent cases have frequently rejected field pre-emption in the absence of statutory language expressly requiring it." For example, in Sprietsma v. Mercury Marine (2002), the Court refused to find that the Federal Boat Safety Act preempted the field of "safety regulation of recreational boats," despite a statement in a House Report on the Act asserting that it did so. An exception is United States v. Locke (2000), in which the Court reaffirmed its holding in Ray v. Atlantic Richfield Co. (1978) that Congress has preempted the field of oil tanker design and construction. Thus, field preemption still exists, but only in limited circumstances.

Blurring of Categorical Lines

Although the Supreme Court continues to describe its preemption analysis in a categorical manner, as based on express, conflict, and field preemption, those categories (as the Court acknowledges) are not "rigidly distinct." Thus, as already noted above, field preemption may be characterized as a form of conflict preemption, in which the state law conflicts with Congress' intent to preclude all state regulation in a particular field.

Even the line between express and implied preemption is not as distinct as one might expect. Professor Caleb Nelson uses the following example to illustrate the point.[116] Section 2 of the Federal Arbitration Act provides that written agreements to arbitrate are "valid, irrevocable, and enforceable, save upon such grounds as exist at law or in equity for the revocation of any contract."[117] In Southland Corp. v. Keating (1984), the Supreme Court held that section 2 preempts state laws that make arbitration agreements unenforceable. The Court analyzed the case as involving implied preemption rather than express preemption. But as Professor Nelson explains: "§ 2 can readily be recast in the form of an express preemption clause; for most purposes, it is identical to a provision that 'no state or local government shall adopt or enforce any law or policy that makes a written arbitration agreement . . . invalid, revocable, or unenforceable, save upon such grounds as exist at law or in equity for the revocation of any contract.'" The effect of the two provisions is largely the same in this context, but they would be categorized differently under current preemption doctrine.

The blurring of categorical lines is well illustrated by Gade v. National Solid Wastes Management Ass'n (1992). In *Gade*, the issue was whether the Occupational Safety and Health Act ("OSH Act") preempted an Illinois statute that required licensing of workers at hazardous waste facilities. The plurality opinion analyzed the case as involving implied conflict preemption. It held that the state law was preempted as an obstacle to Congress' purpose of "promot[ing] occupational safety and health while at the same time avoiding duplicative, and possibly counterproductive, regulation." But the plurality acknowledged that it "could as easily" have held that the federal standard "'pre-empts the field' for any nonapproved state law regulating the same safety and health issue."

Justice Kennedy concurred, but characterized the case as involving express preemption rather than implied preemption. He relied on section 18(b) of the OSH Act, which requires a state that "desires to assume responsibility for development and enforcement therein of occupational safety and health standards relating to any occupational safety or health issue with respect to which a Federal standard has been promulgated" to "submit a State plan."[118] According to Justice Kennedy, the "most reasonable inference" from the provision is that a state that does not submit a plan is precluded from regulating in the area. The plurality disagreed with Justice Kennedy's categorization ("We cannot agree that the negative implications of the text . . . *expressly* address the issue of federal preemption"), but found the differing categorization to be immaterial because it did not affect the outcome (although "[f]requently . . . the pre-emptive 'label' we choose will carry with it substantive implications for the scope of preemption"). Thus, at least one Justice was willing to fit *Gade* into each of the preemption categories traditionally recognized by the Court—express preemption, implied conflict preemption, and implied field preemption. If nothing else, *Gade* provides good evidence that the traditional categories may be less useful than one might think in analyzing preemption issues.

Express Preemption Clauses and Implied Preemption Analysis

Preemption is based on congressional intent (the "ultimate touchstone" in the words of the Supreme Court). What if Congress expressly addresses preemption in a statute, through an express preemption clause or a preemption saving clause? Does that eliminate the need to undertake implied preemption analysis? Or does it simply add another step: A court first considers whether the statute expressly preempts the state law; if not, it then undertakes standard implied preemption analysis. The answer, at present at least, is that an express preemption provision does not preclude implied preemption analysis.

Early indications were to the contrary. Language in Cipollone v. Liggett Group, Inc. (1992) suggested that an express preemption provision precluded analysis under implied preemption doctrines. After describing the court of appeals' finding that state common-law claims were impliedly preempted by federal law, the Supreme Court in *Cipollone* stated that "the pre-emptive scope of [the statute] is governed entirely by the express language in § 5" of the Act. The Court explained that "'there is no need to infer congressional intent to pre-empt state laws from the substantive provisions' of the legislation" when Congress expressly addresses preemption. The negative implication of an express preemption clause is that only state statutes addressed by the clause are preempted; others are not. Therefore, according to the Court, "[W]e need only identify the domain expressly preempted by each of those sections." A concurring opinion by Justice Blackmun agreed completely: "We resort to principles of implied pre-emption . . . only when Congress has been silent with respect to pre-emption."

In dissent, Justice Scalia took issue with the majority's "new rule" (among a number of other objections he raised to the Court's analysis). He acknowledged that an express preemption provision might dispel any possibility of field preemption, as "[t]he existence of an express pre-emption provision tends to contradict any inference that Congress intended to occupy a field broader than the statute's express language defines." But the same is not true for conflict preemption, for which the Court's rule is unprecedented and "works mischief." Justice Scalia gave the following example:

> If taken seriously, it would mean, for example, that if a federal consumer protection law provided that no state agency or court shall assert jurisdiction under state law over any workplace safety issue with respect to which a federal standard is in effect, then a state agency operating under a law dealing with a subject other than workplace safety (e.g., consumer protection) could impose requirements entirely contrary to federal law—forbidding, for example, the use of certain safety equipment that federal law requires.

When combined with the presumption against preemption, "the result is extraordinary": "The statute that says anything about pre-emption must say everything; and it must do so with great exactitude." It would take a "most sporting" Congress to "dare to say anything about pre-emption." Instead, the proper approach, in

Justice Scalia's view, is to construe the express preemption clause according to "its ordinary meaning," which may mean either a broad or narrow interpretation, depending on the text.

The issue arose again in Medtronic, Inc. v. Lohr (1996), in which the Court considered whether the express preemption clause in the Medical Device Amendments of 1976 preempted state common-law damages claims for defective medical devices.[119] The Court cited *Cipollone* as establishing that "the pre-emptive language of [the Act] means that we need not go beyond that language to determine whether Congress intended the MDA to pre-empt at least some state law." The Court proceeded to hold that none of the plaintiffs' claims was preempted by the Act, without considering further the possibility of implied preemption. The dissenting Justices (joined by Justice Scalia) agreed they did not need to go beyond the express preemption clause, but would have found the damage claims within the scope of the clause.

The Supreme Court backed away from *Cipollone* in Freightliner Corp. v. Myrick (1995), in which it held that a highway safety standard suspended by a court did not preempt state tort law causes of action. In *Freightliner*, persons injured in accidents with tractor trailer trucks sued the manufacturers of the trucks alleging that the trucks were defective because they were not manufactured with anti-lock brakes. The National Highway Traffic Safety Administration safety standard that allegedly preempted the state lawsuit had been suspended by a lower federal court, however, and the Supreme Court had little difficulty holding that the absence of a federal safety standard did not preempt state law. In so holding, the Court rejected as "without merit" the argument, based on *Cipollone*, that "implied pre-emption cannot exist when Congress has chosen to include an express pre-emption clause in a statute." According to the Court, *Cipollone* did not "announc[e] a categorical rule precluding the co-existence of express and implied pre-emption." Although an "inference that an express pre-emption clause forecloses implied pre-emption" may have been reasonable in *Cipollone*, the case did "not establish a rule" to that effect.

The Court's next tobacco preemption case—Lorillard Tobacco Co. v. Reilly (2001)—relied on the *Cipollone* "inference" in holding that the Federal Cigarette Labeling and Advertising Act preempted Massachusetts regulations on cigarette advertising. The Court addressed only the express preemption clause in the statute, quoting *Freightliner* to the effect that "an express definition of the pre-emptive reach of a statute . . . supports a reasonable inference . . . that Congress did not intend to pre-empt other matters."

But in Sprietsma v. Mercury Marine (2002), the Court returned to the *Freightliner* approach, rejecting an argument that the express preemption clause in that case precluded implied preemption analysis. The Court first held that the express preemption clause in the Federal Boat Safety Act ("FBSA") did not preempt a state tort claim against an outboard motor manufacturer (a conclusion reinforced by the Act's preemption savings clause). The Court then proceeded to consider whether the FBSA impliedly preempted the tort claim, ultimately holding that it did not. The Court quoted from *Freightliner* and from Geier v. American Honda Motor Co. (2000) (a case involving a preemption savings clause), stating flatly that "Congress' inclusion of an express pre-emption clause 'does *not* bar the ordinary workings of conflict preemption principles.'" Thus, the Supreme Court's most recent statement on the matter is that an express preemption clause does not preclude a federal statute from impliedly preempting state law when the two conflict (although it may well preclude field preemption arguments).

An analogous question arises in connection with preemption savings clauses—clauses that expressly save certain state laws from preemption. What effect does such a clause have on implied preemption analysis? Although the Court left the issue open in *Freightliner,* it resolved the issue in *Geier*, in which it held that "the saving clause (like the express pre-emption provision) does *not* bar the ordinary working of conflict pre-emption principles." The Court reiterated that conclusion in Buckman Co. v. Plaintiffs' Legal Committee (2001), rejecting the respondent's argument that the Court "should be reluctant to find a pre-emptive conflict here because Congress included an express pre-emption provision in the MDA." According to the *Buckman* Court: "To the extent respondent posits that anything other than our ordinary pre-emption principles apply under these circumstances, that contention must fail in light of our conclusion last Term in *Geier* v. *American Honda Motor Co.* that neither an express pre-emption provision nor a saving clause 'bars the ordinary working of conflict pre-emption principles.'"

PRESUMPTION AGAINST PREEMPTION

In areas "which the States have traditionally occupied," the Supreme Court has adopted a presumption against preemption—that is, the Court requires (or at least says it requires) a stronger showing before it will find state law preempted than it does in other areas. (Rice v. Santa Fe Elevator Corp., 1947) The justification for the presumption is to preserve state authority in areas in which states traditionally have had the primary power to regulate. Because preemption doctrine "define[s] the sphere of control between federal and state law when they conflict, or appear to conflict,"[120] the Supreme Court's application of the doctrine has important implications for the relative reaches of state and federal power. When the Court applies preemption doctrine broadly, a given federal statute preempts more state laws, thus expanding the reach of the federal government at the expense of the states. When the Court applies preemption doctrine narrowly, the same federal statute preempts fewer state laws, restricting the reach of the federal government and leaving available a broader range of action for the states. Application of a presumption against preemption would reduce the scope of federal preemption, leaving states relatively greater authority vis-à-vis the federal government.

The classic statement of the "presumption against preemption" is from Rice v. Santa Fe Elevator Corp. (1947) (citations omitted):

Congress legislated here in a field which the States have traditionally occupied. So we start with the assumption that the historic police powers of the States were not to be superseded by the Federal Act unless that was the clear and manifest purpose of Congress. Such a purpose may be evidenced in several ways. The scheme of federal regulation may be so pervasive as to make reasonable the inference that Congress left no room for the States to supplement it. Or the Act of Congress may touch a field in which the federal interest is so dominant that the federal system will be assumed to preclude enforcement of state laws on the same subject. Likewise, the object sought to be obtained by the federal law and the character of obligations imposed by it may reveal the same purpose. Or the state policy may produce a result inconsistent with the objective of the federal statute. It is often a perplexing question whether Congress has precluded state action or by the choice of selective regulatory measures has left the police power of the States undisturbed except as the state and federal regulations collide.

The Supreme Court regularly cites the presumption against preemption in implied preemption cases.[121] In addition, the Court has relied on the presumption in interpreting express preemption clauses (as well as preemption savings clauses) in federal statutes. In Cipollone v. Liggett Group, Inc. (1992), the Supreme Court stated that "we must construe these [express preemption] provisions in light of the presumption against pre-emption of state police power regulations." That presumption, according to the Court, "reinforces the appropriateness of a narrow reading" of such a clause. A court "must fairly but—in light of the strong presumption against preemption—narrowly construe" the statutory language. The Court likewise applied the presumption against preemption in construing express preemption clauses in Medtronic, Inc. v. Lohr (1996) and Lorillard Tobacco Co. v. Reilly (2001), relying on *Cipollone* in both cases. Indeed, in *Medtronic* the Court emphasized that the "approach is consistent with both federalism concerns and the historic primacy of state regulation of matters of health and safety." The Court also commonly has applied the presumption against preemption in interpreting the express preemption and preemption savings clauses in ERISA[122]—the Employee Retirement Income Security Act.

Congress presumably can make the presumption inapplicable by providing, for example, that federal preemption "shall be broadly and liberally construed to ensure that disparate State or local requirements or standards do not affect the uniformity and comprehensiveness of the standards promulgated under" a statute.[123] Moreover, even if applicable, it is only a *presumption* against preemption. The presumption can be overcome when Congress has a "clear and manifest purpose" to preempt state law. An express preemption clause certainly can evidence such a purpose (Egelhoff v. Egelhoff, 2001). Other possibilities are listed in *Rice*. Indeed, the Supreme Court holds state laws preempted with sufficient regularity even when the presumption against preemption applies that some have questioned whether it might not in fact be a presumption *in favor* of preemption.[124]

In deciding whether the presumption against preemption applies, the Court considers two questions. The first is whether Congress is legislating in an area in which states traditionally have regulated. The Court has not adopted a test for identifying areas traditionally regulated by the states, but it has linked the requirement to the state police power (the broad power of states to regulate for the health, safety, and welfare of their citizens).[125] A classic description of the police power is found in the Vermont Supreme Court's opinion in Thorpe v. Rutland & Burlington R.R. Co. (1854):

> This police power of the state extends to the protection of the lives, limbs, health, comfort, and quiet of all persons, and the protection of all property within the state. According to the maxim, *Sic utere tuo ut alienum non lædas* [Use your own property so as not to injure that of another], which being of universal application, it must of course, be within the range of legislative action to define the mode and manner in which every one may so use his own as not to injure others.

As such, the Supreme Court has identified a number of areas traditionally regulated by the states. The following list is by no means an exhaustive one:

- Health and safety—e.g., New York State Conference of Blue Cross & Blue Shield Plans v. Travelers Insurance Co. (1995); Hillsborough County v. Automated Medical Laboratories, Inc. (1985).
- Tort and accident law—e.g., Silkwood v. Kerr-McGee Corp. (1984).
- Employment—e.g., De Canas v. Bica (1976).
- Family law—e.g., Hisquierdo v. Hisquierdo (1979).
- Competition law (laws regulating monopolies and cartels)—e.g., California v. ARC America Corp. (1989).
- Public utilities—e.g., Pacific Gas & Electric Co. v. State Energy Resources Conservation & Development Comm'n (1983).
- Advertising—e.g., Lorillard Tobacco Co. v. Reilly (2001).

Examples of areas in which the states have not traditionally regulated are much less common. One recent example may be Buckman Co. v. Plaintiffs' Legal Committee (2001). The plaintiff in *Buckman* sought damages for fraud, alleging that the defendant made misrepresentations to the federal Food & Drug Administration in obtaining approval of its orthopedic bone screws. In holding that the claim was preempted by federal law, the Court rejected any presumption against preemption in the case. According to the Court, "[p]olicing fraud against federal agencies" is not an area of traditional state regulation. "To the contrary, the relationship between a federal agency and the entity it regulates is inherently federal in character because the relationship originates from, is governed by, and terminates according to federal law."

If the area is one traditionally regulated by the states, the presumption against preemption applies unless the federal government historically has had a significant presence in the area as well. One such case is United States v. Locke (2000), which held that the extensive federal regulatory scheme governing oil tankers preempted regulations adopted by the State of Washington in response to the *Exxon Valdez* oil spill. The Court found that the presumption against preemption did not apply in *Locke* because "national and international maritime commerce" was not an area traditionally occupied by the states. To the contrary, "Congress has legislated in the field from the earliest days of the Republic, creating an extensive federal statutory and regulatory scheme." In holding the presumption inapplicable, the Court revisited Rice v. Santa Fe Elevator Corp. (1947), in particular the excerpt from *Rice* quoted above as the classic statement of the presumption against preemption. Even though the second sentence in the excerpt is commonly quoted in support of a broad presumption against preemption, "[t]he qualification given by the word 'so' and the preceding sentence[ ] in *Rice* are of considerable consequence," the Court reasoned. The presumption is triggered only when Congress has legislated "in a field which the States have traditionally occupied," not "when the State regulates in an area where there has been a history of significant federal presence." The key word is "occupied." It is not enough that the area is one in which states have traditionally regulated. Instead, the area must be one in which the states traditionally have had primary regulatory authority.

Crosby v. National Foreign Trade Council (2000), decided shortly after *Locke,* seemed to be a likely case for the Court to hold the presumption inapplicable as well. *Crosby* involved a challenge to a Massachusetts law that barred state entities from buying goods and services from companies doing business with Burma (Myanmar). The Court held the law preempted by federal legislation that imposed sanctions on Burma. One would have expected the Court to reject application of the presumption against preemption in the case. Although presumably state governments have traditionally regulated their own buying practices, this would not be an area "occupied" by the states because of the central and long-standing federal role in foreign relations. Instead, the Court declined to rule on the issue, "leav[ing] for another day consideration in this context of a presumption against preemption." It assumed for the sake of argument that the presumption applied, and held that the Massachusetts law was preempted anyway.

In other cases, the Court simply fails to apply the presumption against preemption without addressing whether it is applicable. In Southland Corp. v. Keating (1984), for example, the Supreme Court held that the Federal Arbitration Act applies in state court and preempts conflicting state law. The majority opinion did not discuss the presumption against preemption, even though contract law presumably is an area traditionally regulated by the states. When the

Court reconsidered *Southland* in Allied-Bruce Terminix Cos. v. Dobson (1995), Justice Thomas—in dissent—unsuccessfully relied on the presumption against preemption to argue that *Southland* should be overruled. The *Allied-Bruce* majority did not discuss the presumption, instead reaffirming *Southland* as "well-established law."

Commentators have criticized the Court's use of a presumption against preemption on a variety of grounds. Some argue that the presumption is unjustified, either as a matter of constitutional text or constitutional structure. According to Professor Caleb Nelson, the *non obstante* provision at the end of the Supremacy Clause "rejects a general presumption that federal law does not contradict state law" (in ordinary statutes such provisions override the usual presumption against implied repeal of one statute by another).[126] Professor Viet Dinh argues that by "systematically favor[ing] one result over another," the presumption against preemption "would disrupt the constitutional division of power between federal and state governments, rewrite the laws enacted by Congress, or both."[127] Others assert that the Court does not faithfully apply the presumption against preemption and that in fact the Court's cases more accurately should be seen as reflecting a presumption in favor of preemption.[128] Still others contend that the presumption is not strong enough and that it should be replaced with a "clear statement" rule "requiring that Congress speak clearly and explicitly whenever it preempts state legislation outside those areas that the Constitution reserves for Congress alone."[129] A clear statement rule, however, would have its own problems.[130] In short, it seems that no one is happy with the presumption except perhaps the Supreme Court itself.

TRENDS IN PREEMPTION DECISIONS

Because preemption cases depend so much on the individual federal statute involved, it is hard to get a sense for how, if at all, the Supreme Court's application of that doctrine has evolved over time. Given the "federalism revival" under the Rehnquist Court, one would expect the Court to have become less likely to hold state statutes preempted in recent years. As Professor David O'Brien explains, "A Court composed of Justices who genuinely value 'dual federalism' arguably would strongly favor the states in the area of implied federal preemption," and, thus, "one might have expected the Rehnquist court to cut back on federal preemption."[131]

Examining preemption doctrine gives conflicting indications. On the one hand, the presumption against preemption in areas traditionally occupied by the states should reduce the scope of federal preemption. If the Supreme Court has come to rely more faithfully on the presumption, it should be less likely to find state law preempted. On the other hand, implied preemption doctrines such as obstacle and field preemption remain available as potentially broad bases for preempting state law, and the Court has been willing in at least some cases to construe congressional purposes broadly. If the Court continues to rely on either of these preemption categories, it may be no less likely to find preemption than in the past. In short, from examining preemption doctrine alone it is difficult to identify any trends.

An alternative is to examine preemption decision making in the aggregate: to compare outcomes in Supreme Court preemption cases over time. There are important limitations to such a comparison that make drawing firm conclusions difficult. Not only is the sample of cases the Supreme Court faces by no means standard, but the Court itself sets its agenda by deciding what cases to review. Moreover, the parties control the flow of cases to the Court, and can either decline to seek review or can settle a case outright. As a result, differences in outcomes over time may be due to differences in the cases before the Court rather than differences in the Court's decision making. Nonetheless, with that sizable caveat, taking a look at the Supreme Court's preemption decisions in the aggregate may provide some insights.

Table 3 summarizes the outcomes in the Supreme Court's preemption cases from 1921–2003.[132] Overall, of 173 preemption decisions, the Court held state laws preempted in 89, or 51%, of the cases. The data reveal remarkably little difference over time, and certainly provide no indication of a federalism revival in preemption cases. The Rehnquist Court (1986–2003) held the state law preempted in 49% of the cases in which it decided a preemption issue, exactly the same percentage as the Burger Court (1969–1986). The Rehnquist Court was only slightly less likely to hold a state law preempted from 1993–2003 (48%) than from 1986–1993 (51%). The Warren Court (1953–1969) was more likely than either the Burger Court or the Rehnquist Court to hold a state law preempted (59% of the time), but with such a small sample the difference may simply be due to chance.

The results in Table 3 include both express preemption cases and implied preemption cases. Professor O'Brien, however, suggests that implied preemption cases provide a more meaningful test of the Court's views on federalism in the preemption context than do express preemption cases. He explains:

> In contrast to express congressional preemptions, the Court has greater leeway to affirm states' interests in cases involving implicit statutory preemptions. Siding with the states in such cases is also arguably less institutionally costly: The Court neither thwarts express congressional intention nor directly challenges Congress by erecting a barrier, such as the Tenth Amendment. In other words, when ruling on implicit preemptions, the Court need not second-guess Congress nor simply do the national government's bidding.[133]

Table 4 reports the outcomes in Supreme Court implied preemption cases from 1921–2003. The most striking result is that the Rehnquist Court, and in particular the Rehnquist Court in the last ten years, has been more likely to hold state laws

Table 3
Supreme Court Preemption Decisions

Court	Number	State Law Preempted	State Law Not Preempted
Taft Court (1921–1930)	—	—	—
Hughes Court (1930–1941)	5	3 (60%)	2 (40%)
Stone Court (1941–1946)	3	1 (33%)	2 (66%)
Vinson Court (1946–1953)	4	3 (75%)	1 (25%)
Warren Court (1953–1969)	29	17 (59%)	12 (41%)
Burger Court (1969–1986)	57	28 (49%)	29 (51%)
Rehnquist Court (1986–2003)	75	37 (49%)	38 (51%)
1986–1993*	[35]	[18 (51%)]	[17 (49%)]
1993–2003*	[40]	[19 (48%)]	[21 (53%)]
Total	173	89 (51%)	84 (49%)

Source: David M. O'Brien, "The Supreme Court and Intergovernmental Relations: What Happened to 'Our Federalism'?," 9 *Journal of Law & Politics* (1993), 609, 622, & 629 tables 3 & 6, updated by author.

*The bracketed figures are subtotals for the years 1986–1993 and 1993–2003. The subtotals add to the total for the Rehnquist Court (1986–2003).

Table 4
Supreme Court Preemption Decisions—Implied Preemption Only

Court	Number	State Law Preempted	State Law Not Preempted
Taft Court (1921–1930)	—	—	—
Hughes Court (1930–1941)	5	3 (60%)	2 (40%)
Stone Court (1941–1946)	3	1 (33%)	2 (66%)
Vinson Court (1946–1953)	4	3 (75%)	1 (25%)
Warren Court (1953–1969)	26	17 (65%)	9 (35%)
Burger Court (1969–1986)	47	23 (49%)	24 (51%)
Rehnquist Court (1986–2003)	44	25 (57%)	19 (43%)
1986–1993*	[21]	[11 (52%)]	[10 (48%)]
1993–2003*	[23]	[14 (61%)]	[9 (39%)]
Total	129	72 (56%)	57 (44%)

Source: David M. O'Brien, "The Supreme Court and Intergovernmental Relations: What Happened to 'Our Federalism'?," 9 *Journal of Law & Politics* (1993), 609, 623, & 629 tables 4 & 6, updated by author.

*The bracketed figures are subtotals for the years 1986–1993 and 1993–2003. The subtotals add to the total for the Rehnquist Court (1986–2003).

preempted than the Burger Court, and, indeed, almost as likely as the Warren Court. The Rehnquist Court held state laws preempted in 57% of implied preemption cases, including 61% of the cases from 1993–2003. By comparison, the Burger Court held state laws preempted in 49% of the cases (identical to the percentage when express preemption cases are included), and the Warren Court held state laws preempted in 65% of implied preemption cases. Again, selection bias and small sample sizes caution against drawing firm conclusions from the data. Nonetheless, it is fair to say that nothing in the data indicate a trend toward restricting preemption of state law, and, if anything, the data suggest the opposite. Needless to say, given the Court's increased emphasis on states' rights in other substantive areas, such as the commerce power and the Eleventh Amendment, the results are surprising.

REFORM OF PREEMPTION DOCTRINE

Because of dissatisfaction with current preemption doctrine, various reforms have been proposed (or undertaken), generally by those who favor a narrower reach of federal power vis-à-vis the states. Several presidents, beginning with President Reagan, have regulated administrative agency preemption by use of executive orders. Congress now requires a statement in congressional reports on the extent to which proposed legislation would preempt state law.[134] But Congress has not acted on other bills that would have made more significant changes in preemption doctrine. Still other proposals have come from commentators and advocacy groups, some of which would alter preemption doctrine dramatically.

One complication should be noted: Preemption issues can cut across traditional political lines, making predictions about legislative change (and the outcomes of court cases, for that matter[135]) difficult. Conservatives tend to favor states' rights and less government regulation of business. To the extent a federal statute would preempt a state law viewed as imposing "excessive" regulations on businesses, conservatives might support federal preemption even though it would reduce state power to regulate. Conversely, liberals, who tend to favor a stronger federal government and more government regulation, might in such a case advocate leaving the matter to the states.[136] In short, the politics of preemption, like the legal doctrine, also can be a "muddle."

Executive Orders

In 1987, President Reagan promulgated Executive Order 12612, which directed administrative agencies to give greater consideration to federalism principles in their actions.[137] Among other things, the order sought to constrain agencies in the exercise of their power to preempt state laws, as consistent with the "fundamental federalism principles" underlying the Constitution. Section 4 of Executive Order 12612 set out a number of requirements for agencies to follow before taking any action to preempt state law. First, the order permitted federal agencies to construe federal statutes as preempting state law only when (1) the statute contains an express preemption clause; (2) "there is some other firm and palpable evidence compelling" a finding of preemption; or (3) the state law "directly conflicts" with the federal statute. Second, when a federal statute does not itself preempt state law, the order allowed agencies to adopt regulations that would preempt state law only when expressly authorized by the statute or "some other firm and palpable evidence" indicates Congress so intended. Third, the agency must limit any preemption by regulation to the "minimum level necessary to achieve the objectives of the statute." Finally, the agency was to consult with state officials as soon as practicable when preemption issues arise, and give state officials notice and an opportunity to participate in proceedings that may result in preemption of state law.

The order also precluded agencies from proposing legislation to Congress that would preempt state law, unless preemption was consistent with fundamental principles of federalism and necessary to meet a "clearly legitimate national purpose."[138] Finally, each agency was to designate an official to be responsible for compliance with the order. Among other responsibilities, that official was to determine whether a proposed agency action had a sufficient impact on federalism to require preparation of a "Federalism Assessment." In preparing a Federalism Assessment, the agency must evaluate and report on its compliance with the other requirements of Executive Order 12612 and identify any costs and burdens a proposed policy would impose on the states. The order required the agency to "consider any such Assessment in all decisions involved in promulgating and implementing the policy."

Executive Order 12612 continued in force through the administration of President George H.W. Bush and into the Clinton presidency. On May 14, 1998, however, President Clinton issued his own federalism order—Executive Order 13083—that took a significantly different approach to federalism from the Reagan order, emphasizing federal supremacy over states' rights.[139] For example, section 3 of the Clinton order identified nine "[m]atters of national or multi-state scope that justify Federal action," such as when multiple states are involved, when "uniform national standards" are needed, when states have "not adequately protected individual rights and liberties," when federal regulation would be less expensive, and so on. The order's justifications for federal regulation were in sharp contrast to the Reagan order's repeated emphasis that "the presumption of sovereignty should rest with the individual States."[140] Most significantly for present purposes, the Clinton order jettisoned altogether the Reagan order's restrictions on preemption of state law. It also eliminated the requirement of a formal

Federalism Assessment, although the order did require consultation with state and local officials and an assessment of their concerns in any proposed regulation. The order was to take effect 90 days following its issuance.

State and local government groups reacted vocally (albeit somewhat slowly) to Executive Order 13083, complaining in particular about the Clinton administration's failure to consult with them before promulgating the order.[141] Congress also got into the act. The Regulatory Affairs Subcommittee of the House Committee on Government Reform and Oversight held hearings on the order,[142] and the Senate unanimously passed a "sense of the Senate" resolution calling for President Clinton to repeal the order.[143] On August 5, 1998, shortly before Executive Order 13083 was to take effect, President Clinton suspended the order "in order to enable full and adequate consultation with State and local elected officials."[144]

A year later, President Clinton promulgated a new federalism order, Executive Order No. 13132.[145] This order backtracked from the previous Clinton order and more closely followed the Reagan order.[146] The order dropped the listing of matters justifying federal action from the previous Clinton order, and reinstituted the special requirements for preemption from the Reagan order. The requirements were softened somewhat from the Reagan order—permitting an agency to construe a statute as preempting state law only on the basis of an express preemption clause or "some other clear evidence" of congressional intent—but nonetheless very similar. Likewise, the revised Clinton order required a "federalism summary impact statement" in proposed rules, similar but not identical to the Federalism Assessment in the Reagan order. Thus, the result of the consultation between the Clinton administration and state and local governments largely was to maintain the status quo, which continues to the present. As of the time this book went to press, President George W. Bush had not issued his own federalism order.

Although the federalism executive orders put in place a structure to protect the interests of states in the administrative process, the limited available evidence suggests that the orders have had little impact in practice. A 1999 study by the General Accounting Office found that of the 11,414 final rules issued by agencies between April 1996 and December 1998, only 26 percent (3016) even mentioned the Executive Order (usually in a preamble stating that no Federalism Assessment was necessary) and only five rules (0.04 percent!) contained a Federalism Assessment.[147] There is no evidence that compliance was better under other presidents. Perhaps compliance with the other requirements of the orders has been better, or perhaps agencies have simply stopped issuing preemptive regulations. But, again, there is no evidence on either point. Supporters of federal legislation that would codify the federalism orders have cited the apparently limited compliance with the orders as one reason legislation is needed.

Federal Legislation

One congressional effort to reform preemption doctrine is a provision in the Unfunded Mandates Reform Act of 1995 ("UMRA"), enacted as Public Law No. 104-4.[148] The provision requires congressional committees to include with any report on a bill or joint resolution "an explicit statement on the extent to which the bill or joint resolution is intended to preempt any State, local, or tribal law, and, if so, an explanation of the effect of such preemption."[149] After reiterating the statutory requirement, the Senate Committee report on the provision added that "[t]o the maximum extent possible, this intention to preempt should also be clear in the statutory language."[150] No such "clear statement rule" appears in the text of UMRA, however.

As a result, it is now commonplace for congressional committee reports to indicate their "[c]ompliance with Public Law 104-4." The following preemption assessment is from the House Report on a bill to encourage donations of food to nonprofit organizations:

> H.R. 2428 contains one mandate on state and local governments as defined in Public Law 104-4. The bill would preempt civil and criminal liability laws of state and local governments that deal with the donation of food and grocery products to nonprofit organizations. As a result of the preemption, states and localities could lose some income from civil and criminal penalties. However, based on information from the National Association of Attorneys General and Second Harvest, a national network of food banks, CBO estimates that any such loses would be negligible.[151]

Although some preemption assessments are more elaborate,[152] the vast majority assert simply that "[t]his bill is not intended to preempt any State, local, or tribal law."[153]

Other congressional attempts at preemption reform would go well beyond the preemption assessments required by UMRA, but have not been adopted. The Federalism Act of 1999, for example, included several provisions that would have altered current preemption doctrine in important ways.[154] Section 7 of the bill sought to codify central elements of the Reagan (and second Clinton) executive order, locking them in by statute rather than leaving their existence up to the discretion of each individual president. The bill required agencies to consult with potentially affected state and local governments and to publish a federalism impact statement with proposed and final rules. Section 8 provided for a federalism impact assessment for proposed legislation similar to that required under UMRA.

More significantly, section 9 set out rules of construction that "would appear to abolish the doctrine of field preemption and impose significant new limits on conflict preemption"[155] (in subsection (a)) as well as providing a statutory basis for the presumption against preemption (in subsection (c)). The text of the proposed provision was as follows:

(a) Statutes. No Federal statute enacted after the effective date of this Act shall preempt, in whole or in part, any State or local government law, ordinance, or regulation, unless the statute expressly states that such preemption is intended or unless there is a direct conflict between such statute and a State or local law, ordinance, or regulation so the two cannot be reconciled or consistently stand together.

(b) Rules. No Federal rule issued after the effective date of this Act under any provision of law enacted after that effective date shall preempt, in whole or in part, any State or local government law, ordinance, or regulation, unless the statute under which the rule is issued, or another statute, expressly states that such preemption is intended.

(c) Favorable construction. Any ambiguity in this Act, or in any other Federal rule issued or Federal statute enacted after the date of the enactment of this Act, shall be construed in favor of preserving the authority of State and local governments.

Finally, section 10 of the bill provided for biennial reports on federal rules, federal statutes, and federal and state court decisions (presumably construing federal rules and statutes) that preempt state laws.

Other Reform Proposals

Even more extensive reforms have been suggested by commentators and advocacy groups. Several were discussed earlier, such as replacing obstacle preemption with a narrower logical contradiction test and replacing the presumption against preemption with a clear statement rule. A broad ranging position paper on "federalism reform," issued by the Heritage Foundation (a conservative think tank) in response to President Clinton's original federalism order, suggests other possibilities.[156] As a short-term strategy, the position paper recommended codifying President Reagan's federalism order "so that future Administrations cannot thwart the spirit of the Constitution." As a mid-term strategy, it supported construing the commerce power narrowly so as to reduce the power of Congress to enact preemptive legislation.

Finally, as a long-term strategy, the paper proposed a more "radical reform option": giving states a veto over federal laws or regulations that preempt state law or otherwise restrict state authority. Under the proposal, a supermajority (two-thirds) of the states could veto a federal law within three to five years after passage. Not all federal laws would be subject to veto. Even proponents of such a "states' rights veto" acknowledged that states should not be permitted to veto foreign policy or national security measures, and that the veto should be inapplicable to federal treaties. But if federal officials "still found it easy to put in place rules and regulations that run contrary to the true spirit and intent of the Constitution" after other reforms are tried, this option "would ensure the Founders' original balance of powers was restored and protected."

This proposal for a state veto over federal law turns the original Virginia Plan for the Constitution on its head. As explained in Part I, an important element of the Virginia Plan (as well as of James Madison's conception for a new national government) was a congressional negative—that is, a veto by Congress over state laws inconsistent with the Constitution. The Constitutional Convention rejected the congressional negative and replaced it with the Supremacy Clause. A state veto over federal legislation, whether by supermajority or otherwise, was no part of the Founders' design. Certainly the constitutional landscape has changed since ratification (with the direct election of senators and the expansion of the commerce power, for example). But, if nothing else, the suggestion that a states' rights veto is necessary to "ensure the Founders' original balance of powers" is ironic in the extreme.

AN APPLICATION: FEDERAL ARBITRATION ACT PREEMPTION

It is difficult to get a sense of the complexities of preemption doctrine without considering how the doctrine applies in a particular subject area. This section briefly examines how preemption doctrine applies under the Federal Arbitration Act ("FAA").[157] The FAA makes arbitration agreements, whether entered into before or after a dispute arises, "valid, irrevocable, and enforceable, save upon such grounds as exist at law or in equity for the revocation of any contract."[158] In Southland Corp. v. Keating (1984), the Supreme Court first held that the FAA applies in state court and preempts state law,[159] a holding it reaffirmed in Allied-Bruce Terminix Cos. v. Dobson (1995) (the case that was the culmination of the dispute described at the beginning of this Part). A central principle of FAA preemption is nondiscrimination: State laws are preempted only if they treat arbitration clauses differently from how they treat other contracts. Beyond that central principle, however, many fundamental questions are still unanswered, despite over half a dozen Supreme Court cases in the last twenty years dealing with FAA preemption.[160]

Several points are settled about FAA preemption.[161] First, state laws that invalidate arbitration agreements by treating arbitration differently from how they treat contracts generally are preempted. The Supreme Court's arbitration cases to date have dealt almost exclusively with these sorts of state laws. In *Southland*, for example, the Court held preempted a California law that invalidated agreements to arbitrate claims under the state's Franchise Investment Law (which was enacted to protect franchisees from—allegedly—abusive practices by franchisors). In *Allied-Bruce*, the Court held preempted an Alabama law that made all predispute arbitration agreements unenforceable. In each case the state law had two key characteristics: (1) it did not apply to contracts generally; and (2) it invalidated the parties' arbitration agreement, in whole or in part, so that the parties ended up going to court instead of arbitration to resolve their dispute.

Second, general contract law defenses, which apply to all contracts and not just arbitration agreements, generally are not preempted. The statutory basis for this principle is the final clause in section 2 of the FAA, which permits courts to invalidate an arbitration agreement "upon such grounds as exist at law or in equity for the revocation of any contract." Thus, a court can refuse to enforce an arbitration agreement when it finds that the parties did not agree to arbitrate, that a party was tricked into agreeing to arbitrate, that a party materially breached the arbitration agreement, and so on.[162] The Supreme Court explained the distinction in *Allied-Bruce*:

> States may regulate contracts, including arbitration clauses, under general contract law principles and they may invalidate an arbitration clause "upon such grounds as exist at law or in equity for the revocation of *any* contract." 9 U.S.C. § 2 (emphasis added). What States may not do is decide that a contract is fair enough to enforce all its basic terms (price, service, credit) but not fair enough to enforce its arbitration clause. The Act makes any such state policy unlawful, for that kind of policy would place arbitration clauses on an unequal "footing," directly contrary to the Act's language and Congress' intent.

Thus, as construed by the Supreme Court, the FAA only preempts state laws that discriminate against arbitration agreements.

A number of other issues remain unsettled in the lower courts, however. State laws that single out arbitration clauses may be preempted, while generally applicable contract defenses are not. What about state laws that apply to some contract provisions (including arbitration clauses) but not all? An example is a state law that invalidates contract clauses providing for court hearings or arbitration proceedings to be held in another state. The statute does not single out arbitration clauses—it applies to contract clauses providing for out-of-state court hearings as well. But the statute does not apply to all contracts. Lower courts are split on whether such state laws fall within the final clause of section 2 and avoid preemption.[163]

Further, the Supreme Court has suggested that in some circumstances even generally applicable contract law defenses might be preempted. But what those circumstances are is not clear. A court may not, according to the Court in Perry v. Thomas (1987), "rely on the uniqueness of an agreement to arbitrate as a basis for a state-law holding that enforcement would be unconscionable, for this would enable the court to effect what we hold today the state legislature cannot." In other words, a court cannot refuse to enforce an arbitration clause on unconscionability grounds (i.e., because it is too unfair) solely because it precludes the parties from having their dispute resolved in court. But the Supreme Court has not addressed whether other applications of general contract law defenses to arbitration clauses also might be preempted. For example, lower courts have invalidated arbitration clauses on the ground that other aspects of the clause were unconscionable (such as that the clause required the consumer to arbitrate but permitted the business to go to court, or specified an unfair process for selecting the arbitrators). Such courts (when they even addressed the preemption issue) generally have rejected preemption challenges to their holdings (e.g., Ticknor v. Choice Hotels International, Inc., 9th Cir. 2001). The Supreme Court, however, has yet to define when, if ever, those holdings go so far as to be preempted by the FAA.

A final unsettled issue is whether (and if so, under what circumstances) state laws that regulate the arbitration process, rather than invalidating the parties' agreement, are preempted. A number of states have adopted laws that, while they apply only to arbitration, do not invalidate the parties' arbitration agreement. Instead, the laws regulate how the arbitration proceeding will be conducted. California, for example, has promulgated detailed disclosure requirements for neutral arbitrators, requiring them to disclose a wide variety of circumstances that might give rise to potential conflicts of interest.[164] The Supreme Court has not yet decided the extent to which, if at all, the FAA preempts such state laws. In Green Tree Financial Corp. v. Bazzle (2003), the Court granted review to consider whether the FAA preempts a state rule authorizing courts to order that arbitration proceed on a class-wide basis (i.e., like a class action in court). But the Court resolved the case on other grounds, without deciding this preemption issue. Commentators have suggested a variety of approaches to dealing with such "second generation" FAA preemption cases—ranging from no preemption to total preemption.[165] At present, the proper approach to analyzing such cases is unresolved.

* * * * *

The Supreme Court has sought in recent years to clarify its preemption doctrine. But while describing that doctrine may have gotten simpler, applying it has not. As this discussion of Federal Arbitration Act preemption suggests, determining whether a particular state statute is preempted can be a complex undertaking with no certain outcome. The Supreme Court surely will have a steady (even if not increasing) caseload of preemption cases for decades to come.

Federal Immunity from State Law

INTRODUCTION

On August 21, 1992, several federal agents encountered Randy Weaver, his friend Kevin Harris, and Weaver's teenage son Sammy, while scouting out Weaver's property in advance of arresting him on federal weapons charges.[166] Shots were exchanged (although what triggered the shoot-out is uncertain[167]), killing Sammy Weaver and a deputy U.S. Marshal. Weaver and Harris withdrew to Weaver's ranch, where they holed up with Weaver's wife (Vicki) and children. The ranch and property were located at Ruby Ridge, Idaho.

FBI Agent Lon Horiuchi was part of the hostage rescue team sent to Ruby Ridge following the shoot-out. Horiuchi was a trained FBI marksman who could hit a one-quarter inch target from 220 yards away. When Horiuchi arrived, he was briefed on what had happened, including that Weaver was a veteran of the Special Forces and a separatist who hated the federal government. Horiuchi also was briefed on the "rules of engagement," which authorized the team to shoot any armed adult male so long as no child would be injured by the shot. The rules were a departure from the standard FBI rules of engagement, which permitted an FBI agent to use deadly force only in self-defense or to prevent serious harm to another.

The next day, Horiuchi staked out a position several hundred yards from the Weaver cabin. He was armed with a high-powered rifle and telescopic sight. At about 6:00 in the evening, Horiuchi saw two men and a young woman (Harris, Weaver, and Weaver's teenage daughter, Sara) run toward a rock outcropping near the cabin. One of the men was carrying a rifle. After watching the group move through the trees for several minutes, Horiuchi saw the man with the gun look toward the sky. Thinking that the man might shoot at an FBI helicopter surveying the area, Horiuchi fired a shot that lightly wounded him (although at the time Horiuchi thought the shot had missed). The group then ran back toward the cabin. The man now carrying the rifle was the last of the three running toward the cabin.[168] Believing that the group was taking up a defensive position, where they could shoot out but Horiuchi could not shoot in (because of the risk of hitting the children), Horiuchi prepared to fire again. As the man approached the cabin, Horiuchi fired a shot toward the open door, leading his target. The shot struck the man in the shoulder—but only after hitting Vicki Weaver, who was standing out of sight in the doorway holding an infant. The shot hit Weaver in the head, killing her instantly.

The Justice Department's Office of Professional Responsibility conducted an internal investigation of the shooting. It concluded that while Horiuchi's first shot was "objectively reasonable," the second shot—the one that killed Vicki Weaver—was an unconstitutional use of excessive force. Nonetheless, the Justice Department decided not to file federal criminal charges against Horiuchi because it could not establish beyond a reasonable doubt that he had acted wilfully, a necessary element for a federal civil rights violation.[169]

Thereafter, the State of Idaho charged Horiuchi with involuntary manslaughter, alleging that Horiuchi killed Vicki Weaver "in a reckless, careless or negligent manner."[170] As the Justice Department explained in a subsequent press release, the state crime of involuntary manslaughter requires a different showing of intent from a federal civil rights violation, recklessness rather than wilfulness.[171] Horiuchi pleaded not guilty to the state charges. After a preliminary hearing in state court, Horiuchi removed the case to federal court as permitted by federal law.[172]

Once in federal court, Horiuchi sought to have the state indictment dismissed. He relied on a further implication of the Supremacy Clause: that, under appropriate circumstances, it protects the federal government and its instrumentalities from interference by the states. The general principle was stated by the Supreme Court in McCulloch v. Maryland (1819): "[T]he States have no power, by taxation or otherwise, to retard, impede, burden, or in any manner control, the operations of the constitutional laws enacted by Congress to carry into execution the powers vested in the general government." Professor Laurence Tribe states that the doctrine—known variously as intergovernmental immunity, Supremacy Clause immunity, or simply federal immunity from state law—is "best understood as posing an issue essentially of federal preemption."[173] But Supremacy Clause immunity differs from general preemption doctrine in that it deals with attempts to apply state law directly against the federal government, where the risk of interference with federal functions is the greatest.

This Part first discusses federal immunity from state taxes, the most commonly litigated use of Supremacy Clause immunity. State taxes are invalid when they are imposed directly on the federal government or its instrumentalities and when they discriminate against the federal government or those who deal with it. This Part then considers federal immunity from state regulation, where analogous principles govern. Finally, it examines federal immunity from state criminal law, the basis for Horiuchi's motion to dismiss the manslaughter charges brought against him by the State of Idaho. This is the least developed area of federal immunity, as illustrated by the difficult time the courts had in resolving Horiuchi's claim of immunity.

FEDERAL IMMUNITY FROM STATE TAXES

The most commonly litigated issue of federal immunity involves taxes: To what extent must the federal government, or parties who deal with the federal government, pay state taxes on their activities? Since the Supreme Court first considered the issue in McCulloch v. Maryland (1819), it "has never questioned the propriety of absolute federal immunity from state taxation" (United States v. New Mexico, 1982), although it has struggled mightily at times in defining its scope.

Background

Federal immunity from state taxes was first recognized in McCulloch v. Maryland (1819), discussed in detail in Part I. In *McCulloch*, the Supreme Court held invalid a Maryland stamp tax on bank notes issued by the Bank of the United States. The Bank's charter did not address whether it had to pay state taxes. But because (in Chief Justice Marshall's famous dictum) "the power to tax involves the power to destroy," the Court held that the Supremacy Clause required the invalidation of the Maryland tax. A state that taxes the federal government is taxing an entity created in part by nonresidents of that state, Marshall reasoned, over whom the state has no authority. The distinction (one that "always exists, and always must exist," according to Marshall) is "between the action of the whole on a part, and the action of a part on the whole—between the laws of a government declared to be supreme, and those of a government which, when in opposition to those laws, is not supreme."

On its facts, the holding of *McCulloch* was limited to state taxes that discriminated against the federal government—the stamp tax applied only to the Bank of the United States, not to other banks in the state. In cases after *McCulloch*, however, the Supreme Court recognized a broad protection for federal entities even from nondiscriminatory state taxes. In Dobbins v. Commissioners of Erie County (1842), for example, the Court held that a generally applicable local tax could not constitutionally be applied to the income of a federal employee, in this case the captain of a federal revenue cutter ship. The Court reasoned that application of state taxes to federal income would require Congress to increase salaries to offset the amount of the tax, and that the captain of the revenue ship, no less than the ship itself (which the state conceded it could not tax), should be protected from state interference. Citing *McCulloch*, the Court held that "the state governments cannot lay a tax upon the constitutional means employed by the government of the Union to execute its constitutional powers."

Eventually, federal immunity from state taxes became linked with state immunity from federal taxes under the general heading of "intergovernmental immunity." The notion was reciprocity: State governments should be free from federal taxation to the same extent the federal government was free from state taxation. Thus, in Collector v. Day (1871), the Court held that because states could not tax the income of federal employees, Congress could not tax the income of state employees (in the case, a state court judge). It began by affirming the correctness of *Dobbins*, and then concluded that "upon the same construction of that instrument [i.e., the Constitution], and for like reasons," the federal government is prohibited from taxing the income of a state employee. Under the Constitution, states retained the sovereign power to tax "in respect to which the State is as independent of the general government as that government is independent of the States." As a result, "[t]he supremacy of the general government . . . in respect to the question before us, cannot be maintained"; "[t]he two governments are upon an equality."

With the growth of the federal government in the 1930s and the perceived need for more government spending during the Great Depression, states began to chafe at the increasing tax revenue lost due to federal immunity. Thereafter, the Court cut back on the extent of federal tax immunity, overruling a number of prior cases in the process. Thus, in Helvering v. Mountain Producers Corp. (1938), the Court overruled Gillespie v. Oklahoma (1922), which had struck down a state tax on income from land leased from a federal instrumentality. In Alabama v. King & Boozer (1941), the Court overruled Panhandle Oil Co. v. Mississippi ex rel. Knox (1928) and upheld a state sales tax on purchases by a contractor that had a cost-plus contract with the United States. Today, *Panhandle* is best known for Justice Oliver Wendell Holmes's rejoinder (in dissent) to the Marshall dictum in *McCulloch*: "The power to tax is not the power to destroy while this Court sits." And in Graves v. New York ex rel. O'Keefe (1939), the Court expressly overruled Collector v. Day and implicitly overruled *Dobbins*[174] in upholding application of New York's income tax to a federal employee's income. According to Justice Frankfurter concurring in *Graves*, Holmes's rejoinder in *Panhandle* "brushed away by one stroke" of his pen the "web of unreality spun from Marshall's famous dictum," laying the groundwork for the Court's modern approach to federal tax immunity.

Federal tax immunity was to become unlinked from state tax immunity as well. As the Supreme Court recognized in South Carolina v. Baker (1988), the authority for the two immunities is different (the Supremacy Clause for federal tax immunity and "constitutional structure and a concern for protecting state sovereignty" for state tax immunity), the "underlying political theory" of the immunities is different (referring back to *McCulloch*'s distinction between "the action of a part on the whole" and "the action of the whole on a part"), and the scope of the immunities is different ("federal tax immunity has always been greater than the States' immunity").

In an often-quoted passage, the Supreme Court in *Baker* described the current scope of federal tax immunity as follows:[175]

> [U]nder current intergovernmental tax immunity doctrine, the States can never tax the United States directly but can tax any private parties with whom it does business, even though the financial burden falls on the United States, as long as the tax does not discriminate against the United States or those with whom it deals. A tax is considered to be directly on the Federal Government only "when the levy falls on the United States itself, or on an agency or instrumentality so closely connected to the Government that the two cannot realistically be viewed as separate entities." (citations omitted)

The description can usefully be restated as involving three steps of analysis. First, is the legal incidence of the state tax on the federal government itself? This "legal incidence" test defines when a tax is directly on the federal government. It focuses not on the party that bears the economic burden of the tax (its "economic incidence") but instead on the party that state law directs to bear the burden (its legal incidence). If the legal incidence of the tax is on the federal government, the state tax is invalid. Second, if not on the federal government itself, is the legal incidence of the tax on a federal instrumentality? Some entities are so closely tied to the federal government that they have the same immunity from state taxes. If the legal incidence of the tax is on a federal instrumentality, the tax is invalid. Third, does the state tax discriminate against the federal government or parties who deal with the federal government? State taxes that treat the federal government or those who deal with it less favorably than other groups are invalid. The rest of this section discusses each of these steps in more detail.

Legal Incidence Test

The general principle is that states may not impose taxes "directly" on the federal government (United States v. New Mexico, 1982). Thus, a state cannot collect property taxes on a military base, personal property taxes on military equipment, or a gross receipts tax on federal tax revenues. When a state seeks to tax some aspect of federal operations directly, the federal government is immune from the tax. Federal immunity does not extend, however, to private parties who deal with the federal government (unless the private party somehow qualifies as a federal instrumentality, as discussed in the next section). These private parties generally are subject to state taxes just like the rest of us.

When the private parties are engaged in business, they will seek to pass on the taxes to their customers by charging higher prices.[176] That is true whether their customers are other private parties or the federal government. They may not be successful in raising prices enough to pass on the full amount of the tax; their ability to do so will depend on what the market will bear. But to the extent they succeed, the customer will bear at least part of the burden of the tax. This is the "economic incidence" of a tax: which party or parties actually bear the financial burden of a tax after market prices adjust to reflect the amount of the tax.[177]

Not surprisingly, the party that is legally obligated to pay the tax is not necessarily the party that ends up bearing the financial burden of the tax. In other words, the economic incidence of a tax can be very different from its statutory incidence ("the distribution of tax payments based on the legal obligation to remit taxes to the government").[178] One example is payroll taxes. The statutory incidence of payroll taxes is shared equally between the employee and the employer. Economists have "confirmed repeatedly," however, that the economic incidence of payroll taxes is wholly on employees: In other words, employers reduce the wages of employees by the full amount of the tax, so that its full financial burden is borne by employees.[179] By comparison, the economic incidence of property taxes seems to be shared by tenants and landlords, even though the statutory incidence of the tax is solely on the landlord.[180]

Does the fact that the federal government bears the economic burden of a state tax give a private party immunity from paying the tax? The answer is no. In James v. Dravo Contracting Co. (1937), the Supreme Court flatly rejected the proposition that a state tax is unlawful if the economic incidence of the tax is on the federal government. The tax at issue in *Dravo Contracting* was a West Virginia tax on a contractor's gross receipts from federal contracts. The Court first noted that, depending on "the state of the competitive market," the contractor might not be able to pass on the tax to the federal government—in other words that it was not even clear that the federal government bore the economic burden of the tax. But even if it did, the Court held that the tax was valid nonetheless. If such a tax "'affects the federal government at all, it at most gives rise to a burden which is consequential and remote and not to one that is necessary, immediate, or direct'" (quoting Trinityfarm Construction Co. v. Grosjean, 1934). To the extent state taxes such as this one become too burdensome, the Court explained, Congress has the power to intervene.

Rather than on its economic incidence, the legality of a tax under the Supremacy Clause depends on its legal incidence. The legal incidence of a tax is like its statutory incidence in that it depends on what state law, rather than economics, dictates about who bears the burden of the tax. But legal incidence is a "term of art" that may have a different meaning than statutory incidence in certain cases.

The Court first applied the legal incidence test in Alabama v. King & Boozer (1941) to reject a claimed immunity from state tax. King & Boozer sold lumber to private contractors that were building a military base. The federal government paid the contractors on a cost-plus basis, such that any sales tax they paid on the lumber would be charged directly to the federal government. Alabama law imposed a 2 percent sales tax on the sale of the lumber, naming the seller (King & Boozer) as the taxpayer but requiring the seller "to add to the sales price and collect from the purchaser the amount due by the taxpayer on account of said tax." King & Boozer, joined by the United States, challenged the tax in Alabama state court. The trial court upheld the tax, but the Alabama Supreme Court reversed, invalidating the tax. The court concluded that the contractors building the army base were sufficiently connected to the government that the tax was effectively "laid on a transaction by which the United States secures the things desired for governmental purposes." The United States Supreme Court granted certiorari and reversed, upholding the tax.

Under *Dravo Contracting*, the mere fact that the tax was passed on to the government under a cost-plus contract alone was not enough to make it unlawful, as the federal government admitted. Instead, the government argued that the tax was invalid because the legal incidence of the tax fell on the government. The Court accepted that a tax would be invalid if its legal incidence were on the United States. But in this case the legal incidence was on the contractors: The contractors ordered and paid for the lumber (being reimbursed by the government), and thus were the "purchasers" subject to the tax. The control exercised by the federal government over the purchase—approval of all aspects of the transaction—was immaterial. "[H]owever extensively the Government may have reserved the right to restrict or control the action of the contractors in other respects," the Court explained, "neither the reservation nor the exercise of that power gave to the contractors the status of agents of the Government to enter into contracts or to pledge its credit." In a companion case, the Court upheld application of a state use tax to federal contractors on a similar rationale (Curry v. United States, 1941).

Subsequently, the Court applied the legal incidence test in upholding application of local property taxes to property owned by the federal government, but used by private parties. Ordinarily, federally owned property would be immune from property taxes. But here, local governments sought to avoid the immunity by putting the legal incidence of the tax not on the federal government, but on the value of the property to the private party. In a trilogy of cases from Michigan, the Supreme Court agreed, rejecting the claim of immunity (United States v. City of Detroit, 1958 (real property tax on factory leased from federal government); United States v. Township of Muskegon, 1958 (real property tax on factory used under federal permit); City of Detroit v. Murray Corp., 1958 (personal property tax on materials and work in progress under federal contract)). As the Court explained in United States v. Boyd (1964), "The use by the contractor for his own private ends—in connection with commercial activities carried on for profit—is a separate and distinct taxable activity." The Court subsequently applied the principle to uphold a property tax imposed on United States Forest Service workers living in housing provided and owned by the federal government (United States v. County of Fresno, 1977). Because the legal incidence of the tax was on the value to the workers of the federally provided housing, the tax was valid.

Not all applications of the legal incidence test are quite so straightforward, as shown by the Supreme Court's decision in Kern-Limerick, Inc. v. Scurlock (1954). The facts of *Kern-Limerick* were essentially the same as *King & Boozer*, except that in *Kern-Limerick*, the contract between the federal government and the federal contractor provided that the government was the purchaser of the goods and that the contractor as purchasing agent had no liability for the purchase price.[181] The Court concluded that the economic incidence of the tax was no different from the economic incidence of the tax in *King & Boozer*: In both cases, the federal government bore the economic burden. But because of the contract provisions in *Kern-Limerick*, the legal incidence of the tax fell on the United States, not the contractor, and so Supremacy Clause immunity precluded the state from imposing the tax. The Court acknowledged that the contract in *Kern-Limerick* "differs in form but not in economic effect on the United States," and that the government may have chosen that form "to conserve Government funds" (i.e., to avoid payment of state taxes). But that was not enough to undercut federal immunity.

The problem with *Kern-Limerick*, as explained by Professor Laurence Tribe, is not so much federalism (although it does restrict the state power to tax) but separation of powers: Which branch of the federal government should have the power to define federal immunity from state taxes?[182] Ordinarily, Congress is the body that has the power to expand or contract federal tax immunity, as is discussed in more detail below. But under *Kern-Limerick*, administrative agencies (and, indeed, relatively low-level federal employees in administrative agencies) have control over the scope of federal tax immunity. When the agency includes certain provisions in the contract, the federal contractor is immune from state tax; when the provisions are not included, the contractor is subject to state tax.

According to Professor Tribe, the Supreme Court has consistently (except for *Kern-Limerick*) refused to "allow[] the executive to define the state tax consequences for persons who contract with the federal government,"[183] and accordingly *Kern-Limerick* should be overruled. The Supreme Court has not yet done so explicitly, but in United States v. New Mexico (1982), according to Tribe, the "Court virtually read it out of existence."[184] *New Mexico*, like *Kern-Limerick*, addressed the liability of federal contractors for state taxes. (The setting of *New Mexico* is described in detail in the next section.) But in *New Mexico*, the Supreme Court rejected a finding of immunity, distinguishing *Kern-Limerick* on the grounds that the contractors made purchases in their own names; did not inform sellers "that the Government is the only party with an independent interest in the purchase"; did not need advance approval by the government for purchases; and were not formally designated purchasing agents by the federal government.

As a result, even if not yet overruled, *Kern-Limerick* seems largely to be limited to its facts.

Determining when the legal incidence of a tax falls on the federal government thus is a question "shrouded in considerable uncertainty."[185] The Supreme Court has rejected as "error" the view that a party necessarily bears the legal incidence of a tax when it is responsible for paying the amount of the tax to the state (United States v. Mississippi Tax Comm'n, 1975). Thus, when state law requires a seller to pass on a sales tax to the buyer, "[i]t would appear to be indisputable" that the buyer bears the legal incidence of the tax, even though it is the seller who must pay the tax to the state (First Agricultural National Bank v. State Tax Comm'n, 1968). The same is true when state law imposes a tax in the form of a markup on alcoholic beverages and requires the wholesaler to pass on the tax to the retailer (United States v. Mississippi Tax Comm'n, 1975).

Beyond uncertainty over how it should be applied, commentators are divided on the usefulness of the legal incidence test. The test has been criticized as essentially unconnected with any policy goal that might be achieved by federal immunity. As one commentator has written, "[I]t appears that legally incident taxes do not impose significantly greater burdens on the federal government than do taxes economically but not legally incident on the government."[186] The commentator contends that the legal incidence test should be abolished and replaced with a simple nondiscrimination standard, perhaps supplemented with a noninterference standard of the sort described below. On the other hand, Professor Tribe concludes that the "legal incidence rule seems a fairly good one." He contends:

> It signals a return to the principal purpose of the immunity doctrine: "forestalling 'clashing sovereignty' by preventing the States from laying demands directly on the Federal Government." At the same time, it comports with federalism by "giving full range to each sovereign's taxing authority." In addition, it reserves to Congress the authority to adjust the competing symbolic and fiscal claims of federal autonomy and state revenue needs.[187]

Indeed, according to Professor Tribe, concerns that the legal incidence test might be unduly formalistic are particularly ironic, given that the test replaced much more formalistic standards that went before.

To evaluate the legal incidence test, it is helpful to consider some alternative standards that might be used to define when the federal government is immune from state tax. Aside from a standard of complete immunity, the broadest alternative is the economic incidence test: A state tax is unlawful when the economic burden of the tax falls on the federal government, regardless of whether the government is responsible for paying it under state law. The Supreme Court has firmly rejected such a test. Next, is the legal incidence test, under which a state tax is unlawful when state law provides that the burden of the tax falls on the federal government, regardless of who bears the economic burden of the tax. The potential confrontation test is similar to the legal incidence test. Under it, a state tax is unlawful when state law makes the federal government responsible for paying the tax, such that if the tax is not paid, the state can initiate a collection action against the federal government. This test is based on the potential for a confrontation in the form of state efforts to collect its taxes. It differs from the legal incidence test because of cases such as *Mississippi Tax Comm'n* and *First Agricultural National Bank*, which hold that the federal government can bear the legal incidence of a tax even when it is not responsible for paying the tax to the state.

The final two tests focus on actual, rather than potential, effects of state taxes. Under the actual interference test, a state tax is invalid if the economic burden of the tax falls on the federal government, but only if the burden is such that it actually interferes with federal operations. It is like the economic incidence test, except that it requires the burden of the tax to be greater (the economic incidence test thus could be called a potential interference test). Finally, the actual confrontation test would invalidate a state tax only if state law makes the federal government responsible for paying the tax, and the state initiates collection efforts (i.e., there is an actual, as opposed to potential, confrontation between the two sovereigns).

Considering these alternative standards, it is difficult to justify the legal incidence test as avoiding "conflicting sovereignty." Both the potential confrontation test and the actual confrontation test would seem preferable to the legal incidence test in this regard. If instead the Court is trying to protect the federal government from excessive tax burdens, either the economic incidence test or the actual interference test would seem more on point. But both those tests require difficult factual evaluations in determining whether, and the extent to which, the federal government in fact bears the economic burden of a state tax. The legal incidence test, while difficult to apply, requires only legal determinations, not factual ones, about the burden of a tax. As a result, it may be that the best justification for the legal incidence test (to the extent there is one) is administrative convenience: The legal incidence test is easier to apply, and more within the traditional competence of courts, than the alternatives. Of course, if a test is not substantively useful, the fact that it is easy to apply is a lame justification.

Federal Instrumentalities

Some entities, although not technically the federal government itself, are so closely linked to the federal government that they are treated as part of the federal government and thus protected by federal tax immunity as well. The United States military, including military post exchanges (United States v. Mississippi Tax Comm'n, 1975), and cabinet-level federal departments plainly are federal instrumentalities.[188] According to the leading treatise on state taxation, "[f]ederal employees acting within the scope of their official function clearly are federal instrumentalities. The federal government cannot act except through its employees, whether they be the President of the United States or an army private."[189] The Court in McCulloch v. Maryland (1819)—albeit without discussion—held that the federally chartered Bank of the United States was a federal instrumentality, rejecting the State of Maryland's argument to the contrary. Conversely, private contractors engaged in "commercial, profit-making considerations" using their own expertise are not federal instrumentalities even when operating under a cost-plus contract with the federal government, and thus are fully subject to (nondiscriminatory) state taxes on their activities (United States v. Boyd, 1964).

Other cases are not so clear cut. The American Red Cross is one example. When Colorado sought to impose an unemployment compensation tax on the Red Cross, the Red Cross asserted that it was a "federal instrumentality" and thus was immune from the tax. A three-judge trial court found in favor of the Red Cross, and the Supreme Court affirmed (Department of Employment v. United States, 1966). Although setting out "no simple test for ascertaining whether an institution is so closely related to governmental activity as to become a tax-immune instrumentality," the Court determined that "the Red Cross is clearly such an instrumentality." The Court cited the following facts as decisive: (1) the Red Cross was chartered by Congress; (2) it is subject to supervision by the federal government and a regular financial audit by the Department of Defense; (3) the President appoints the principal officer and seven of the other forty-nine governors of the Red Cross; (4) the Red Cross receives substantial "material benefits" from the government (such as its headquarters building), although it is financed primarily by private contributions; (5) the Red Cross provides services "indispensable" to the military, satisfies American obligations under the Geneva Conventions, and provides disaster aid to the states; and (6) the federal government repeatedly has "recognized and acted in reliance upon the Red Cross' status virtually as an arm of the Government." Although Red Cross employees are not government employees and the day-to-day activities of the Red Cross are not controlled by the government, the Court found this no different from some other recognized federal instrumentalities.

By contrast, the Court rejected a claim by several federal contractors to be treated as federal instrumentalities in United States v. New Mexico (1982). The contractors were under contract with the Department of Energy to perform various management and construction duties at the federal government's Sandia and Los Alamos Labs in New Mexico. The contracts, like many federal contracts, were on a cost-plus basis—the contractor was to be paid its costs plus a fixed fee—and described the contractors as agents of the United States. Title to any property purchased passed directly from the seller to the federal government, and the risk of any loss was borne solely by the government. The contracts provided for an "advanced funding" mechanism whereby any purchases arranged by the contractors were paid directly by the federal government. The contractors' own funds were not used in the transactions.

The contractors paid New Mexico taxes on the fees paid to them by the federal government. But they argued that payments under the advanced funding mechanism were immune from state tax. The federal government conceded that the legal incidence of the state taxes was on the contractors, but contended that the contractors were federal instrumentalities. The Supreme Court rejected the argument, holding that the contractors were not immune from state tax. In describing what it takes for a party to be treated as a federal instrumentality, the Court used phrases such as: the private party "must actually 'stand in the Government's shoes'" (quoting City of Detroit v. Murray Corp. (1958) (opinion of Frankfurter, J.)); be "'virtually . . . an arm of the Government'" (quoting *Department of Employment*); be "'integral parts of [a governmental department]'"; and be "'arms of the Government deemed by it essential for the performance of governmental functions'" (quoting Standard Oil Co. v. Johnson (1942)). On the facts of the case, the contractors were distinguishable from federal employees. The contractors remained "independent taxable entities" with distinct professional interests and a "limited and carefully defined" relationship with the federal government.

At one time, the federal government's immunity from state taxes provided the basis for exempting Indian tribes from state taxes as well. That seems no longer to be the case. In Mescalero Apache Tribe v. Jones (1973), the Court explained the decline of the doctrine as follows:

> The intergovernmental-immunity doctrine was once much in vogue in a variety of contexts and, with respect to Indian affairs, was consistently held to bar a state tax on the lessees of, or the product or income from, restricted lands of tribes or individual Indians. The theory was that a federal instrumentality was involved and that the tax would interfere with the Government's realizing the maximum return for its wards. This approach did not survive; its rise and decline in Indian affairs is described and reflected in *Helvering* v. *Mountain Producers Corp.*, 303 U.S. 376 (1938); *Oklahoma Tax Comm'n* v. *United States*, 319 U.S. 598 (1943); and *Oklahoma Tax Comm'n* v. *Texas Co.*, 336 U.S. 342 (1949), where the Court cut to the bone the proposition that restricted Indian lands and the proceeds from them were—as a matter of constitutional law—automatically exempt from state taxation.

In *Mescalero* itself, the Court "decline[d] the invitation to resurrect the expansive version of the intergovernmental-immunity doctrine that has been so consistently rejected in modern times," leaving the scope of tribal immunity instead to be determined by Congress.

The Court later stated that *Mescalero* "effectively eliminated" the federal-instrumentality doctrine "as a basis for immunizing Indians from State taxation" (Moe v. Confederated Salish & Kootenai Tribes of the Flathead Reservation,

1976). More recently, however, the Court has indicated that Indian tribes share the tax immunity of the federal government when it comes to reservation lands held in trust by the United States[190] (Cotton Petroleum Corp. v. New Mexico, 1989). So perhaps some role for the doctrine remains.

A party that is a federal instrumentality has the same Supremacy Clause immunity from state taxes as the federal government itself: If the legal incidence of the tax is on a federal instrumentality, the tax is invalid.

Discriminatory State Taxes

Finally, even state taxes not "directly" on the federal government are invalid if they discriminate against the federal government or those who deal with it (Memphis Bank & Trust Co. v. Garner, 1983). This nondiscrimination requirement can be traced back to McCulloch v. Maryland (1819), which on its facts invalidated a state tax that discriminated against the Bank of the United States. Although in later cases the Supreme Court extended *McCulloch* to invalidate nondiscriminatory taxes, the baseline has remained that the Supremacy Clause precludes states from imposing taxes that discriminate against the federal government.[191]

The question, then, is when does a state tax discriminate against the federal government or those who deal with it? *McCulloch* presented a clear case of discrimination: The bank note tax was imposed only on the Bank of the United States and no other entity in the state. In addition, although unusual, a state tax imposed only on government instrumentalities (both state and federal) but not private parties likely also would constitute unlawful discrimination.[192] By exempting all private entities from the tax, the state would face virtually no political pressure to hold down the amount of the tax: Private entities would not pay it, and the state could increase payments to state entities to offset the amount of the tax.

The Supreme Court's discrimination cases have focused on state taxes that treat those who deal with the federal government differently from those who deal with the state government. An illustration is Davis v. Michigan Department of the Treasury (1989).[193] The state of Michigan, like a number of other states, exempted the retirement benefits of state employees from state income tax. Retirees receiving retirement benefits from the federal government did not receive a similar exemption, nor did retired employees of private companies. Davis, a retired federal employee, sought a refund of his state taxes arguing that the Michigan exemption discriminated against federal retirees in violation of federal law.[194]

Michigan conceded that its "tax system discriminates in favor of retired state employees and against retired federal employees," but offered two justifications for the discrimination. Before examining the justifications, the Supreme Court explained that it would not defer to the state classifications the way it would under the Equal Protection Clause (when it merely requires that the state have a rational basis for treating one class differently from another).[195] State policy justifications, which may well be sufficient under rational basis review, are insufficient here because the federal government's interests must be considered as well. Discrimination that otherwise would be unconstitutional under the Supremacy Clause can be justified only by "significant differences" between federal retirees and state retirees.

The state argued first that discriminating in favor of state retirees was justified by the state's interest in attracting and retaining qualified employees. But that argument is precisely the type of state policy justification that the Court deemed irrelevant: "The State's interest in adopting the discriminatory tax, no matter how substantial, is simply irrelevant to an inquiry into the nature of the two classes receiving inconsistent treatment." The state's second argument was that the differing tax treatment was justified because state retirement benefits were significantly lower than federal retirement benefits. This justification, at least, identified a difference between state retirees and federal retirees. But the Court rejected it as well, because "undoubtedly" there are many federal retirees who receive lower benefits than state retirees. If the true rationale for the exemption were to benefit employees with lower retirement benefits, it would not distinguish based on the source of the benefits (federal vs. state) but rather based on the amount of the benefits. Accordingly, the Court held that the Michigan tax was invalid.[196]

Justice Stevens in dissent took a different approach, arguing that the tax was not discriminatory because it "draws no distinction between the federal employees or retirees and the vast majority of voters in the State." He cited data showing that the tax applied to roughly 4.5 million Michigan taxpayers, including 24,000 federal retirees, while excluding only 130,000 state retirees. Because the tax applied virtually to all potential taxpayers in the state, there was no reason to be concerned about excessive taxation. To the contrary, "'[t]he political check against abuse of the taxing power found lacking in *M'Culloch*, where the tax was imposed solely on the Bank of the United States, is present where the State imposes a nondiscriminatory tax only on its constituents or their artificially owned entities'" (quoting United States v. County of Fresno, 1977). In addition, comparing federal retirees to state retirees was "peculiarly inappropriate," according to Justice Stevens, because the state can respond simply by increasing the benefits of state retirees to offset any additional tax. Finding unconstitutional discrimination under these circumstances "trivializes the Supremacy Clause."

The majority rejected both arguments. First, the Court relied on precedent: In Phillips Chemical Co. v. Dumas Independent School District (1960), the Court likewise invalidated as discriminatory a generally applicable state property tax that applied to lessees of federal property but excluded lessees of state property. The Court in *Davis* explained that "[t]he danger that a State is engaging in impermissible discrimination against the Federal Government is greatest when the State acts to benefit itself and those in privity with it." Second, the Court identified what it saw as a key difference between tax exemptions for state retirees and increased retirement benefits. If the state paid higher benefits to its retirees to offset the loss of the tax exemption, the retiree would be subject to federal taxes on the additional benefits.[197] By adopting a discriminatory tax exemption for state retirees, the state avoided giving the federal government a cut. As such, the Court concluded: "Taxes enacted to reduce the State's employment costs at the expense of the federal treasury are the type of discriminatory legislation that the doctrine of intergovernmental tax immunity is intended to bar."

Following *Davis*, states faced difficult choices as to how to correct the discriminatory taxation of federal retirees.[198] A state could extend the exemption for state retirement benefits to federal retirement benefits.[199] This approach eliminated the discrimination but cost the state tax revenues.[200] A state could end the exemption for state retirement benefits, subjecting those benefits to the same tax as federal retirement benefits.[201] This approach eliminated the discrimination and increased tax revenues, but at the expense of alienating a politically active group in the state (retired and current state employees). Third, a state could do a combination of the above: increase the exemption for federal retirees and reduce it for state retirees, making nobody completely happy.[202]

Two states—Oregon and Montana—adopted a variation on the second option by ending the exemption for state retirees but simultaneously increasing their retirement benefits to offset the tax increase.[203] Federal retirees challenged those programs, with conflicting results. In Sheehy v. Public Employees Retirement Division (Mont. 1993), the Montana Supreme Court invalidated the state's "annual retirement adjustment payment" to state retirees to offset the amount of increased taxes. Characterizing the payment as a "partial tax rebate denominated otherwise in an attempt to evade the requirements of federal law," the court (not surprisingly) found it unlawful. By contrast, in Ragsdale v. Department of Revenue (Ore. 1995), the Oregon Supreme Court upheld Oregon's program, distinguishing *Sheehy* on the grounds that: (1) the Oregon payments were available to all state retirees, not just those living in Oregon (and paying Oregon taxes); and (2) the payments came from the Oregon retirement fund, not the general treasury (into which income tax payments were made). The United States Supreme Court has not yet addressed the issue, so the range of permissible responses remains unresolved.[204]

One final (but important) point: In determining whether a state tax discriminates against the federal government, the Supreme Court is more willing to look at the economic burdens of the tax and related taxes than it is when deciding whether a tax is directly on the federal government. For example, in Washington v. United States (1983), the State of Washington imposed a tax solely on sales by contractors to the federal government. The legal incidence of the tax was on the contractors, so it was lawful under the first step of federal immunity analysis. But the United States challenged the tax as discriminatory because Washington had no sales tax on contractors who dealt with parties other than the federal government.

The Supreme Court upheld the tax, relying on the fact that Washington's general sales tax (with a legal incidence on buyers) applied to all transactions other than those with the federal government. According to the Court, "The important consideration . . . is not whether the State differentiates in determining what entity shall bear the legal incidence of the tax, but whether the tax is discriminatory with regard to the economic burdens that result." Put otherwise, the Court saw the sales tax on federal contractors, not as discrimination, but as a permissible way to accommodate the formalism of the legal incidence rule. The Court has shown a similar willingness to look beyond the form of a state tax in the context of state property taxes, where it has upheld taxes on the value of a lessee's interest in public property as nondiscriminatory because private property owners were subject to the state's general property tax on their interests (United States v. County of Fresno, 1977; United States v. City of Detroit, 1958).

Congress and Federal Tax Immunity

The doctrine of federal immunity is an implied protection of the federal government and federal instrumentalities. If Congress is silent on the extent of federal immunity from state law, the doctrine applies. But Congress has the power to create express immunities for federal instrumentalities, based on its "power to preserve and protect functions validly authorized—the power to make all laws necessary and proper for carrying into execution the powers vested in the Congress" (Carson v. Roane-Anderson Co., 1952). If it does so, then the statute, rather than constitutional immunity, sets the standard for evaluating the legality of the state law. The Supremacy Clause still is implicated, but the legal theory is preemption rather than Supremacy Clause immunity.

The "most significant"[205] federal law establishing an immunity from state taxes is Rev. Stat. § 3701,[206] which provides that "[s]tocks and obligations of the United States Government are exempt from taxation by a State or political subdivision of a State." Section 3701 creates a "sweeping" exemption from state taxes (American Bank & Trust Co. v. Dallas County, 1983), albeit "no broader than that which the Constitution requires" (First National Bank v. Bartow County Board of Tax Assessors, 1985). Another federal statute that creates an immunity from state taxes is 4 U.S.C. § 111 (the Public Salary Tax Act of 1939),[207] which consents to state taxation of federal employees' wages, but only so long as the state tax is nondiscriminatory. As noted above, in Davis v. Michigan Department of the Treasury (1989), the Supreme Court construed the provision as "coextensive" with the nondiscrimination prong of Supremacy Clause immunity.

Conversely, Congress can subject federal instrumentalities to state taxes by waiving their Supremacy Clause immunity. In Jefferson County v. Acker (1999), the Court construed a county ordinance as imposing a nondiscriminatory income tax on federal judges, to which Congress had consented in 4 U.S.C. § 111. Similarly, in Director of Revenue v. CoBank ACB (2001), the Court found that Congress had waived any immunity of banks for cooperatives (banks that loaned money to farm cooperative associations) by subjecting such banks to suit. The Farm Credit Act designated banks for cooperatives as "federally chartered instrumentalities of the United States,"[208] but the lower courts were split on whether the banks were federal instrumentalities immune from state tax. The Supreme Court declined to reach the issue, holding instead that Congress had waived any such immunity. Even though technical amendments to the governing statute had eliminated the provision expressly making the banks liable for state taxes, there was no indication that Congress intended to change that rule.

FEDERAL IMMUNITY FROM STATE REGULATIONS

The Supreme Court stated in Mayo v. United States (1943) that "the activities of the Federal Government are free from regulation by any state." Certainly on the facts of *Mayo*, the statement is overly broad, as that case involved a state administrative order directing the federal government to stop distributing fertilizer without a state-required label (an "actual confrontation" as described above). The Court in Hancock v. Train (1976) later made clear that the Supremacy Clause does not "bar[ ] all state regulation which may touch the activities of the Federal Government." Indeed, the legal principles governing federal immunity from state regulations are largely analogous to those governing federal immunity from state taxes. The plurality opinion in North Dakota v. United States (1990) described those principles as taking a "functional approach" that is "accommodating" to the legislative powers of both sovereigns (states and the federal government) and yet "respectful" of federal supremacy—a description that applies to federal immunity from state taxes as well.

The analytical framework is essentially the same as for state taxes. A state regulation is unlawful if it directly regulates the federal government or a federal instrumentality, or if it discriminates against the federal government or those who deal with it.

First, states may not directly regulate the federal government. As the Court stated in Goodyear Atomic Corp. v. Miller (1988), "It is well settled that the activities of federal installations are shielded by the Supremacy Clause from direct state regulation unless Congress provides 'clear and unambiguous' authorization for such regulation" (quoting Environmental Protection Agency v. California ex rel. State Water Resources Control Board, 1976). Although the legal incidence rule does not apply to state regulations, a similar principle seems to govern. Thus, the mere fact that a state regulation imposed on private parties increases costs to the federal government does not invalidate the regulation. For example, state price controls on the sale of milk are valid, even though they burden the federal government by increasing the price it pays for milk (Penn Dairies, Inc. v. Milk

Control Comm'n, 1943). However, state environmental permit requirements, as applied to federally owned power plants, are invalid, even when the facility is operated by a federal contractor (Hancock v. Train, 1976; Environmental Protection Agency v. California ex rel. State Water Resources Control Board, 1976). In such a case, the regulation is treated as directly on the federal government.[209]

In several cases, the Court has seemed to go beyond this distinction, holding invalid generally applicable state regulations as applied to those dealing with the federal government.[210] In *North Dakota*, the plurality opinion distinguished those cases as based on federal preemption, rather than Supremacy Clause immunity. The four dissenting Justices would have relied on those cases to find an immunity for those who deal with the federal government "when a state law actually and substantially interferes with specific federal programs." They reasoned that state regulations "present a wider range of possibilities for interference with federal activities than do taxes," and that there is no reason to presume that nondiscriminatory regulations are "equally harmless" as nondiscriminatory taxes.

Second, federal immunity from state regulations (like federal immunity from state taxes) extends to federal instrumentalities as well as the federal government itself. In the context of state regulation, the Court has made clear that federal contractors generally are not federal instrumentalities (Penn Dairies, Inc. v. Milk Control Comm'n, 1943). Presumably the same standards apply as with state taxes in determining whether a party should be treated as a federal instrumentality protected by Supremacy Clause immunity.

Third, state regulations that discriminate against the federal government or those who deal with it are invalid. As with state taxes, "the entire regulatory system should be analyzed to determine whether it is discriminatory 'with regard to the economic burdens that result'" (North Dakota v. United States, 1990 (plurality opinion) (quoting Washington v. United States, 1983)). In *North Dakota*, the Court rejected a claim that the state regulatory scheme—which required that special labels be affixed to alcoholic beverages shipped directly to military bases (indicating that it was for consumption on the base only)—discriminated against those who dealt with the federal government. The plurality reasoned that the federal government has the option either to buy from in-state wholesalers (not subject to the labeling requirement) or buy from out-of-state wholesalers (subject to the labeling requirement) and thus is better off, not worse off, than other retailers in the state. The dissent would have held the regulation discriminatory because in-state wholesalers were not subject to a comparable labeling requirement. Justice Scalia, concurring, agreed with the plurality, but relied on the special authority given states to regulate importation of alcoholic beverages provided by the Twenty-First Amendment.

As with state taxes, Congress can subject the federal government to a greater or lesser degree of state regulation than otherwise permitted by the Supremacy Clause. The Court has been more explicit in stating that federal authorization for state regulation must be "clear and unambiguous" (Hancock v. Train, 1976; Environmental Protection Agency v. California ex rel. State Water Resources Control Board, 1976). Likewise, Congress can extend federal immunity from state regulation beyond that implied from the Supremacy Clause.

One remaining question is whether there are any state regulations to which the federal government or federal instrumentalities remain subject. For example, do mail carriers have to abide by speed limits when delivering mail? Professor Laurence Tribe argues that Supremacy Clause immunity "obviously cannot include 'a general immunity from state law' . . . for all federal agents or instrumentalities acting within the scope of their agency or carrying on their functions as federal instruments."[211] In his view, the federal government should be presumptively subject to generally applicable state regulations (and perhaps even state taxes), except that "no state may command federal officials, instrumentalities, or agents to take action in derogation of their validly delegated federal responsibilities." The rationale for this approach, according to Professor Tribe (which he admits applies to state regulations but not state taxes) is that state law can provide a comprehensive set of background rules, filling gaps when Congress has not yet addressed a particular topic (such as the "'mode of turning at the corners of streets'") (quoting Johnson v. Maryland, 1920, discussed in detail in the next section).

So understood, the suggestion is consistent with the Court's cases on federal immunity from state regulations (and state criminal law), and likely reflects how the federal government behaves in practice—expecting federal employees to drive the speed limit, for example. But the Court's state tax cases contain no similar suggestion, and the gap-filling function served by state regulations does not seem applicable to state taxes. Lower courts are split over whether federal employees are subject to state hotel, car rental, and sales taxes while acting in the course of their federal employment, with some holding employees immune and others rejecting immunity.[212] The leading treatise favors the former position: that federal employees, as federal instrumentalities, are immune from such taxes.[213] As noted above, Professor Tribe is ambivalent on the issue, at one point suggesting that the federal government is not entitled to a general immunity from state taxes, while at another recognizing that the gap-filling rationale does not apply to state taxes.[214] It remains to be seen how the Supreme Court will resolve the conflict.

FEDERAL IMMUNITY FROM STATE CRIMINAL LAW

That brings us back to the question with which this Part started: When is a federal official immune, not from state taxes or state regulatory law, but from state criminal law? This is the least well developed area of Supremacy Clause immunity, and much uncertainty remains. The state interest in applying its own law is likely to be at its highest: The federal official has committed an act that presumably would be a crime if done by someone who was not employed by the federal government.

At the same time, a state's ability to interfere with federal actions remains high, and the consequences for a convicted federal official dramatic.

In re Neagle

The leading case is In re Neagle (1890), in which the Supreme Court first recognized Supremacy Clause immunity as a defense to a state criminal prosecution. The *Neagle* case has been described as a "classic of law and order in the wild west,"[215] and is worth a slight digression to take a closer look at the events giving rise to the case.[216] Neagle was a federal marshal assigned to protect United States Supreme Court Justice Stephen J. Field while Field was riding circuit in California. As a Circuit Justice, Field issued a ruling that affected a hotly contested divorce proceeding between William Sharon and Sarah Althea Hill, who thereafter remarried her lawyer, David Terry (whom Field had sworn in as Chief Justice of the California Supreme Court more than thirty years earlier). Hill alleged that she and Sharon were married, and produced a document that purported to be a marriage contract. Sharon asserted that Hill was merely his mistress and that the document was a forgery.

On September 3, 1888, as Field was reading a decision that was to require Hill (now Mrs. Terry) to turn in the purported marriage contract to be cancelled, she jumped up and yelled, "Judge, are you going to take the responsibility of ordering me to deliver up that marriage contract?" After Field asked her to sit down, she continued: "You have been paid for this decision!" Field then ordered her removed from the courtroom. When the courtroom marshal approached her, Mrs. Terry slapped him. Mr. Terry then got into the act, telling the marshal, "Don't touch my wife," and punching the marshal in the face when the marshal tried to remove Mrs. Terry from the room. After she was finally removed to the marshal's office, Mr. Terry tried to force his way through to her, at one point pulling out a bowie knife. Neagle, who was simply a bystander at that point, took the knife from Terry. All the time, Field continued to read the court's opinion, seeming little disturbed by the altercation.

The Terrys were both sentenced to several months in jail for contempt of court. While in jail they both made various threats against Field. Because of the threats, Neagle was assigned to Field as a bodyguard when Field returned to California in 1889 to sit again as a Circuit Justice. On August 13, 1889, Field and Neagle boarded a train from Los Angeles to San Francisco. The Terrys boarded the same train in Fresno. The next morning, when the train stopped in Lathrop, Field and Neagle got off to eat breakfast at the stationhouse. Shortly thereafter, Mr. Terry came in and sat at a different table. When Terry saw Field, he came over to Field's table. Standing behind Field, Terry then hit him twice: according to some witnesses, lightly with the back of his hand, as if challenging him to a duel; according to others, violently with a clenched fist. Neagle responded by shooting Terry in the chest, and then again in the head as he fell, killing him on the spot. Neagle later testified that he thought Terry was pulling a knife, but no weapon was found on the body.

A local sheriff arrested Neagle for murder, holding him in the Stockton jail. A few days later, another sheriff went to San Francisco to arrest Field as an accomplice. After telling the sheriff that "I am in your custody" and that "I am not excused from the proper processes of law," Field obtained a (previously arranged) writ of habeas corpus, which ordered him "released" from custody before leaving the hotel room.

Neagle, too, thereafter obtained habeas corpus relief, releasing him from state custody. The Supreme Court affirmed the order releasing him, concluding that Neagle could not be prosecuted under state law for his actions. (Justice Field was still on the Court at the time, but did not participate in the decision.) Because no statute authorized the executive branch to assign U.S. Marshals to protect Justice Field, the Court analyzed at length the implied power of the executive branch to do so. The federal government, "declared to be within its sphere sovereign and supreme," necessarily must have the power to protect federal judges from threats arising out of the exercise of their duties. A person who harms a judge of course can be prosecuted, the Court explained, but preventing the harm from happening in the first place is more "efficient" (and no doubt greatly preferred by federal judges!). Although both state governments and the federal government have the power to execute their own laws (state governments by enforcing their criminal laws, the federal government by protecting judges who enforce criminal and other laws), in the event of conflict the Supremacy Clause dictates that federal law controls.

The Court quoted at length from Tennessee v. Davis (1880), which considered the constitutionality of a federal statute authorizing the removal of state criminal prosecutions of federal officials from state court to federal court. According to the Court, "[a] more important question can hardly be imagined," for "[u]pon its answer may depend the possibility of the general government's preserving its own existence." The Court continued (quoting in part from Martin v. Hunter's Lessee, 1816), using language often cited in federal immunity cases:

> "[T]he general government must cease to exist whenever it loses the power of protecting itself in the exercise of its constitutional powers." It can act only through its officers and agents, and they must act within the States. If, when thus acting, and within the scope of their authority, those officers can be arrested and brought to trial in a State court, for an alleged offence against the law of the State, yet warranted by the Federal authority they possess, and if the general government is powerless to interfere at once for their protection,—if their protection must be left to the action of the State court,—the operations of the general government may at any time be arrested at the will of one of its members. . . .
>
> We do not think such an element of weakness is to be found in the Constitution. The United States is a government with authority extending over the whole territory of the

Union, acting upon the States and upon the people of the States. While it is limited in the number of its powers, so far as its sovereignty extends it is supreme. No State government can exclude it from the exercise of any authority conferred upon it by the Constitution, obstruct its authorized officers against its will, or withhold from it, for a moment, the cognizance of any subject which that instrument has committed to it.

Thus, the Court concluded, the executive without doubt had the power to appoint Neagle to protect Justice Field, a power that trumped the state's power to enforce its criminal laws under the proper circumstances.

On the facts of this case, those circumstances were met. Federal law authorized Neagle to protect Justice Field—indeed, Neagle had a duty to protect the Justice. In carrying out that duty, Neagle "did no more than what was necessary and proper for him to do." As a result, the Court wrote, "[h]e is innocent of any crime under the laws of the state, or of any other authority whatsoever." Later in the opinion, in summarizing its findings, the Court reiterated that Neagle's actions were authorized by federal law and that Neagle "was correct in his belief" that, without his actions, Field would have been killed As a result, in the Court's words, Neagle was "not liable to answer in the courts of California" for shooting Terry.

Other Supreme Court Cases

Subsequent Supreme Court cases have treated *Neagle* as establishing Supremacy Clause immunity from state criminal law but also have identified some limits. The Court reaffirmed *Neagle* in Ohio v. Thomas (1899), in which the State of Ohio charged the director of a federal disabled veterans home with unlawfully serving margarine to the veterans without posting a state-required notice. The director was convicted and fined $50 (and ordered imprisoned until the fine was paid). The lower federal courts granted the director's petition for habeas corpus relief, concluding that the state tribunal had no jurisdiction. The Supreme Court affirmed, relying on Tennessee v. Davis and *Neagle*. Federal law gave the director authority to determine the foods served to veterans in the home, and the decision to serve margarine was within that authority. Indeed, by approving the budget for the veteran's home, which was calculated based on the price of margarine rather than the price of butter, Congress, "in effect, provided oleomargarine as part of the rations for the inmates of the home." Accordingly, the director was not subject to the state law.

In United States ex rel. Drury v. Lewis (1906), however, the Court refused to grant habeas corpus relief to a soldier who shot and killed a civilian suspected of stealing materials from a federal arsenal. The evidence was conflicting: Some witnesses testified that the soldier had warned the suspect to stop and had fired only when the suspect disregarded the warning; others testified that the suspect had surrendered before he was shot. The soldier was charged with murder (and the officer who ordered the arrest with manslaughter) in Pennsylvania state court. The Supreme Court rejected the government's argument that the defendants were immune from state prosecution because they were under a federal duty to arrest the suspect for larceny. The parties conceded that if the suspect had surrendered, as some evidence indicated, "it could not reasonably be claimed that the fatal shot was fired in the performance of a duty imposed by the Federal law." Accordingly, the Court held, the state court had jurisdiction to try the defendants on state charges.

Drury establishes that Supremacy Clause immunity under *Neagle* is not absolute. A federal official is not immune from state law for acts not done in pursuance of his or her official duties. The principle is an obvious one: Otherwise, federal employees would not be subject to state law for acts in their private capacities, as opposed to their official capacities, which certainly could not be the law. *Drury* illustrates that even while "on the job," federal officials can take actions that will not be treated as acts of a federal instrumentality immune from state law.

Subsequently, in Johnson v. Maryland (1920), a post office employee was convicted by the state for driving his mail truck over a post road without a Maryland drivers licence. The Supreme Court reversed the conviction, holding that the employee was immune from the license requirement. The Court traced the doctrine of Supremacy Clause immunity back to McCulloch v. Maryland (1819), reading that case as establishing "the entire absence of power on the part of the States to touch," by taxation at least, federal instrumentalities. It also relied on *Neagle*, explaining that even state laws against murder cannot "control" the actions of federal officials "acting under and in pursuance of" federal law. The Court emphasized, however, that a federal employee acting within the scope of employment is not completely immune from state law. When federal law does not address a particular issue, federal employees may well have to comply with "general rules that might affect incidentally the mode of carrying out employment," such as a state law "regulating the mode of turning at the corners of streets" or perhaps common law negligence liability. But the Maryland law prohibiting driving without a license was not merely a "general rule of conduct," but instead "require[d] qualifications in addition to those that the Government has pronounced sufficient." As such, the federal employee was immune from its application.

Since *Johnson*, the Supreme Court has not directly addressed the scope of Supremacy Clause immunity from state criminal law. The governing legal precedents in this area thus predate the significant reduction in Supremacy Clause immunity in other areas, particularly state taxation, that began in the 1930s. Whether the Court might similarly cut back on federal immunity from state criminal laws is uncertain. More recent Supreme Court cases have considered Supremacy Cause immunity only in the course of deciding other issues. In Mesa v. California (1989), for example, the issue was whether two postal workers charged with traffic violations while on duty could remove the prosecutions from state court to federal court. Kathryn Mesa was charged with manslaughter and driving outside a laned roadway after the mail truck she was driving collided with (and killed) a bicyclist. Shabbir Ebrahim was charged with speeding and failure to yield after the mail truck he was driving collided with a police car. The Supreme Court held that removal from state court to federal court was permissible only when the defendant raised a defense based on federal law—such as that he or she was immune from prosecution under the Supremacy Clause. Importantly, the Court accepted (as apparently the parties did) that neither Mesa nor Ebrahim had such a federal defense under the facts of their respective cases, and thus held that removal was improper.

Although the Supreme Court in *Mesa* did not discuss further the immunity defense, the court of appeals had concluded that "[t]here is no colorable [i.e., plausible] claim that federal immunity protects the officials' acts, as there was when a federal officer received a speeding ticket while hurrying to stage a raid on a suspected illegal still" (California v. Mesa, 9th Cir. 1987). It explained in a brief footnote:

> The doctrine of federal immunity insulates a federal officer from state prosecution if the officer's acts "are both (1) authorized by the laws of the United States and (2) necessary and proper to the execution of his responsibilities." *Morgan v. California*, 743 F.2d 728, 731, 733 (9th Cir. 1984) (holding that the defendant had not "demonstrated how it would be necessary and proper for him to drive while under the influence in order to carry out his federal duty of meeting with an informant"); *see In re* Neagle, 135 U.S. 1 (1890).

Under the court of appeals' interpretation, then, the federal employees were not entitled to immunity because their actions were not necessary and proper to carrying out their federal duties.

Ambiguities in Current Doctrine

This Supreme Court precedent leaves important questions unanswered about the application of Supremacy Clause immunity from state criminal laws. As seen above, the lower federal courts have derived from *Neagle* a two-part test. To establish immunity from a state criminal prosecution under that test, a federal official must establish that: (1) the official had the authority to perform the disputed act; and (2) the official did no more than necessary and proper in performing the act.[217] Both parts of the test contain important ambiguities.[218]

At least three interpretations are possible of the requirement that the federal official have authority to perform the disputed act. First, the requirement might be read as limiting immunity to cases in which the federal official has a duty, not merely the discretion, to act. This reading is suggested by the Court's finding in *Neagle* that not only did Neagle have the authority to act to protect Justice Field, but he had a duty to do so. Second, the requirement might mean that immunity is available only when the official has authority to do the particular type of act for which he or she is being prosecuted. Third, the requirement might be only that the act at issue be within the official's scope of authority generally. As stated by Seth Waxman, the distinction is whether this element "demand[s] that the federal officer have authority to perform the *specific* act in question, or . . . require[s] only that the officer's actions fall within the *general* scope of his duties."[219]

As for the "necessary and proper" prong of the test, again there are several possibilities: (1) the federal official honestly believed his or her actions were necessary and proper (a subjective standard); (2) the federal official reasonably believed the actions were necessary and proper (an objective standard); (3) the belief must be both honest and reasonable; or (4) the actions must in fact have been both necessary and proper, without regard to the federal official's belief. The Supreme Court in *Neagle* seemed to apply the latter standard, finding that Neagle was "correct" in his evaluation of the threat posed to Field. But lower courts applying *Neagle* have focused on the nature of the federal official's belief, generally requiring the belief both be honestly held and objectively reasonable.[220]

Idaho v. Horiuchi Revisited

Given these precedents, what was the result of Idaho's attempt to prosecute Agent Horiuchi for shooting Vicki Weaver at Ruby Ridge? Recall that Horiuchi removed the Idaho prosecution to federal court and sought to have the criminal charges dismissed on the basis of Supremacy Clause immunity.

The federal district court granted Horiuchi's motion and dismissed the charges (Idaho v. Horiuchi, D. Idaho 1998). After reciting the two-part test courts have derived from *Neagle*—that (1) the federal official was acting within the scope of his or her duties; and (2) the official did no more than was "necessary and proper" in carrying out those duties—the court found the test satisfied. As for the first element of the test, Idaho essentially conceded that Horiuchi acted within the scope of his duties with the FBI. As for the second element of the test, the court stated that the key issue was whether Horiuchi "employed means which he could not honestly consider reasonable in discharging his duties or otherwise acts out of malice or criminal intent." This statement of the standard conflates the subjective and objective elements of the test: to require the official to "honestly consider" an act "reasonable" seems to make the subjective element of honesty controlling over the objective element of reasonableness. But the court's recital of its conclusion treats the elements as separate requirements, as most lower courts have done. Thus, the district court concluded:

> The record supports Mr. Horiuchi's subjective belief that the threat to his or other lives honestly existed; that he intended only to shoot the third individual (Mr. Harris); and that the State has provided no evidence of malice or criminal intent. The record also supports a

finding that the means by which Mr. Horiuchi carried out his duties were objectively reasonable based on the circumstances then existing at Ruby Ridge on August 22, 1992, and that he did not see Mrs. Weaver behind the door or in the doorway when he fired at Mr. Harris running into the cabin.

Because Horiuchi honestly and reasonably believed firing the second shot was necessary and proper, the district court held that he was immune from prosecution under the Supremacy Clause.

On appeal, a panel of the Ninth Circuit affirmed the district court in a split (2–1) decision (Idaho v. Horiuchi, 9th Cir. 2000). The majority and the dissent agreed that the essential facts were undisputed and that to be immune from prosecution Horiuchi had to honestly and reasonably believe his actions were necessary and proper. There was no dispute about application of the subjective "honesty" standard; the majority and dissent differed, however, on whether Horiuchi's actions were objectively reasonable. The majority concluded that the evidence was sufficient to uphold the district court's finding of reasonableness:

Faced with a dangerous armed man who was running to an area where he would present a greater danger, Horiuchi had less than a few seconds to make a decision. . . . Harris was a suspect in the shooting of a federal marshal; he was threatening a helicopter; he was running to a place where he could rearm, regroup, and take up a defensive position. Horiuchi could not see Vicki Weaver standing behind the open door with the curtains closed. He had no reason to believe that a woman holding a baby would be standing outside the threshold of the cabin, but hidden by the open door, after her husband had been shot at by an unknown agent. Horiuchi saw no danger to others, and he shot. He only intended to hit Harris.

The dissent disagreed, arguing that "taking up a defensive position" did not justify shooting a fleeing suspect. The cabin was surrounded by armed FBI agents, who could have taken a variety of other actions to flush out the Weavers. Instead, Horiuchi shot without warning and without affording a chance to surrender. By adopting what the dissent called "the 007 standard for the use of deadly force," the majority opinion weakened the standard of behavior governing law enforcement personnel in a way that "should make us all feel less secure."

The majority and dissent also differed on the relationship between Supremacy Clause immunity, which was at issue in the case, and qualified immunity, which is a defense to a suit for damages against a government official who allegedly violated an individual's constitutional rights. The majority concluded that the standard for Supremacy Clause immunity must be lower—that is, easier for a defendant to establish—than the standard for qualified immunity because it protects federal employees from criminal conviction, a much harsher sanction. Qualified immunity, by contrast, merely protects employees from having to pay money damages in a civil lawsuit. Judge Alex Kozinski, in dissent, argued that "*precisely* the same test applies as to both: Did the officer act constitutionally?" Either the federal official's acts were lawful or they were not. If unlawful, according to Judge Kozinski, the state's interest in enforcing its criminal laws should prevail over the federal government's interest in unimpeded actions for its agents. The disagreement over the relationship between Supremacy Clause immunity and qualified immunity was important here because the Ninth Circuit already had rejected Horiuchi's qualified immunity defense (at least at a preliminary stage of the proceedings) in a damages action brought by Kevin Harris (Harris v. Roderick, 9th Cir. 1997).[221] As a result, according to the dissent, the majority's decision conflicted with prior circuit precedent.

The Ninth Circuit granted Idaho's petition for rehearing en banc.[222] Before the en banc court, the parties and amici ("friends of the court"—nonparties who submit briefs to the court) presented an array of viewpoints on the proper scope of federal immunity from state criminal laws. At one end of the spectrum, Idaho argued that Supremacy Clause immunity should be abolished altogether. According to Idaho, immunity is an "archaic anomaly" under which the federal government "is the king and [Horiuchi] is its Sheriff of Nottingham, who may do no wrong when he does its bidding."[223] Alternatively, Idaho argued that Horiuchi's actions were objectively unreasonable and so not protected by Supremacy Clause immunity in any event.

At the other end of the spectrum, five former U.S. Attorneys General filed an amicus brief arguing that federal officials acting within the scope of their employment should be absolutely immune from state criminal prosecution.[224] Under this view, federal employees could be subject only to federal criminal sanctions for wrongdoing while on the job, but not state criminal sanctions. Because all agreed that Horiuchi was acting within the scope of his federal authority, the Idaho criminal charges should be dismissed, the Attorneys General argued.

Finally, Horiuchi and the federal government as amicus argued for an intermediate position that largely tracked the two-part test courts of appeals have derived from *Neagle*: Was Horiuchi acting within the scope of his duties and did he reasonably believe that his actions were necessary and proper to carrying out those duties?[225] Under this test, Horiuchi would lose the protection of Supremacy Clause immunity if he acted outside the scope of his employment or if he took "measures so extreme that no reasonable officer could have deemed them appropriate."[226]

The en banc court held in favor of the state, rejecting the immunity defense. The majority reiterated the two-part test used by the panel but found numerous disputed issues of material fact: whether the FBI helicopter was in any danger had the man with the gun reached the cabin; whether Horiuchi was in fact following the FBI rules of engagement; whether a warning would have been futile (or even dangerous); whether Horiuchi reasonably believed his second shot was at the same person he had shot at previously; whether Horiuchi was aware of Vicki Weaver standing behind the open door; and whether there was any risk that Randy

Weaver would escape. The court directed the district court to determine the disputed factual issues necessary for resolving Horiuchi's immunity defense (if he were to renew the defense on remand) before conducting a trial on the underlying criminal charge. The dissenting judges disagreed that any material facts were in dispute, and would have found that Horiuchi had established his Supremacy Clause immunity defense.

After the en banc court upheld the state prosecution, the Ninth Circuit requested briefing on whether the full Ninth Circuit should rehear the case. Shortly thereafter, the Idaho county prosecutor (a different prosecutor from the one who had originally begun the prosecution) announced that he would seek to drop the charges against Horiuchi. The prosecutor explained that given all the surrounding circumstances, the state was unlikely to be able to prove guilt beyond a reasonable doubt.[227] As a result, the court of appeals vacated its opinion (along with all the other opinions in the case) as moot—that is, not involving an ongoing controversy. Because the court of appeals vacated the opinions, at the end of the day nothing was left of the opinions in the case. Indeed, the court of appeals' opinions even were removed from the official case reports of the court.[228] The result is, as stated by former Solicitor General Seth Waxman, "In the universe of American jurisprudence, *Idaho v. Horiuchi* became a black hole."[229]

So how should the Ninth Circuit have resolved the issue? In a recent article in the *Yale Law Journal*, Waxman and Professor Trevor W. Morrison argue that courts should construe the scope of Supremacy Clause immunity to be coextensive with qualified immunity in section 1983 actions (federal statutory claims that impose liability for constitutional violations by state officials) and in implied causes of action alleging constitutional violations by federal officials (Bivens v. Six Unknown Named Agents of Federal Bureau of Narcotics, 1971).[230] They give two justifications for this conclusion. First, federal employees are entitled to "fair warning" when their actions may be criminal. They should be able to look to federal law rather than the multitude of state laws in making that determination. Second, as a general matter, state law is preempted only when it conflicts with federal law. Qualified immunity, which protects federal (and state) officials from civil liability in circumstances in which liability would interfere with their governmental duties, thus defines when application of state criminal law would conflict with federal law.

Although Waxman and Morrison recognize "another class of cases bearing more directly on the issue of Supremacy Clause immunity,"[231] they give those cases surprisingly little attention. Those cases are the ones discussed throughout this Part, dealing with federal immunity from state taxation and regulation. They address the same issue as *Horiuchi*—federal immunity from state law—albeit in somewhat different contexts.[232] Although only a handful of Supreme Court cases address federal immunity from state criminal law, substantially more address federal immunity from state tax and regulatory law. The approach of these cases, described at length above, would seem applicable in the criminal context as well, with appropriate modifications.

Those cases establish as a starting point that states cannot apply their criminal laws so as to discriminate against federal officials. For example, Supremacy Clause immunity would preclude Idaho from applying substantive criminal law standards to Horiuchi that differ from those the state applies to prosecutions of state law enforcement officials. This immunity from discriminatory state prosecutions would be available even assuming Horiuchi had acted unreasonably in firing the second shot, just as it is available for federal contractors who are not federal instrumentalities. Presumably Waxman and Morrison would reach the same conclusion, although their qualified immunity standard does not seem to contemplate such a case.

Beyond the baseline nondiscrimination standard, only the federal government and federal instrumentalities are entitled to Supremacy Clause immunity. Federal employees generally are treated as federal instrumentalities when acting within the scope of their duties with the federal government. When they act outside the scope of their duties, they are not immune from state law. As the Supreme Court noted in United States ex rel. Drury v. Lewis, when the actions of federal employees violate the Constitution,[233] one would be hard pressed to say that those actions are within the scope of their duties. In such circumstances, the employees no longer would be treated as federal instrumentalities for immunity purposes, and would be subject to state criminal prosecution for their actions. So construed, the approach suggested by Waxman and Morrison is consistent with the more general principles of Supremacy Clause immunity.

Indeed, Waxman and Morrison essentially deal with a special case of Supremacy Clause immunity—the extent to which federal officials are subject to state criminal liability when their actions arguably violate the United States Constitution. *Horiuchi*, *Drury*, and *Neagle*—which all involved allegations that law enforcement officials had used excessive force—were cases of this sort. But cases like *Johnson* and Ohio v. Thomas show that immunity issues can arise even when there is no allegation that the federal official acted in violation of the Constitution. Instead, in such cases, the issue is not whether the official violated the Constitution, but whether the action was within his or her scope of authority. The framework established by cases addressing federal immunity from state law thus applies not only to state taxes and regulations, but to state criminal law as well.

Further, state criminal law might provide background rules that govern when the federal government has not acted, as the discussion of state speed limits in *Johnson* suggests. I agree with Waxman and Morrison, however, that the degree of immunity is subject to ultimate control by Congress, at least in the vast majority of cases.[234] When acting within its powers under the Constitution, Congress can expand the scope of immunity beyond that provided by the Supremacy Clause. In most cases, Congress can waive that immunity as well, subjecting the federal government and federal instrumentalities to state law—criminal, regulatory, and tax. Ample support for both propositions can be found in cases dealing with federal immunity from state taxes.

Treaties as the Supreme Law of the Land

INTRODUCTION

In March 1995, Napoleon Beazley was sentenced to death for killing John Luttig[235] during a carjacking. According to court opinions,[236] Beazley shot Luttig twice, the second time at point blank range, after Beazley had thrown Luttig to the ground. Before the carjacking, Beazley told a friend that he wanted to steal a car and "to see what it [was] like to kill somebody." Afterwards, Beazley described the experience as "a trip." At the time of the murder, Beazley was only 17 years old.

Texas, like twenty-one other states, permits the execution of juvenile offenders—those who were under the age of 18 at the time they committed the crime.[237] The Supreme Court has upheld the practice under the Eighth Amendment, so long as the juvenile was at least 16 at the time of the crime.[238] The United States is one of only four countries known to have executed juvenile offenders since 2000. Of the other three—Iran, Pakistan, and the Democratic Republic of the Congo ("DRC")—one (Pakistan) recently abolished the juvenile death penalty and another (the DRC) has imposed a moratorium on all executions.[239]

The state courts affirmed Beazley's death sentence on direct appeal and denied his requests for post-conviction relief. Beazley then petitioned for a writ of habeas corpus in federal court, arguing that his death sentence was unconstitutional. Among other arguments, Beazley contended that the juvenile death penalty violated both the International Covenant on Civil and Political Rights ("ICCPR") and norms of customary international law. The ICCPR is an international treaty ratified by the United States following Senate approval in 1992.[240] It provides that a "[s]entence of death shall not be imposed for crimes committed by persons below eighteen years of age." The Supremacy Clause plainly states that treaties are the "supreme Law of the Land." Does the ICCPR preclude Texas from executing defendants such as Beazley? The juvenile death penalty also arguably is contrary to customary international law—what countries customarily do (or do not do) when they act out of a sense of legal obligation. The Supremacy Clause does not mention customary international law (referred to as the "law of nations" at the time the Constitution was drafted). Does customary international law nonetheless preempt state law and render Beazley's death sentence unlawful as a matter of U.S. law?

This Part first looks at the preemptive effect of treaties. It analyzes the long-standing distinction between self-executing and non-self-executing treaties, how the presumption against preemption applies to treaties, and the last-in-time rule permitting subsequently enacted statutes to override previously ratified treaties. It also examines the "myth," dating back to the ratification debates and fostered by the wording of the Supremacy Clause, that treaties are co-equal to the Constitution and can override the individual rights protections of the Constitution. Second, this Part briefly considers whether executive agreements—international agreements that do not follow the constitutionally required procedures for treaties—have the same preemptive effect as treaties. Third, it discusses the extent to which customary international law preempts state law. Finally, it considers how these aspects of international law apply to the domestic legality of the juvenile death penalty. The short answer is that Beazley did not prevail on his claims and was executed on May 28, 2002.[241]

TREATIES

Treaties are agreements among nations. They can be bilateral (between two countries), such as the Treaty of Peace between the United States and Great Britain ending the Revolutionary War, or multilateral (among multiple countries), such as the United Nations Charter and the Nuclear Non-Proliferation Treaty.[242] Under Article II of the Constitution, the President has the power to make treaties, with the "Advice and Consent of the Senate, . . . provided two thirds of the Senators present concur."[243] In other words, treaties must be approved by a two-thirds vote in the Senate to be ratified. The House of Representatives has no formal role in the treaty ratification process, a common source of complaint by Anti-Federalists during the ratification of the Constitution.

Once ratified, treaties can give rise both to international obligations and to domestic obligations on the part of the United States. It is the domestic obligations that are of interest here. Under the terms of the Supremacy Clause, "all Treaties made, or which shall be made, under the Authority of the United States, shall be the supreme Law of the Land." (The "which shall be made" language was included to make clear that both future treaties and treaties existing at the time the Constitution was ratified—especially the Treaty of Peace—would be supreme to state law.) Thus, treaties, like federal statutes, can preempt conflicting state laws. As the Supreme Court stated in United States v. Belmont (1937): "Plainly, the external powers of the United States are to be exercised without regard to state laws or policies. The supremacy of a treaty in this respect has been recognized from the beginning.... [T]his rule in respect of treaties is established by the express language of cl. 2, Art. VI, of the Constitution ...." Indeed, the Court first invalidated a state law as contrary to a federal treaty in Ware v. Hylton (1796) (described in detail in Part I) in which the Supreme Court held that a Virginia statute that conflicted with the Treaty of Peace was invalid.

A more recent example is El Al Israel Airlines, Ltd. v. Tseng (1999). In *Tseng*, the plaintiff sued El Al asserting claims for assault and false imprisonment based on an allegedly intrusive airline security search. Because the plaintiff alleged only psychic injuries, not bodily injury, as a result of the search, her claim did not meet the requirements of the Warsaw Convention governing liability of international airlines.[244] The question in *Tseng* was whether the Warsaw Convention provided the exclusive remedy for air passengers against international airlines—in other words, whether the Convention preempted causes of action based on state law that might otherwise be brought. The Supreme Court held that the Convention was exclusive, reasoning that "[r]ecourse to local law would undermine the uniform regulation of international air carrier liability that the [Warsaw] Convention was designed to foster."

Self-Executing Treaties vs. Non-Self-Executing Treaties

Not all treaties, however, preempt state law. The Supreme Court has distinguished between self-executing treaties—treaties that have legal effect within the United States immediately upon being ratified—and non-self-executing treaties—treaties that have legal effect within the United States only after Congress enacts legislation implementing the treaty obligations. The distinction is a long-standing one. In Foster v. Neilson (1829), Chief Justice John Marshall explained:

> Our constitution declares a treaty to be the law of the land. It is, consequently, to be regarded in the Courts of justice as equivalent to an act of the legislature, whenever it operates of itself without the aid of any legislative provision. But when the terms of the stipulation import a contract, when either of the parties engages to perform a particular act, the treaty addresses itself to the political, not the judicial department; and the legislature must execute the contract before it can become a rule for the Court.

Accordingly, the Court held that a provision in a treaty with Spain governing Spanish land grants in Florida, which Spain had ceded to the United States, was not self-executing. (Interestingly, in a later case, and after examining the

Spanish-language version of the treaty, the Court reconsidered its decision in *Foster* and held the treaty to be self-executing (United States v. Percheman, 1833).)

Because treaties are contracts between nations, as with other contracts the intent of the parties determines their effect. Thus, the intent of the parties to a treaty is central in determining whether the treaty is self-executing. As the Restatement (Third) of Foreign Relations Law of the United States indicates, a treaty is "'non-self-executing' . . . if the agreement manifests an intention that it shall not become effective as domestic law without the enactment of implementing legislation."[245] In addition, courts may consider the intent of the United States government (as opposed to all the signatory governments to the treaty), including statements by the President in submitting the treaty to the Senate and indications by the Senate upon voting for ratification of the treaty.[246]

Courts and commentators are divided on how to deal with treaties that are silent on self-execution. A number of commentaries, including the Restatement (Third) of Foreign Relations Law, favor a presumption in favor of self-execution.[247] The majority of court cases, however, "presume to some extent that treaties are *not* self-executing."[248]

The subject has been extensively debated in the academic literature. Professor Carlos Manuel Vázquez has argued that by making treaties (like federal statutes and the Constitution) the "supreme Law of the Land," the Supremacy Clause makes treaties "enforceable by the courts without prior legislative transformation into domestic law."[249] Professor Vázquez further contends that the Framers sought to overcome state failures to abide by treaties under the Articles of Confederation by giving treaties immediate effect without waiting for legislative implementation. Professor Jordan J. Paust is more blunt: "The distinction found in certain cases between 'self-executing' and 'non-self-executing' treaties is a judicially invented notion that is patently inconsistent with express language in the Constitution affirming that '*all* Treaties . . . shall be the supreme Law of the Land.'"[250] By contrast, Professor John C. Yoo reads the constitutional history as supporting a rule of non-self-execution for treaties when the subject of the treaty would fall within Congress' Article I powers to legislate. At a minimum, according to Professor Yoo, the history supports "a clear statement requirement that treaties are non-self-executing unless the treatymakers openly declare otherwise."[251]

Certainly the Supremacy Clause does away with the question under the Articles of Confederation of whether *states* have to implement treaties before they take effect. That possibility, the subject of debate and federal action in connection with the Treaty of Peace with Great Britain, is conclusively rejected by the Supremacy Clause. Beyond that, however, the resolution of the self-execution debate is less clear, at least with respect to preemption of state law. On the one hand, the text of the Supremacy Clause itself does not distinguish between self-executing and non-self-executing treaties. On the other hand, Congress regularly qualifies federal statutes with preemption savings clauses, which suggests some ability on the part of the participants in the legislative process (and by analogy the treaty process) to restrict the preemptive effect of enactments on state law. In the end, the disagreement among academics and the courts is likely to persist, with the courts, of course, getting the ultimate say on the matter.

Presumption Against Preemption

In areas traditionally occupied by the states, the Supreme Court has adopted a presumption against preemption of state law by federal statutes. The presumption applies not only in cases of implied preemption, but also in cases of express preemption, when interpreting a statute that by its terms preempts particular state laws. The presumption does not apply, however, in areas in which the federal government historically has had a significant presence. Given the strong federal presence in foreign relations matters, one would expect the presumption against preemption not to apply. In Crosby v. National Foreign Trade Council (2000), the Court passed up a chance to rule on that question, holding that a Massachusetts law forbidding state agencies to buy from companies doing business with Burma was preempted even if the presumption against preempted applied.

The case law is mixed on whether the presumption against preemption applies to federal treaties. In a pair of older cases, the Court suggested that the presumption against preemption would apply. Thus, in Guaranty Trust Co. v. United States (1938), the Court stated that "[e]ven the language of a treaty wherever reasonably possible will be construed so as not to override state laws or to impair rights arising under them." Similar language appears in United States v. Pink (1942), which cited *Guaranty Trust* as authority for the presumption: "It is, of course, true that even treaties with foreign nations will be carefully construed so as not to derogate from the authority and jurisdiction of the States of this nation unless clearly necessary to effectuate the national policy." However, in *Pink* the Court went on to hold that "state law must yield when it is inconsistent with, or impairs the policy or provisions of, a treaty or of an international compact or agreement."

More recently, the Court severely limited application of the presumption against preemption in cases of treaty preemption. In *Tseng*, the Court emphasized that American treaty partners focus on "the nation-state, not subdivisions within one nation." Thus, it concluded, "[o]ur home-centered preemption analysis"—including the presumption against preemption—"should not be applied, mechanically, in construing our international obligations." Justice Stevens dissented, not because the issue in the case was particularly important, but because of the majority's departure from ordinary preemption analysis. His position was that the presumption against preemption should apply even in cases of treaty preemption. The rest of the Court, however, disagreed.

"Last-in-Time" Rule

The Supremacy Clause lists both treaties and federal statutes as supreme to state law. As between treaties and federal statutes, which controls in the event of a conflict? Arguably, the Supremacy Clause does not answer that question. The fact that both treaties and federal statutes are supreme to state law does not necessarily mean they are equal to each other. As Professor Louis Henkin says, "3 and 2 are both 'supreme' to 1 but they are not equal."[252]

In Whitney v. Robertson (1888), however, the Supreme Court adopted what is known as the "last-in-time rule": When statutes and treaties conflict (just as when two federal statutes conflict), whichever was enacted most recently controls. Moreover, the Court relied on the Supremacy Clause (at least in part) as authority for its holding:

> By the Constitution, a treaty is placed on the same footing, and made of like obligation, with an act of legislation. Both are declared by that instrument to be the supreme law of the land, and no superior efficacy is given to either over the other. When the two relate to the same subject, the courts will always endeavor to construe them so as to give effect to both, if that can be done without violating the language of either; but, if the two are inconsistent, the one last in date will control the other: provided, always, the stipulation of the treaty on the subject is self-executing.

Despite the uncertainty about the constitutional authority for the last-in-time rule, the rule "appear[s] to be firmly established."[253]

Most commonly, the last-in-time rule operates so that a later enacted federal statute overrides an earlier ratified treaty. In Breard v. Greene (1998), for example, the Supreme Court considered a Paraguayan national's habeas challenge to his conviction and death sentence based on the failure of Virginia officials to inform him after his arrest that he had the right to contact the Paraguayan Consulate. The petitioner asserted that such a right was established by the Vienna Convention on Consular Relations (in effect in the United States from 1969), and that, as the supreme law of the land, the Convention excused his failure to raise the claim in state court. The Court refused to excuse the defendant's procedural default. It relied in part on the Antiterrorism and Effective Death Penalty Act, enacted in 1996, which denies habeas petitioners an evidentiary hearing on their claims, including claimed treaty violations, if the petitioner fails to develop an adequate factual record in state court. The defendant's "ability to obtain relief based on violations of the Vienna Convention is subject to this subsequently enacted rule," the court explained in holding Breard's claims procedurally barred.[254]

On rare occasion, the rule can work in the opposite direction, with the later ratified treaty overriding an earlier enacted statute. One example is Cook v. United States (1933),[255] in which the Supreme Court held that a 1924 treaty between the

United States and Great Britain modified a 1922 statute authorizing Coast Guard inspections of certain foreign ships.

The last-in-time rule deals only with the domestic effect of a treaty to which the United States is a party. The United States remains subject to any international obligations resulting from the treaty until it is validly terminated. Thus, when Congress enacts a law overriding a provision of a treaty, the law may both eliminate the domestic effect of the treaty and violate international obligations under the treaty at the same time.

Treaties and Constitutional Rights

In 1952, not long before being named Secretary of State, John Foster Dulles made a remarkable statement on the supremacy of treaties. Dulles told a bar association audience in Louisville, Kentucky, that treaties are "more supreme than ordinary laws for congressional laws are invalid if they do not conform to the Constitution, whereas treaty law can override the Constitution."[256] He continued by citing examples of ways in which treaties could "override the Constitution": "Treaties . . . can take powers away from the Congress and give them to the President; they can take away powers from the States and give them to the Federal Government or to some international body, and they can cut across the rights given the people by their constitutional Bill of Rights."

Although Dulles did not cite the basis for his view that "a treaty can override the Constitution," his remarks suggest that he relied on the text of the Supremacy Clause itself. While the Clause makes the "Constitution, and the Laws of the United States which shall be made *in Pursuance thereof*" the "supreme Law of the Land," it includes "all Treaties made, or which shall be made, *under the Authority of the United States*" as supreme law (emphasis added).[257] This difference in wording—with treaties not required to be made "in Pursuance" of the Constitution—has given rise to "a myth" (reflected in Dulles' remarks) "that treaties are equal in authority to the Constitution and not subject to its limitations."[258]

This myth—which is no more than a myth—persists in any number of circles even today. Circulating the Internet are assertions, by those who fear the loss of American sovereignty to global government, that "[t]he UN Treaty and all other treaties are included in the Constitution of the United States."[259] At the other end of the political spectrum, commentators have suggested that the United States acts unlawfully when it does not meet its financial obligations to the United Nations[260] and that Congress could not by statute "legalize assassinations" of foreign officials because a prohibition on assassinations "had entered into customary international law."[261] Both statements could be true as a matter of domestic law only if treaties and customary international law have the same status as the Constitution. The pedigree of the view that treaties are equal to the Constitution is a long one that, as Part I notes, can be traced back to the state ratifying debates on the Constitution: One of the grounds on which the Anti-Federalists opposed ratification was that the treaty power would permit the President and the Senate to repeal the Constitution.

The modern origins of the myth date to Missouri v. Holland (1920), in which the Supreme Court upheld the Migratory Bird Treaty Act of 1918 against a challenge that it interfered with states' rights under the Tenth Amendment.[262] The Act implemented a treaty between the United States and Great Britain by regulating the hunting, capture, and sale of migratory birds covered by the treaty. The Court rejected Missouri's challenge to the treaty in an opinion by Justice Oliver Wendell Holmes. Justice Holmes began by making the very argument on which Dulles relied: that "Acts of Congress are the supreme law of the land only when made in pursuance of the Constitution, while treaties are declared to be so when made under the authority of the United States." The rest of the opinion, however, provides indications that the Court was not making what Professor David Currie calls the "horrifying suggestion" that the treaty power was not limited by the Constitution at all.[263] Thus, the Court in *Holland* continued that "[w]e do not mean to imply that there are no qualifications to the treaty-making power," and made clear that the Migratory Bird Treaty was not contrary to any express prohibition in the Constitution. (The Tenth Amendment provides that the powers not delegated to the federal government are reserved to the states or the people. Here, at issue was the treaty power, one of the powers delegated to the federal government.) But the damage was done: The myth was given new life.

Thereafter, in Reid v. Covert (1957), the Supreme Court sought to undo the damage by clarifying that a treaty could not override individual rights protected by the Constitution. The issue in *Reid* was whether spouses of military personnel could be tried by military court martial—that is, without a right to jury trial and other constitutional protections. The government argued that the court martial of military spouses was permissible as necessary and proper to the treaty power: A treaty between the United States and Great Britain granted U.S. military courts exclusive jurisdiction over military personnel and dependants. A plurality of the court (four justices) rejected the argument for the "obvious and decisive" reason that no treaty "can confer power on the Congress, or on any other branch of Government, which is free from the restraints of the Constitution." After quoting the text of the Supremacy Clause, the plurality opinion continued:

> There is nothing in this language which intimates that treaties and laws enacted pursuant to them do not have to comply with the provisions of the Constitution. Nor is there anything in the debates which accompanied the drafting and ratification of the Constitution which even suggests such a result. These debates as well as the history that surrounds the adoption of the treaty provision in Article VI make it clear that the reason treaties were not limited to those made in "pursuance" of the Constitution was so that agreements made by the

United States under the Articles of Confederation, including the important peace treaties which concluded the Revolutionary War, would remain in effect. It would be manifestly contrary to the objectives of those who created the Constitution, as well as those who were responsible for the Bill of Rights—let alone alien to our entire constitutional history and tradition—to construe Article VI as permitting the United States to exercise power under an international agreement without observing constitutional prohibitions.

The plurality distinguished Missouri v. Holland as based on the Tenth Amendment, which by its terms was subject to the powers delegated to the federal government by the Constitution. The plurality concluded: "To the extent the United States can validly make treaties, the people and the States have delegated their power to the National Government and the Tenth Amendment is no barrier."

Periodically, the Court has reiterated the point. In Boos v. Barry (1988), the Court struck down as contrary to the First Amendment a District of Columbia law restricting the display of signs near foreign embassies that would bring the foreign government into "public disrepute." Such restrictions based on the content of the speech are highly suspect under the First Amendment and will be upheld only if they serve a compelling state interest and are narrowly tailored to achieve that interest. The argument in *Boos* was that protecting foreign diplomats as required by international law was a compelling government interest. While acknowledging the importance of complying with international law, the Court stated that "it is well-established" that the federal government is subject to the constraints of the United States Constitution in carrying out its international obligations.

Most recently, the Court made the point again in dicta in American Insurance Ass'n v. Garamendi (2003) (described in detail in the next section). After stating that treaties and executive agreements preempt state law, the Court made clear that both are "[s]ubject, that is, to the Constitution's guarantees of individual rights," citing both Reid v. Covert and Boos v. Barry as authority.

In short, the Supremacy Clause does not give treaties the same status as the Constitution itself. In their domestic applications, treaties, like federal statutes, are subject to the Constitution's protections for individual rights.[264] Dulles' fears, and their modern reincarnations, are based on a myth.

EXECUTIVE AGREEMENTS

Not all agreements between the United States and other countries are "treaties" within the meaning of the Constitution—that is, not all are approved by two-thirds of the Senate. The President also enters into what are called "executive agreements" with other countries. Executive agreements, like treaties, create legal obligations on the part of the United States. But executive agreements are far more common: From 1939 to 1989, the United States entered into 702 treaties and 11,698 executive agreements.[265] Scholars have identified three types of executive agreements: congressional-executive agreements (agreements entered into by the President with the prior or subsequent approval of both the Senate and the House of Representatives); treaty-authorized executive agreements (agreements entered into by the President under the authority of a previously ratified treaty); and sole executive agreements (agreements entered into by the President without any congressional approval).[266]

Although some have raised questions about the constitutionality of congressional-executive agreements, "it is now widely accepted that the Congressional-Executive agreement is available for wide use, even general use, and is a complete alternative to a treaty."[267] One well known example of a congressional-executive agreement is NAFTA, the North American Free Trade Agreement,[268] which was approved by both houses of Congress after being negotiated by the President. Treaty-authorized executive agreements likewise seem relatively uncontroversial, having been authorized in advance by a duly ratified treaty. Sole executive agreements raise the most serious constitutional questions, because the President avoids Congress altogether in entering into such an international agreement.

But the Supreme Court has held that even sole executive agreements preempt conflicting state law (at least in cases involving settlement of claims). The first case in which it so held was United States v. Belmont (1937). In *Belmont*, the United States sought to recover property assigned to it by the Soviet Union in connection with American recognition of the USSR and the settlement of claims between the governments (the "Litvinov Assignment"). The Court rejected the argument that permitting the United States to recover the property was contrary to the public policy of New York (where the bank deposit at issue was located) because "no state policy can prevail against the international compact here involved." After concluding that the sole executive agreement was within the President's power, the Court continued: While the supremacy of a treaty over state law "is established by the express language of cl. 2, Art. VI, of the Constitution, the same rule would result in the case of all international compacts and agreements from the very fact that complete power over international affairs is in the national government and is not and cannot be subject to any curtailment or interference on the part of the several states."

The Court reaffirmed *Belmont* in United States v. Pink (1942), another case involving the Litvinov Assignment, in which it stated that "[a] treaty is a 'Law of the Land' under the supremacy clause" and "[s]uch international compacts as the Litvinov Assignment have a similar dignity." Accordingly, "state law must yield when it is inconsistent with or impairs the policy or provisions of a treaty or of an international compact or agreement."

Finally, the Court again recited the preemptive force of executive agreements in American Insurance Ass'n v. Garamendi (2003). At issue in *Garamendi* was a challenge to California's Holocaust Victim Insurance Relief Act ("HVIRA"), which required insurance companies to disclose information on insurance policies sold in Europe from 1920 through 1945. The purpose of the Act was to help survivors of the Holocaust and their descendants recover proceeds from insurance policies confiscated by Nazi Germany or simply not paid to beneficiaries. The Court held that the California law was invalid because it interfered with the federal government's ability to conduct American foreign relations (but not because it was preempted by any particular federal statute or international agreement). In so holding, the Court considered executive agreements the United States had entered into with Germany, France, and Austria setting up voluntary compensation funds. The Court explained that the President had the power to enter into sole executive agreements and that settlement of claims by Americans against foreign governments "is a particularly longstanding practice" and "indisputab[ly]" within the President's power. Such executive agreements "are fit to preempt state law, just as treaties are, and if the agreements here had expressly preempted laws like HVIRA, the issue would be straightforward." But because the executive agreements did not purport to preempt state laws, the Court instead invalidated the law under the dormant foreign relations power. The four dissenting Justices likewise recognized that "executive agreements directed at claims settlement may sometimes preempt state law."

Thus, even though the Supremacy Clause mentions only treaties and not other international agreements, courts treat executive agreements like treaties as the "supreme Law of the Land."

CUSTOMARY INTERNATIONAL LAW

Treaties and executive agreements are not the only sources of international law. In addition, international obligations can arise from "customary international law," defined as "a general and consistent practice of states followed by them from a sense of legal obligation."[269] Classic examples of customary international law are prohibitions against torture and genocide, which, according to international legal scholars, bind even countries that have not agreed to the prohibitions by treaty.

At the time the Constitution was ratified, customary international law was one aspect of the "law of nations" (others included maritime law, conflict-of-laws rules, and the law merchant). Once the United States became an independent sovereign, it was subject to whatever international obligations flowed from customary international law. As Chief Justice John Jay wrote in Chisholm v. Georgia (1793): "[T]he *United States* had, by taking a place among the nations of the earth, become amenable to the laws of nations; and it was their interest as well as their duty to provide, that those laws should be respected and obeyed; in their national character and capacity, the *United States* were responsible to foreign nations for the conduct of each State, relative to the laws of nations . . . ."

The domestic (as opposed to international) obligations that resulted were less clear. The only reference to the "law of nations" in the Constitution is in Article I, which gives Congress the power to "define and punish . . . Offences against the Law of Nations."[270] The Supremacy Clause does not mention the law of nations as part of the "supreme Law of the Land." Moreover, it includes as supreme law "the Laws of the United States which shall be made in Pursuance" of the Constitution, and, presumably, customary international law is not made in pursuance of the United States Constitution.[271] Nonetheless, some roughly contemporaneous materials support treating the law of nations as part of the law of the land (although perhaps not the "supreme Law of the Land"). In Federalist No. 3, for example, John Jay appeared to equate treaties and the law of nations, writing that "under the national Government, treaties and articles of treaties, as well as the law of nations, will always be expounded in one sense, and executed in the same manner."[272] During the debate over the Neutrality Proclamation of 1793, Alexander Hamilton under the pseudonym Pacificus refers to the "law of Nations" as "a part" of "the laws of the land."[273] On the other hand, Justices Chase and Iredell both concluded in Ware v. Hylton (1796) that the law of nations did not override the Virginia law confiscating British debts—in their view it was a matter to be addressed in the Treaty of Peace.

The "modern position" is that customary international law, despite the textual and historical uncertainty, is federal law that preempts state law under the Supremacy Clause. As the Restatement (Third) of the Foreign Relations Law of the United States explains, "Customary international law is considered to be like common law in the United States, but it is federal law." Thus, "while not mentioned explicitly in the Supremacy Clause," customary international law also is "supreme over State law."[274] Despite the widespread acceptance of customary international law as supreme federal law in the academic literature, no Supreme Court case has held that customary international law preempts conflicting state law.[275] Professor Peter Spiro has described the modern position as "a specter that never ruled beyond the pages of the Restatement and the law reviews."[276]

Recently, the modern position has come under strong criticism even in the academic literature. Professors Curtis Bradley & Jack Goldsmith argue that customary international law is not federal law but rather part of the "general common law."[277] As such, it does not preempt conflicting state law. The Bradley & Goldsmith argument has prompted harsh responses from international law scholars, who have decried it as "seriously in error"[278] and "utterly mistaken."[279] One reason for the heated debate is that the status of customary international law has become increasingly important in recent years because of its growing focus on individual rights rather than simply the relationship between countries. Challenges to the juvenile death penalty as violating customary international law illustrate the point. Because of the changing nature of customary international law, there is likely to be increasing legal development in this area in the future.

INTERNATIONAL LAW AND THE JUVENILE DEATH PENALTY

How have courts so far applied these principles to international law challenges to the juvenile death penalty? To date, the challenges have been unsuccessful.[280] In Napoleon Beazley's case, for example, the court of appeals rejected Beazley's argument based on the International Covenant on Civil and Political Rights as waived (because he had not raised it in a timely fashion in the state courts), but in doing so discussed the merits of the claim. The court held that the ICCPR was not self-executing based on the Senate's declaration upon ratification that the substantive provisions of the treaty were "not self-executing."[281] Although Beazley argued that the non-self-execution declaration was contrary to the provisions of the ICCPR, the court rejected the claim as "nonsensical, to say the very least." The court of appeals also relied on the fact that the Senate qualified its approval of the treaty by reserving the right for the United States "to impose capital punishment on any person . . . duly convicted under existing or future laws permitting the imposition of capital punishment, including such punishment for crimes committed by persons below eighteen years of age."[282] Such reservations are commonplace (one estimate is that 15 percent of all treaties entered into by the United States have been ratified subject to some condition imposed by the Senate[283]) and ordinarily given effect by the courts. As for the claim that the juvenile death penalty violates customary international law, the court rejected it on procedural grounds (although noting that the district court found "the norms of international law . . . *not* controlling" because of the Senate reservations on the ICCPR and the Supreme Court cases upholding the juvenile death penalty as constitutional).

Other courts likewise have rejected challenges to the juvenile death penalty on international law grounds, although in some cases with judges dissenting from the ruling.[284] The United States Supreme Court has not yet addressed the challenges. The closest it has come is in denying review in Domingues v. Nevada (1999) (which is not a decision on the merits of the issue). Before denying review, the Supreme Court requested the views of the U.S. Solicitor General (the Justice Department official in charge of the government's litigation before the Supreme Court), who recommended that the Court deny the petition for certiorari.[285] The Solicitor General relied principally on the Senate reservation to the ICCPR, arguing that the Senate has the constitutional authority to condition its consent to treaties and that such reservations "become part of the treaty insofar as the treaty is to be applied in United States courts." Because of the reservation for the juvenile death penalty, the Court did not need to consider the Senate's non-self-execution declaration. Finally, the Solicitor General recognized that the customary international law issue "raise[d] numerous issues of considerable difficulty, with potentially far-reaching significance." But even if the juvenile death penalty is contrary to customary international law, the United States has persistently objected and thus is not bound by any such rule. (In any event, the lack of any lower court opinion or record on the subject made this an inappropriate case to consider the issue.) The position of the United States government, then, is that neither the ICCPR nor customary international law preclude imposition of the death penalty on juvenile offenders. The Supreme Court followed the Solicitor General's recommendation and declined review. Whether it will agree with the recommendation on the merits awaits an appropriate case.

The use of customary international law (and treaties for that matter) in capital cases is not limited to challenges to the juvenile death penalty. Capital defendants now rely on customary international law to attack more broadly the institution of the death penalty itself. If the death penalty violates customary international law (a position which even supporters concede is premature[286]), a straightforward implication of the modern position is that state death penalty laws are invalid. As Professor Ernest A. Young says, however, "It is hard to imagine the courts taking such an argument for preemption seriously."[287] Indeed, courts have routinely rejected such arguments by capital defendants.[288] Nonetheless, at least until the U.S. Supreme Court steps into the fray, advocates will continue to look not only to domestic law but also to international law for arguments against the legality of the death penalty. The Supremacy Clause, which makes at least some forms of international law the "supreme Law of the Land," is the ultimate authority for (and against) those arguments.

ENDNOTES

1. The factual description that follows comes principally from the district court's opinion in Glassroth v. Moore (M.D. Ala. 2002) and the court of appeals' opinion in Glassroth v. Moore (11th Cir. 2003).

2. A picture of the monument is reprinted as Appendix A to the district court's opinion in Glassroth v. Moore (M.D. Ala. 2002), and also can be found on various web sites. Appendix B to the district court's opinion quotes the inscriptions around the sides of the monument, and Appendix C includes the text of Chief Justice Moore's remarks at the unveiling ceremony.

3. Jonathan Ringel, "Alabama Chief Justice: Not Bound by U.S. Rulings," *Fulton County Daily Report* (Dec. 20, 2002), at <www.law.com>.

4. Stan Bailey, "Monumental Showdown Looms," *Birmingham News* (Aug. 15, 2003), at <www.al.com>.

5. "Ten Commandments Monument Walled Off from Public in Building," *Sarasota Herald Tribune* (Aug. 21, 2003), at <www.heraldtribune.com>. In a column in the *Wall Street Journal*, Moore wrote that "[w]e must acknowledge God in the public sector because the state constitution explicitly requires us to do so. . . . As the chief justice of the state's supreme court I am entrusted with the sacred duty to uphold the state's constitution. I have taken an oath before God and man to do such, and I will not waver from that commitment." Roy S. Moore, "In God I Trust: Why I'm Standing Up for the Ten Commandments in Alabama," *Wall St. J.* (Aug. 25, 2003).

6. Todd Kleffman & Ken Spear, "Protesters Removed, Monument Stays," *Montgomery Advertiser* (Aug. 21, 2003), at <www.montgomeryadvertiser.com/NEWS/StoryLocalmonument21w.htm>.

7. In re Compliance with Writ of Injunction of the United States District Court for the Middle District of Alabama, Order No. 03–01 (Ala. Aug. 21, 2003).

8. Stan Bailey, "Moore Barred from Duties," *Birmingham News* (Aug. 23, 2003), at <www.al.com>; see Complaint, In re Moore (Ala. Ct. Jud. Aug. 22, 2003), available at <news.findlaw.com/hdocs/docs/religion/inremoore82203cmp.pdf>.

9. "Ten Commandments Monument Moved," CNN.com (Aug. 27, 2003), at <www.cnn.com>.

10. For a broader treatment, see Saikrishna B. Prakash & John C. Yoo, "The Origins of Judicial Review," 70 *U. Chi. L. Rev.* (2003) 887, which was very useful in preparing this section.

11. Larry D. Kramer, "Foreword: We the Court," 115 *Harv. L. Rev.* (2001) 4, 63.

12. James S. Liebman & William F. Ryan, "'Some Effectual Power': The Quantity and Quality of Decisionmaking Required of Article III Courts," 98 *Colum. L. Rev.* (1998) 696, 764.

13. William P. Murphy, *The Triumph of Nationalism* (Chicago: Quadrangle Books, 1967) 220.

14. Prakash & Yoo, 70 *U. Chi. L. Rev.* 911 n.88.

15. See Bradford R. Clark, "The Supremacy Clause as a Constraint on Federal Power," 71 *Geo. Wash. L. Rev.* (2003) 91, 91 ("Today it is widely accepted that the Constitution authorizes courts to review and invalidate state laws that conflict with federal statutes").

16. Oliver Wendell Holmes, *Collected Legal Papers* (New York: Peter Smith, 1952) 295–296.

17. Prakash & Yoo, 70 *U. Chi. L. Rev.* 912.

18. Henry M. Hart, Jr., "Professor Crosskey and Judicial Review," 67 *Harv. L. Rev.* (1954) 1456, 1470.

19. Caleb Nelson, "Preemption," 86 *Va. L. Rev.* (2000) 225, 249.

20. Tung Yin, "A Justice's Contempt for Rule of Law," *Iowa City Press-Citizen* (Aug. 20, 2003), at <www.press-citizen.com/opinion/082003/guestedit.htm> ("if the Alabama Constitution requires him to install the Ten Commandments monument in the state courthouse, then the Alabama Constitution must give way to the establishment clause if, as federal judges have thus far ruled, that clause so requires").

21. 1 Laurence H. Tribe, *American Constitutional Law*, 3rd ed. (New York: Foundation Press, 2000) 257.

22. Charles Alan Wright & Mary Kay Kane, *Law of Federal Courts*, 6th ed. (St. Paul: West Group, 2002) § 14 (discussing political questions).

23. Not only the other justices on the Alabama Supreme Court, but also the governor and attorney general of Alabama criticized Moore for his refusal to comply with the court order. See "Statement by Gov. Bob Riley on the Ten Commandments Monument" (Aug 21, 2003), at <www.governorpress.state.al.us/pr/pr-2003–08-21–01-monument.asp> ("Because we are a society of laws, the Alabama Supreme Court has a duty to comply with the federal court order, whether they agree with it or not."); "Statement of Attorney General Bill Pryor Regarding the Order of the Alabama Supreme Court to Require the Judicial

Building Manager to Comply with the Federal Injunction" (Aug. 21, 2003), at <www.ago.state.al.us/news_template.cfm?Record_ID=768> ("The rule of law means that no person, including the Chief Justice of Alabama, is above the law. The rule of law means that when courts resolve disputes, after all appeals and arguments, we all must obey the orders of those courts even when we disagree with those orders. The rule of law means that we can work to change the law but not to defy court orders.").

24. See Ronald A. Cass, *The Rule of Law in America* (Baltimore: Johns Hopkins University Press, 2001) 4 ("The first element states the central thesis of the classic conception of the rule of law: in a government of laws, not of men, individuals—including individuals exercising governmental power—must obey laws.").

25. Michael Stokes Paulsen, "The *Merryman* Power and the Dilemma of Autonomous Executive Branch Interpretation," 15 *Cardozo L. Rev.* (1993) 81, 93 n.41 (adding that such a reading is a "much less natural[]" one). For another perspective, see 1 Tribe, *American Constitutional Law* 257 ("[T]he Court [in *Cooper*] need not be understood to say anything more than that *Brown* [*v. Board of Education*] and its progeny, including the case at hand, are binding in the same way that any other judicial decision is binding, so that state officials who interfere with enforcement of a judgment, or act to undermine its goals, are acting unlawfully. On this view, *Brown* need not be seen as itself 'part' of the Constitution, but as a constitutional judgment, an exercise of judicial power entitled to respect under the Supremacy Clause not because it *is* the Constitution but because it is an exercise of power *under* the Constitution . . . .").

26. E.g., Akhil Reed Amar, "Intratextualism," 112 *Harv. L. Rev.* (1999) 748, 765–766 (citing parallels between Supremacy Clause and Article III of the Constitution); John Harrison, "The Constitutional Origins and Implications of Judicial Review," 84 *Va. L. Rev.* (1998) 333, 364; and Herbert Wechsler, "Toward Neutral Principles of Constitutional Law," 73 *Harv. L. Rev.* (1959) 1, 3–5.

27. Clark, 71 *Geo. Wash. L. Rev.* 92.

28. See, e.g., Alexander M. Bickel, *The Least Dangerous Branch: The Supreme Court at the Bar of Politics* 8–12 (Indianapolis: Bobbs-Merrill Co., 1962); 2 William Winslow Crosskey, *Politics and the Constitution in the History of the United States* (Chicago: University of Chicago Press, 1953) 982–1007.

29. Bickel, *The Least Dangerous Branch* 9–10.

30. David P. Currie, *The Constitution in the Supreme Court: The First Hundred Years 1789–1888* (Chicago: University of Chicago Press, 1985) 72–73; see also 2 Crosskey, *Politics and the Constitution in the History of the United States* 999 (words "in Pursuance thereof" "were employed in the Supremacy Clause merely to make clear a cleavage, of the temporal kind . . ., between 'the Laws of the United States' which were to be, and those which were *not* to be, elements of 'the supreme Law'").

31. 2 Crosskey, *Politics and the Constitution in the History of the United States* 984–985.

32. Kramer, 115 *Harv. L. Rev.* 10; see also Sylvia Snowiss, *Judicial Review and the Law of the Constitution* (New Haven: Yale University Press, 1990).

33. See 3 John Phillip Reid, *Constitutional History of the American Revolution: The Authority to Legislate* (Madison: University of Wisconsin Press, 1991) 28–29.

34. Prakash & Yoo, 70 *U. Chi. L. Rev.* 903–913.

35. Clark, 71 *Geo. Wash. L. Rev.* 118–119.

36. Kramer, 115 *Harv. L. Rev.* 6.

37. 1 Tribe, *American Constitutional Law* 258.

38. Michael Stokes Paulsen, "The Most Dangerous Branch: Executive Power to Say What the Law Is," 83 *Geo. L.J.* (1994) 217, 292; Paulsen, 15 *Cardozo L. Rev.* 81–83.

39. Kramer, 115 *Harv. L. Rev.* 6–7.

40. 45 U.S.C. §§ 51–60 (creating a federal cause of action permitting employees to recover against interstate railroads for on-the-job injuries).

41. Wright & Kane, *Law of Federal Courts* 292.

42. In Federal Energy Regulatory Comm'n v. Mississippi (1982), the Supreme Court extended *Testa*'s holding to state public utility commissions, reasoning that the role of an administrative hearing officer was "'functionally comparable' to that of a judge" (quoting Butz v. Economou (1978)). The Court concluded: "Any other conclusion would allow the States to disregard both the preeminent position of federal law throughout the Nation . . . and the congressional determination that the federal rights granted by [the federal statute] can appropriately be enforced through state adjudicatory machinery."

43. Wright & Kane, *Law of Federal Courts* 292.

44. The Supreme Court in *Howlett* quoted from Henry M. Hart, Jr., "The Relations Between State and Federal Law," 54 *Colum. L. Rev.* (1954) 489, 508. Professor Hart continued: "For example, state rules about the ways in which claims for relief, or defenses, or counter-defenses, must be asserted may ordinarily be applied also to federal claims and defenses and counter-defenses, providing only that the rules are not so rigorous as, in effect, to nullify the asserted rights."

45. Anthony J. Bellia, Jr., "Federal Regulation of State Court Procedures," 110 *Yale L.J.* (2001) 947, 962.

46. See also Brown v. Western Railway (1949) (holding that "[s]trict local rules of pleading cannot be used to impose unnecessary burdens upon rights of recovery authorized by federal laws").

47. See also St. Louis & San Francisco R.R. v. Brown (1916) (upholding verdict by three-fourths of the jury); Louisville & Nashville R.R. v. Stewart (1916) (same); and Chesapeake & Ohio Railway Co. v. Carnahan (1916) (upholding trial by seven-member jury).

48. Bellia, 110 *Yale L.J.* 962.

49. Richard H. Fallon, Jr. et al., *The Federal Courts and the Federal System*, 5th ed. (New York: Foundation Press, 2003) 450.

50. The academic commentary on the anti-commandeering rule is extensive. For a few selections that address the relationship of the Supremacy Clause to the rule, see Peter Jeremy Smith, "The Anticommandeering Principle and Congress's Power to Direct State Judicial Action: Congress's Power to Compel State Courts to Answer Certified Questions of State Law," 31 *Conn. L. Rev.* (1999) 649 and Martin H. Redish & Steven G. Sklaver, "Federal Power to Commander State Courts: Implications for the Theory of Judicial Federalism," 32 *Ind. L. Rev.* (1998) 71.

51. Liebman & Ryan, 98 *Colum. L. Rev.* 764. For differing views on the relevant history, compare Saikrishna Bangalore Prakash, "Field Office Federalism," 79 *Va. L. Rev.* (1993) 1957, 2007 ("the Founding Generation envisioned commandeering of state courts

in two different manners. First, many thought that the Supremacy Clause required state judges to hear federal claims. Second, some Framers thought that Congress could constitute state courts as inferior federal courts") with Michael G. Collins, "Article III Cases, State Court Duties, and the Madisonian Compromise," 1995 *Wis. L. Rev.* 39, 195 ("As a historical matter, the notion that Congress might make use of the state courts to enforce federal law any time it was arguably necessary and proper to the achievement of some legitimate congressional goal, is inaccurate").

52. 42 U.S.C. § 2021e(d)(2)(c).

53. The Court also distinguished Federal Energy Regulatory Comm'n v. Mississippi (1982), in which it had extended *Testa* to state administrative hearing officers, explaining that "the answer to the question of which state officers *must* apply federal law (only '"judges" within the meaning of the Supremacy Clause') is different from the answer to the question of which state officers *may be required by statute* to apply federal law (officers who conduct adjudications similar to those traditionally performed by judges)." The Court concluded: "We have no doubt that *FERC* would not have been decided the way it was if *non*adjudicative responsibilities of the state agency were at issue."

54. Commentators have argued that the judicial exception is derived, not from the State Judges Clause, but from the Supremacy Clause generally; see Evan H. Caminker, "Printz, State Sovereignty and the Limits of Formalism," 1997 *Sup. Ct. Rev.* 199, 212–217, or Article I of the Constitution; see Redish & Sklaver, 32 *Ind. L. Rev.* 88–90.

55. U.S. Const., amend. XI ("The Judicial power of the United States shall not be construed to extend to any suit in law or equity, commenced or prosecuted against one of the United States by Citizens of another State, or by Citizens or Subjects of any Foreign State.").

56. A.C. Pritchard, "Constitutional Federalism, Individual Liberty, and the Securities Litigation Uniform Standards Act of 1998," 78 *Wash. U.L.Q.* (2000) 435, 477–478.

57. The illustration that follows is based on the facts of Allied-Bruce Terminix Cos. v. Dobson (1995).

58. See Thomas J. Stipanowich, "The Growing Debate over 'Consumerized' Arbitration: Adding Cole to the Fire," *Disp. Resol. Mag.* (Summer 1997) 20; Thomas J. Stipanowich, "Punitive Damages and the Consumerization of Arbitration," 92 *Nw. U.L. Rev.* (1997) 1.

59. 9 U.S.C. § 2.

60. S. Candice Hoke, "Preemption Pathologies and Civic Republican Virtues," 71 *B.U. L. Rev.* (1991) 685, 725.

61. Hoke, 71 *B.U. L. Rev.* 687.

62. Viet D. Dinh, "Reassessing the Law of Preemption," 88 *Geo. L.J.* (2000) 2085, 2085.

63. Jack Goldsmith, "Statutory Foreign Affairs Preemption," 2000 *Sup. Ct. Rev.* 175, 178.

64. Marin R. Scordato, "Federal Preemption of State Tort Claims," 35 *U.C.-Davis L. Rev.* (2001) 1, 7.

65. Nelson, 86 *Va. L. Rev.* 232.

66. Compare Paul M. Bator et al., *The Federal Courts and the Federal System,* 2nd ed. (New York: Foundation Press, 1973) 470–471 (quoting 1953 first edition) ("Federal law is generally interstitial in its nature. It rarely occupies a legal field completely, totally

excluding all participation by the legal systems of the states. This plainly was true in the beginning when the federal legislative product (including the Constitution) was extremely small. It is significantly true today, despite the volume of Congressional enactments, and even within areas where Congress has been very active.") with Fallon et al., *The Federal Courts and the Federal System* 495 ("In the fifty years since the First Edition was published, the expansion of federal legislation and administrative regulation noted in this discussion has accelerated; today one finds many more instances in which federal enactments supply both right and remedy in, or wholly occupy, a particular field. This same period has witnessed a broad extension of federal laws (constitutional and statutory) that protect individual rights and provide remedies for violations thereof. Thus, at present federal law appears to be more primary than interstitial in numerous areas.").

67. U.S. Advisory Commission on Intergovernmental Relations, *Federal Statutory Preemption of State and Local Authority: History, Inventory, and Issues* (Sept. 1992).

68. U.S. Advisory Commission Report 14.

69. David M. O'Brien, "The Supreme Court and Intergovernmental Relations: What Happened to 'Our Federalism'?," 9 *J.L. & Pol.* (1993) 609, 618.

70. Mary J. Davis, "Unmasking the Presumption in Favor of Preemption," 53 *S. Car. L. Rev.* (2002) 967, 969 n.9.

71. Kenneth Starr et al., *The Law of Preemption: A Report of the Appellate Judges Conference* (Chicago: American Bar Association, 1991) 1 n.3.

72. *The Federalism Accountability Act of 1999*, Hearings on S. 1214 Before the Senate Committee on Governmental Affairs, 106th Cong., 1st Sess. 95 (July 14, 1999) (opening statement of Sen. Fred Thompson).

73. During the October 1999 Term, the Court decided four preemption cases: Crosby v. National Foreign Trade Council (2000); Geier v. American Honda Motor Co. (2000); Norfolk Southern Railway Co. v. Shanklin (2000); and United States v. Locke (2000). During the October 2000 Term, the Court decided three preemption cases: Lorillard Tobacco Co. v. Reilly (2001); Egelhoff v. Egelhoff (2001); and Buckman Co. v. Plaintiffs' Legal Committee (2001). During the October 2001 Term, the Court decided two preemption cases: City of Columbus v. Ours Garage & Wrecker Service, Inc. (2002); and Rush Prudential HMO, Inc. v. Moran (2002).

74. During its terms beginning 1985–1987, the Supreme Court issued 453 opinions. See "The Supreme Court, 1985 Term, The Statistics," 100 *Harv. L. Rev.* (1986) 304; "The Supreme Court, 1986 Term, The Statistics," 101 *Harv. L. Rev.* (1987) 362; and "The Supreme Court, 1987 Term, The Statistics," 102 *Harv. L. Rev.* (1988) 350. By comparison, the Court issued only 244 opinions during the terms beginning 1999–2001. See "The Supreme Court, 1999 Term, The Statistics," 114 *Harv. L. Rev.* (2000) 390; "The Supreme Court, 2000 Term, The Statistics," 115 *Harv. L. Rev.* (2001) 539; and "The Supreme Court, 2001 Term, The Statistics," 116 *Harv. L. Rev.* (2002) 453.

75. Stephen A. Gardbaum, "The Nature of Preemption," 79 *Cornell L. Rev.* (1994) 767, 768.

76. 29 U.S.C. § 1001 *et seq.*

77. District of Columbia v. Greater Washington Bd. of Trade (1992) (Stevens, J., dissenting).

78. Scordato, 35 *U.C. Davis L. Rev.* 26 & n.100.

79. Gardbaum, 79 *Cornell L. Rev.* 768.

80. Gardbaum, 79 *Cornell L. Rev.* 770–777.

81. Dinh, 88 *Geo. L.J.* 2091 n.36.

82. Dinh, 88 *Geo. L.J.*. 2090.

83. Letter from James Madison to Thomas Jefferson (Mar. 19, 1787), in 9 Robert A. Rutland, ed., *The Papers of James Madison* (Chicago: University of Chicago Press, 1975) 317, 318.

84. Dinh, 88 *Geo. L.J.* 2090.

85. E.g., Hillsborough County v. Automated Medical Laboratories, Inc. (1985); Capital Cities Cable, Inc. v. Crisp (1984); and Fidelity Federal Savings & Loan Ass'n v. de la Cuesta (1982).

86. E.g., Lorillard Tobacco Co. v. Reilly (2001); Medtronic, Inc. v. Lohr (1996); Cipollone v. Liggett Group (1992); and Gade v. National Solid Wastes Management Ass'n (1992).

87. Karen A. Jordan, "The Shifting Preemption Paradigm: Conceptual and Interpretive Issues," 51 *Vand. L. Rev.* (1998) 1149.

88. Hoke, 71 *B.U. L. Rev.* 735–737 & Figure 1.

89. For an example that predates the time period searched, see 49 U.S.C. § 11501; see also Department of Revenue v. ACF Industries, Inc. (1994) (explaining that § 11501"sets limits upon the taxation authority of state government" and applying the presumption against preemption in interpreting its provisions).

90. Pub. L. No. 101–647, sec. 3611, § 3003(d), 104 Stat. 4789 (Nov. 29, 1990).

91. Pub. L. No. 104–88, sec. 103, § 13902(b)(4), 109 Stat. 803 (Dec. 29, 1995).

92. Pub. L. No. 103–272, sec. 1(d), § 5125, 108 Stat. 745 (July 5, 1994).

93. Pub. L. No. 91–222, 84 Stat. 87 (Apr. 1, 1970).

94. Animal Enterprise Protection Act of 1992, Pub. L. No. 102–346, sec. 2(a), § 43(e), 106 Stat. 928 (Aug. 26, 1992).

95. Pub. L. No. 102–243, sec. 3(a), § 227(e), 105 Stat. 2394 (Dec. 20, 1991).

96. Pub. L. No. 106–274, § 5(h), 114 Stat. 803 (Sept. 22, 2000).

97. Philanthropy Protection Act of 1995, Pub. L. No. 104–62, § 6(c), 109 Stat. 682 (Dec. 8, 1995) ("Notwithstanding subsections (a) and (b), during the 3-year period beginning on the date of enactment of this Act, a State may enact a statute that specifically refers to this section and provides prospectively that this section shall not preempt the laws of that State referred to in this section.").

98. 15 U.S.C. § 1397(k) (recodified at 49 U.S.C. § 30103) ("Compliance with a motor vehicle safety standard prescribed under this chapter does not exempt a person from liability at common law.")

99. Davis, 53 *S. Car. L. Rev.* 1009–1010.

100. 7 U.S.C. § 136v.

101. 7 U.S.C. § 136(aa).

102. 49 U.S.C. § 14501(c)(2)(A) (specifying that express preemption provision "shall not restrict the safety regulatory authority of a State with respect to motor vehicles").

103. 49 U.S.C. § 14501(c)(2)(C) (specifying that express preemption provision "does not apply to the authority of a State or a political subdivision of a State to enact or enforce a law . . . relating to the price of for-hire motor vehicle transportation by a tow truck").

104. Nelson, 86 *Va. L. Rev.* 260–261.

105. See Erwin Chemerinsky, *Constitutional Law: Principles and Policies* (New York: Aspen Law & Business, 1997) 298 (citing *McDermott*) and 1 Tribe, *American Constitutional Law* 1180 (citing *McDermott* and *Southland*, among others).

106. 1 Tribe, *American Constitutional Law* 1182–1189.

107. Chemerinsky, *Constitutional Law: Principles and Policies* 303–304. Professor Chemerinsky contrasts *Pacific Gas & Electric* with *Gade*. I add *Geier* to the mix as well.

108. Chemerinsky, *Constitutional Law: Principles and Policies* 301.

109. Nelson, 86 *Va. L. Rev.* 254–276.

110. Nelson, 86 *Va. L. Rev.* 261.

111. Chemerinsky, *Constitutional Law: Principles and Policies* 292.

112. 1 Tribe, *American Constitutional Law* 1205.

113. 1 Tribe, *American Constitutional Law* 1205.

114. There is some disagreement in the academic literature over whether *Hines* involves obstacle preemption or field preemption. Compare Goldsmith, 2000 *Sup. Ct. Rev.* 187–188 ("The *Hines* Court did not, as many maintain, establish that federal power in foreign relations, or even in immigration, is exclusive of the states. Rather, it held that the Pennsylvania law 'stands as an obstacle to the accomplishment and execution of the full purposes and objectives of Congress.' ") with Starr, *The Law of Preemption* 27 ("*Hines* was in reality an occupying the field case"); Chemerinsky, *Constitutional Law: Principles and Policies* 292 (same). Because subsequent Supreme Court cases, although quoting the obstacle preemption test, seem to treat *Hines* as a field preemption case, I treat it that way here as well. See Rice v. Santa Fe Elevator Corp. (1947); Pennsylvania v. Nelson (1956).

115. Nelson, 86 *Va. L. Rev.* 227 ("The Court has grown increasingly hesitant to read implicit field-preemption clauses into federal statutes."); Goldsmith, 2000 *Sup. Ct. Rev.* 213 (noting "Court's attenuated use of field preemption in general in recent years").

116. Nelson, 86 *Va. L. Rev.* 298–299.

117. 9 U.S.C. § 2.

118. 29 U.S.C. § 667(b).

119. 21 U.S.C. § 360k(a).

120. Davis, 53 *S. Car. L. Rev.* 968.

121. E.g., Johnson v. Fankell (1997); California v. ARC America Corp. (1989); and Hillsborough County v. Automated Medical Laboratories, Inc. (1985).

122. E.g., Rush Prudential HMO, Inc. v. Moran (2002); California Division of Labor Standards Enforcement v. Dillingham Construction, N.A. (1997).

123. Manufactured Housing Improvement Act of 2000, Pub. L. No. 106–569, § 604(2), 114 Stat. 2944 (Dec. 27, 2000).

124. Davis, 53 *S. Car. L. Rev.* 971.

125. See Christopher G. Tiedeman, *A Treatise on the Limitations of the Police Power in the United States* (1886); see also Glenn H. Reynolds & David B. Kopel, "The Evolving Police Power: Some Observations for a New Century," 27 *Hastings Const. L.Q.* (2000) 511.

126. Nelson, 86 *Va. L. Rev.* 292–293.

127. Dinh, 88 *Geo. L.J.* 2092.

128. Davis, 53 *S. Car. L. Rev.* 971.

129. Paul Wolfson, "Preemption and Federalism: The Missing Link," 16 *Hastings Const. L.Q.* (1988) 69, 112–114; Starr, *The Law of Preemption* 40–55; see also Gregory v. Ashcroft (1991).

130. Scordato, 35 *U.C. Davis L. Rev.* 24–29.

131. O'Brien, 9 *J.L. & Pol.* 621.

132. Table 3 reports data collected by Professor David O'Brien, which I have updated. O'Brien includes dormant Commerce Clause cases in his tables reporting outcomes in preemption and implied preemption cases. O'Brien, 9 *J.L. & Pol.* 622–623 tables 3 & 4. Because the subject here is statutory preemption rather than the dormant Commerce Clause, I excluded those cases. For a description of O'Brien's methodology in collecting the data, see 9 *J.L. & Pol.* 621 n.73. I tried to follow his methodology in updating the data, but there is no guarantee that his results and mine are fully comparable.

133. O'Brien, 9 *J.L. & Pol.* 621.

134. 2 U.S.C. § 658b(e).

135. Louise Weinberg, "A Federal-State Conflict of Laws: 'Actual Conflicts'," 70 *Tex. L. Rev.* (1992) 1743, 1751 ("The current majority, appointees of the Reagan and Bush administrations, might care about states' rights, but they also might want to control intrusions of state regulation upon the nations' markets"); Scordato, 35 *U.C. Davis L. Rev.* 4 ("[O]ne can find some strange bedfellows in this area").

136. Scordato, 35 *U.C. Davis L. Rev.* 3.

137. Executive Order 12612 of Oct. 26, 1987, 52 Fed. Reg. 41685 (Oct. 30, 1987).

138. Executive Order 12612, § 5.

139. Executive Order 13083 of May 14, 1998, 63 Fed. Reg. 27651 (May 19, 1998).

140. Executive Order 12612, § 2(i).

141. Letter from George V. Voinovich, National Governors' Ass'n, et al., to William J. Clinton, President of the United States (July 17, 1998), at <www.ncsl.org/statefed/eo13083.htm> (urging withdrawal of Executive Order 13083 and stating that "[n]o state and local government official was consulted in the drafting of E.O. 13083").

142. *Clinton-Gore v. State and Local Governments*, Hearings Before the Subcomm. on Nat'l Econ. Growth, Natural Resources, and Regulatory Affairs of the House Comm. on Gov't Reform and Oversight, 105th Cong., 2d Sess. (July 28, 1998).

143. 144 Cong. Rec. S8747 (July 22, 1998).

144. Executive Order 13095 of Aug. 5, 1998, 63 Fed. Reg. 42565 (Aug. 7, 1998).

145. Executive Order 13132 of Aug. 4, 1999, 64 Fed. Reg. 43255 (Aug. 10, 1999).

146. For a detailed comparison of the three federalism orders, see Jennie Holman Blake, Note, "Presidential Power Grab or Pure State Might? A Modern Debate Over Executive Interpretations on Federalism," 2000 *B.Y.U. L. Rev.* 293, 343 app. B.

147. United States General Accounting Office, *Federalism: Comments on S. 1214—The Federalism Accountability Act of 1999* (July 14, 1999) 3–5 (Statement of L. Nye Stevens Before the Senate Committee on Governmental Affairs).

148. Unfunded Mandates Reform Act of 1995, Pub. L. No. 104–4, sec. 101(a)(2), § 423(e), 109 Stat. 48 (Mar. 22, 1995).

149. 2 U.S.C. § 658b(e).

150. S. Rep. No. 104–1 (1995) 13; S. Rep. No. 104–2 (1995) 10.

151. H.R. Rep. 104–661 (1996) 7 (on the Bill Emerson Good Samaritan Food Donation Act).

152. E.g., H.R. Rep. 104–622 (1996) (on the 1996 securities amendments); S. Rep. No. 104–293 (1996) (on the Securities Investment Promotion Act of 1996).

153. E.g., H.R. Rep. No. 107–678 (2002); H.R. Rep. No. 107–651 (2002).

154. H.R. 2245, 106th Cong., 1st Sess. (1999); see also S. 1214, 106th Cong., 1st Sess. (1999) ("Federalism Accountability Act of 1999").

155. *The Federalism Accountability Act of 1999*, Hearings on S. 1214 Before the Senate Committee on Governmental Affairs, 106th Cong., 1st Sess. (July 14, 1999) 101 (statement of Randall D. Moss, Acting Assistant Attorney General, U.S. Department of Justice); see also *The Federalism Accountability Act of 1999*, Hearings on S. 1214, at 133 (statement of Professor Caleb E. Nelson) ("[T]he statute would preempt all State law that is in 'direct conflict' with it, but not State law that merely hinders the accomplishment of the full purposes and objectives behind it").

156. Adam D. Thierer, "Federalism Reform: Seven Options for Congress," Heritage Foundation Backgrounder #1245 (Jan. 27, 1999), at <www.heritage.org/Research/GovernmentReform/BG1245.cfm>.

157. The discussion in the text is simplified. For a more detailed analysis, see Christopher R. Drahozal, "Federal Arbitration Act Preemption," 79 *Ind. L.J.* 393 (2004).

158. 9 U.S.C. § 2.

159. Despite the passage of twenty years since *Southland* was decided, the case remains controversial. For criticisms of *Southland*, particularly its reliance on the legislative history of the FAA to hold that the Act applies in state court, see, e.g., Ian R. Macneil, *American Arbitration Law: Reformation, Nationalization, Internationalization* (Oxford: Oxford University Press, 1992) 83–147; David S. Schwartz, "Correcting Federalism Mistakes in Statutory Interpretation: The Supreme Court and the Federal Arbitration Act," 67 *Law & Contemp. Probs.* ___ (2004) (forthcoming). For a contrary view on the legislative history of the Act, see Christopher R. Drahozal, "In Defense of *Southland*: Reexamining the Legislative History of the Federal Arbitration Act," 78 *Notre Dame L. Rev.* (2002) 101, 107 ("construing the Act as applicable in state court is more consistent with the legislative history—that is, it leaves fewer ambiguities unexplained—than the Macneil interpretation").

160. See Southland Corp. v. Keating (1984); Perry v. Thomas (1987); Volt Information Sciences, Inc. v. Board of Trustees of the Leland Stanford Junior University (1989); Allied-Bruce Terminix Cos. v. Dobson (1995); Mastrobuono v. Shearson Lehman Hutton, Inc. (1995); and Doctor's Associates, Inc. v. Casarotto (1996).

161. One settled, but complicated, point is that parties can avoid the effects of FAA preemption by incorporating the state law at issue into their contract. Determining when an arbitration agreement incorporates state law by reference has been the subject of a pair of Supreme Court cases: Volt Information Sciences, Inc. v. Board of Trustees of the Leland Stanford Junior University (1989); and Mastrobuono v. Shearson Lehman Hutton, Inc. (1995). For further discussion of the issue, see Drahozal, 79 *Ind. L.J.* 411–415.

162. Although the FAA does not preempt application of general contract law defenses to arbitration agreements, the Supreme Court has held that some such defenses must be resolved by the arbitrator rather than a judge. See Prima Paint Corp. v. Flood & Conklin

Mfg. Co. (1967) (defense of fraud in the inducement of the contract as a whole to be decided by arbitrator) and Howsam v. Dean Witter Reynolds, Inc. (2002) (time limit for bringing claim to be applied by arbitrator rather than judge).

163. Compare Keystone, Inc. v. Triad Systems Corp. (Mont. 1998) (holding that FAA does not preempt Montana statute that applies both to arbitration clauses and court-selection clauses) with Bradley v. Harris Research, Inc. (9th Cir. 2001) (holding that fact that statute applies both to arbitration clauses and court-selection clauses does not save it from preemption by FAA). Given that *Southland* involved a state law that invalidated arbitration clauses and other contract provisions waiving protections of the California Franchise Investment Law (i.e., it did not "single out" arbitration clauses), the Ninth Circuit rather than the Montana Supreme Court has the better of the argument.

164. Judicial Council of California, *Ethics Standards for Neutral Arbitrators in Contractual Arbitration* (effective Jan. 1, 2003). A federal district court has held the disclosure requirements preempted by the FAA. See Mayo v. Dean Witter Reynolds, Inc. (N.D. Cal. 2003).

165. See, e.g., 1 Ian R. Macneil et al., *Federal Arbitration Law* (Boston: Little, Brown & Co., Supp. 1999) chap. 10; Stephen J. Ware, *Alternative Dispute Resolution* (St. Paul: West Group, 2001) 26–43; Stephen L. Hayford & Alan R. Palmiter, "Arbitration Federalism: A State Role in Commercial Arbitration," 54 *Fla. L. Rev.* (2002) 175; Stephen L. Hayford, "Federal Preemption and Vacatur: The Bookend Issues under the Revised Uniform Arbitration Act," 2001 *J. Disp. Resol.* 67; Stephen J. Ware, "Punitive Damages in Arbitration: Contracting Out of Government's Role in Punishment and Federal Preemption of State Law," 63 *Fordham L. Rev.* (1994) 529; Stephen J. Ware, "'Opt-In' for Judicial Review of Errors of Law under the Revised Uniform Arbitration Act," 8 *Am. Rev. Int'l Arb.* (1997) 263. See generally Drahozal, 79 *Ind. L.J.* 416–420.

166. This introduction was suggested by a lecture given by former Solicitor General Seth P. Waxman at the University of Kansas School of Law on January 28, 2002. The lecture is published as "Federalism, Law Enforcement, and the Supremacy Clause: The Strange Case of Ruby Ridge," 51 *U. Kan. L. Rev.* (2002) 141; see also Seth P. Waxman & Trevor W. Morrison, "What Kind of Immunity? Federal Officers, State Criminal Law, and the Supremacy Clause," 112 *Yale L.J.* (2003) 2195. The description of the facts that follows is based largely on Idaho v. Horiuchi (9th Cir. 2000) and Idaho v. Horiuchi (9th Cir. 2001) (en banc), as well as the Waxman lecture.

167. See *The Federal Raid on Ruby Ridge, ID*: Hearings Before the Subcomm. on Terrorism, Tech., and Gov't Info. of the Senate Comm. on the Judiciary, 104th Cong., 1st Sess. (1995) 1095, 1106–1107 (Appendix, Ruby Ridge: Report of the Subcommittee) (finding more plausible that the Marshals fired first and killed Sammy Weaver's dog).

168. At the time of the first shot, Randy Weaver was carrying the gun. As the group approached the cabin, Kevin Harris was carrying the gun.

169. United States Department of Justice, "Evidence from Investigation of 1992 Ruby Ridge Matter Only Sufficient to Charge One Official with Criminal Conduct" (Aug. 15, 1997), at <www.usdoj.gov/opa/pr/1997/August97/337crm.htm>.

170. The relevant part of the state indictment alleged that Horiuchi "did unlawfully, but without malice, kill Vicki J. Weaver, a human being, in the operation of a firearm in a reckless, careless or negligent manner, to wit: discharging the firearm through the front door of the Weaver residence in an attempt to shoot Kevin Harris as he entered the door from

outside, without first determining whether any person other than his intended target was present on the other side of the door" (Idaho v. Horiuchi, D. Idaho 1998).

171. United States Department of Justice, "Justice Department Press Release Regarding Charges Filed Against Lon Horiuchi" (Aug. 21, 1997), at <www.usdoj.gov/opa/pr/1997/August97/342crm.htm>.

172. He relied on 28 U.S.C. § 1442(a)(1), which permits a federal official to remove from state court to federal court a criminal prosecution based on "any act under color of such office or on account of any right, title or authority claimed under any Act of Congress for the apprehension or punishment of criminals or the collection of the revenue."

173. 1 Tribe, *American Constitutional Law* 1220.

174. See United States v. County of Fresno (1977) (explaining that in *Graves* the Supreme Court "sustained a nondiscriminatory tax on the income of a federal employee, thereby overruling *Dobbins* v. *Commissioners of Erie County*").

175. In Cotton Petroleum Corp. v. New Mexico (1989), the Court stated that "[s]hortly after reaching its zenith in the *Gillespie* decision, the doctrine of intergovernmental tax immunity started a long path in decline and has now been 'thoroughly repudiated' by modern case law" (quoting South Carolina v. Baker, 1988). Although the reach of the doctrine has declined, it certainly has not been "thoroughly repudiated." Instead, as the Court made clear in *Baker*, what has been "thoroughly repudiated" is the "general immunity" for income earned by government contractors.

176. A party may also try to pass some taxes backward to suppliers by paying less for a particular good or service.

177. For a detailed (and highly technical) analysis, see Don Fullerton and Gilbert E. Metcalf, "Tax Incidence" (March 2002) (National Bureau of Economic Research Working Paper 8829), at <papers.nber.org/papers/w8829.pdf>.

178. Fullerton & Metcalf, NBER Working Paper 8829, at 1. As will shortly be seen, Supremacy Clause immunity from taxes depends on the "legal incidence" of the tax, which may be, but is not necessarily, the same as its statutory incidence. I will use the phrase "legal incidence" only in the context of federal immunity and the phrase "statutory incidence" otherwise.

179. Fullerton & Metcalf, NBER Working Paper 8829, at 28.

180. E.g., Minnesota Department of Revenue, Tax Research Division, *2003 Minnesota Tax Incidence Study: Analysis of Minnesota's Household and Business Taxes* 28 (March 1, 2003) (estimating that 43 percent of property tax on rental property was borne by owners of rental property, leaving 57 percent borne by tenants through higher rents), at <www.state.mn.us/ebranch/mdor/reports/Incidence%202003/whole_doc_feb2003.pdf>.

181. 2 Jerome R. Hellerstein & Walter Hellerstein, *State Taxation*, 3rd ed. (Boston: Warren Gorham & Lamont, 2001) ¶ 22.02[2], at 22–8.

182. Laurence H. Tribe, "Intergovernmental Immunities in Litigation, Taxation, and Regulation: Separation of Powers Issues in Controversies about Federalism," 89 *Harv. L. Rev.* (1976) 682, 710.

183. Tribe, 89 *Harv. L. Rev.* 710.

184. 1 Tribe, *American Constitutional Law* 1229.

185. 2 Hellerstein & Hellerstein, *State Taxation* ¶ 22.02[2][b], at 22–16.

186. Maureen Mahoney, Note, "Federal Immunity from State Taxation: A Reassessment," 45 *U. Chi. L. Rev.* (1978) 695, 723.

187. 1 Tribe, *American Constitutional Law* 1232.

188. 2 Hellerstein & Hellerstein, *State Taxation* ¶ 22.02[3], at 22–17.

189. 2 Hellerstein & Hellerstein, *State Taxation* ¶ 22.02[3][b], at 22–24.

190. For a discussion of the current scope of tribal immunity from state taxes, see 2 Hellerstein & Hellerstein, *State Taxation* ¶ 22.07. For a broader consideration of Indian tribes and the Supremacy Clause, see Robert N. Clinton, "There is No Federal Supremacy Clause for Indian Tribes," 34 *Az. St. L.J.* (2002) 113.

191. 2 Hellerstein & Hellerstein, *State Taxation* ¶ 22.04, at 22–38 ("[T]he Court has steadfastly adhered to the fundamental principle that the Supremacy Clause bars taxes discriminating against the federal government").

192. 2 Hellerstein & Hellerstein, *State Taxation* ¶ 22.04[6], at 22–55 (explaining that "the Court has not clearly indicated whether a statute that treats those who deal with public or exempt entities (including the federal government) differently from those who deal with the private sector constitutes unconstitutional discrimination"; but concluding that "one suspects that the Court would invalidate" such a tax).

193. For prior cases, see Memphis Bank & Trust Co. v. Garner (1983) (invalidating state tax on bank income that taxed interest from federal obligations but excluded interest from state obligations); Moses Lake Homes, Inc. v. Grant County (1961) (invalidating state tax when property leased from federal government subject to higher valuation than property leased from state government); and Phillips Chemical Co. v. Dumas Independent School District (1960) (invalidating state tax that applied to lessees of federal property but not lessees of state property).

194. The retiree relied on 4 U.S.C. § 111, which consents to state taxes on federal employees' wages, but only so long as the tax is nondiscriminatory. The Supreme Court in *Davis* construed section 111 as "coextensive with the prohibition against discriminatory taxes embodied in the modern constitutional doctrine of intergovernmental tax immunity." Thus, the statutory question was the same as the constitutional question.

195. Unless the disadvantaged group is a suspect class, or the case involves a fundamental right, in which case the Court applies "strict scrutiny."

196. See also Barker v. Kansas (1992) (extending *Davis* to military retirees).

197. For a critique of the Court's reasoning on this point, see David M. Richardson, "Federal Income Taxation of States," 19 *Stetson L. Rev.* (1990) 411, 439 n.168 ("If the taxpayer itemizes his deductions, . . . then the increase in compensation itself will not result in an increase in federal tax liability because the state taxes paid would be deductible for purposes of determining federal taxable income").

198. One issue was whether the *Davis* decision applied retroactively. In Harper v. Virginia Dep't of Taxation (1993), the Court held that it did. For a detailed discussion of the implications of *Harper*, see Eric Rakowski, "*Harper* and Its Aftermath," 1 *Fla. Tax Rev.* (1993) 445; see also Eric Rakowski, *Harper* and Retroactive Remedies: Why States' Fears Are Exaggerated," 4 *State Tax Notes* (1993) 983; Eugene O. Duffy, "Suggested Approach for States After *Harper* Faces 'Host of Legal Barriers,'" 4 *State Tax Notes* (1993) 1246; Eric Rakowski, "Rakowski Responds: There's More to *Harper* than Large Refund Payments," 4 *State Tax Notes* (1993) 1318 (letter to the editor).

199. Alabama, Kentucky, Louisiana, New York, North Dakota, West Virginia, and Wisconsin took this approach. Corina L. Eckl et al., "State Taxation of Public Pensions: The Impact of *Davis v. Michigan*," 47 *Tax Notes* (1990) 1119, 1127.

200. Dan T. Coenen & Walter Hellerstein, "Suspect Linkage: The Interplay of State Taxing and Spending Measures in the Application of Constitutional Antidiscrimination Rules," 95 *Mich. L. Rev.* (1997) 2167, 2178–2181.

201. Arizona, Colorado, Michigan, Mississippi, Missouri, North Carolina, and South Carolina took this approach. Eckl et al., 47 *Tax Notes* 1127.

202. Georgia and Oklahoma took this approach. Eckl et al., 47 *Tax Notes* 1127. Iowa reduced and equalized the tax preference for both state and federal retirees, while New Mexico, Utah, and Virginia adopted income exclusions based on age to replace the pension exclusions. Eckl et al., 47 *Tax Notes* 1127.

203. Coenen & Hellerstein, 95 *Mich. L. Rev.* 2179.

204. Professors Dan T. Coenen and Walter Hellerstein, while acknowledging "room for disagreement about the proper result in *Ragsdale*," conclude that *Sheehy* was correctly decided and *Ragsdale* was wrongly decided. For their reasoning, see Coenen & Hellerstein, 95 *Mich. L. Rev.* 2219–2227.

205. 2 Hellerstein & Hellerstein, *State Taxation* ¶ 22.06[1][a], at 22–59.

206. 31 U.S.C. § 3124. The statute commonly is referred to as Revised Statutes § 3701, which was its designation for many years. 2 Hellerstein & Hellerstein, *State Taxation* ¶ 22.06[1][a], at 22–59.

207. The statute provides: "The United States consents to the taxation of pay or compensation for personal service as an officer or employee of the United States . . . by a duly constituted taxing authority having jurisdiction, if the taxation does not discriminate against the officer or employee because of the source of the pay or compensation." 4 U.S.C. § 111.

208. 12 U.S.C. § 2121.

209. See also Arizona v. California (1931) (state approval not needed before construction of dam authorized by Congress) ("The United States may perform its functions without conforming to the police regulations of a state").

210. See Leslie Miller, Inc. v. Arkansas (1956) (state licensing requirement for contractors as applied to federal contractor); Public Utilities Comm'n v. United States (1958) (state regulation of rates charged by common carriers to federal government); and United States v. Georgia Public Service Comm'n (1963) (state regulation precluding discounts for transport of goods as applied to the federal government).

211. 1 Tribe, *American Constitutional Law* 1223–1224.

212. 2 Hellerstein & Hellerstein, *State Taxation* ¶ 22.02[3][b], at 22–22 to 22–23.

213. 2 Hellerstein & Hellerstein, *State Taxation* ¶ 22.02[3][b], at 22–24.

214. 1 Tribe, *American Constitutional Law* 1223.

215. Idaho v. Horiuchi (9th Cir. 2001) (en banc) (Hawkins, J., dissenting).

216. The description that follows draws from Paul Kens, *Justice Stephen Field: Shaping Liberty from the Gold Rush to the Gilded Age* (Lawrence, KS: University Press of Kansas, 1997) 276–283; Carl Brent Swisher, *Stephen J. Field: Craftsman of the Law* (Washington, D.C.: The Brookings Institution, 1930) 321–361; and Robert Kroninger, "The Justice and the Lady," *Yearbook 1977 Supreme Court Historical Society* 11–19, as well as the Supreme Court's opinion in *Neagle*.

217. Kentucky v. Long (6th Cir. 1988); Clifton v. Cox (9th Cir. 1977); In re McShane (N.D. Miss. 1964).

218. The discussion that follows relies on Susan L. Smith, "Shields for the King's Men: Official Immunity and Other Obstacles to Effective Prosecution of Federal Officials for Environmental Crimes," 16 *Colum. J. Env'l L.* (1991) 1, 38–46; and Waxman, 51 *U. Kan. L. Rev.* 147.

219. Waxman, 51 *U. Kan. L. Rev.* 147.

220. Smith, 16 *Colum. J. Env'l L.* 44 n.140.

221. The decision was an interlocutory appeal from the trial court's denial of Horiuchi's motion to dismiss on qualified immunity grounds. The Ninth Circuit concluded that "it is extremely doubtful . . . that Horiuchi will ever be able to establish that he is entitled to qualified immunity for his conduct in shooting Harris" and that "as the record now stands, he cannot do so."

222. Because of the number of judges on the Ninth Circuit, rehearing en banc is held before eleven active judges (including the chief judge) out of the twenty-eight judges on the court. 9th Cir. R. 35–3. After the "limited" en banc rehearing, the court can rehear the case before all twenty-eight judges if it so decides.

223. Waxman, 51 *U. Kan. L. Rev.* 148 (quoting Brief for Plaintiff-Appellant at 58, Idaho v. Horiuchi, 9th Cir. 2001 (No. 98–30149)).

224. Waxman, 51 *U. Kan. L. Rev.* 148–149 (citing Brief of Amici Curiae William P. Barr *et al.*, Idaho v. Horiuchi, 9th Cir. 2001 (No. 98–30149)).

225. Waxman, 51 *U. Kan. L. Rev.* 149 (citing Brief for Appellee and Brief of the United States of America as *Amicus Curiae* for Appellee, Idaho v. Horiuchi, 9th Cir. 2001 (No. 98–30149)).

226. Waxman, 51 *U. Kan. L. Rev.* 149.

227. "Charges Dropped Against Ruby Ridge FBI Sniper," CNN.com (June 15, 2001), at <www.cnn.com/2001/LAW/06/14/ruby.ridge.02/index.html>.

228. At the time of this writing, however, the court of appeals' opinions remain available at <www.findlaw.com>.

229. Waxman, 51 *U. Kan. L. Rev.* 148.

230. Waxman & Morrison, 112 *Yale L.J.* 2239–2242.

231. Waxman & Morrison, 112 *Yale L.J.* 2218.

232. Other commentators recognize that the cases address variations on the same issue. See, e.g., 1 Tribe, *American Constitutional Law* 1220–1225 (treating together "state attempts to regulate or tax entities with some special link to the federal government or its property"), 1224 n.14 (explaining that rule applied in state regulatory cases "emerged as early as In re Neagle").

233. Or at least when the federal official could not reasonably believe his or her actions were constitutional.

234. Waxman & Morrision, 112 *Yale L.J.* 2252–2255.

235. The victim was the father of Judge J. Michael Luttig of the United States Court of Appeals for the Fourth Circuit. Ronald B. Hurdle & Walter J. Champion, Jr., "The Life and Times of Napoleon Beazley: The Effect (If Any) of the International Covenant on Civil and Political Rights on Texas' 17 & Up Execution Standard," 28 *Thurgood Marshall L. Rev.* (2002) 1, 3 n.4.

236. The description of the facts that follows comes from the opinion of the United States Court of Appeals for the Fifth Circuit in Beazley v. Johnson (5th Cir. 2001), quoting the unpublished opinion of the Texas Court of Criminal Appeals, Beazley v. Texas (Tex. Crim. App. Feb. 26, 1997).

237. Victor L. Streib, *The Juvenile Death Penalty Today: Death Sentences and Executions for Juvenile Crimes, January 1, 1973—June 30, 2003*, at Table 3 (last updated July 1, 2003), at <www.law.onu.edu/faculty/streib/juvdeath.htm>. Given the lengthy appeals process in capital cases, the youngest juvenile offender executed since 1973 was 23 at the time of the execution. Streib, *The Juvenile Death Penalty Today* Table 1.

238. Stanford v. Kentucky (1989) (upholding death penalty as applied to persons 16 or 17 years old at time committed crime); Thompson v. Oklahoma (1988) (striking down death penalty as applied to persons 15 years old at time committed crime). Four Justices have indicated they would hold otherwise were the Court to face the issue again. In re Stanford (2002) (Stevens, J., dissenting from denial of certiorari) (joined by Justices Breyer, Ginsburg, and Souter) ("[O]ffenses committed by juveniles under the age of 18 do not merit the death penalty. The practice of executing such offenders is a relic of the past and is inconsistent with evolving standards of decency in a civilized society. We should put an end to this shameful practice.").

239. Amnesty International, "Death Penalty Facts—Juveniles" (visited June 12, 2003), at <www.amnestyusa.org/abolish/juveniles.html>.

240. International Covenant on Civil and Political Rights, Dec. 19, 1966, art. 6, para. 5, S. Exec. Doc. E, 95–2, at 25 (1978), 999 U.N.T.S. 171, 173 (ratified by the U.S. on June 8, 1992).

241. Streib, *The Juvenile Death Penalty Today* App. A.

242. For a list of treaties to which the United States is a party, see United States Department of State, *A List of Treaties and Other International Agreements of the United States in Force as of January 1, 2002*, at <www.state.gov/s/l/18531.htm>.

243. U.S. Const. art. II, § 2.

244. Convention for the Unification of Certain Rules Relating to International Transportation by Air, Oct. 12, 1929, 49 Stat. 3000, T.S. No. 876 (1934); see Eastern Airlines, Inc. v. Floyd (1991) (holding physical injury required under Article 17 of the Warsaw Convention).

245. American Law Institute, *Restatement (Third) of Foreign Relations Law of the United States* § 111(4)(a) (St. Paul: American Law Institute Publishers, 1987).

246. *Restatement (Third) of Foreign Relations Law of the United States* § 111, comment h.

247. E.g., *Restatement (Third) of Foreign Relations Law of the United States* § 111, reporters' note 5 ("[I]f the Executive Branch has not requested implementing legislation and Congress has not enacted such legislation, there is a strong presumption that the treaty has been considered self-executing by the political branches, and should be considered self-executing by the courts").

248. Curtis A. Bradley, "*Breard*, Our Dualist Constitution, and the Internationalist Conception," 51 *Stan. L. Rev.* (1999) 529, 541–542.

249. Carlos Manuel Vázquez, "The Four Doctrines of Self-Executing Treaties," 89 *Am. J. Int'l L.* (1995) 695, 698–700; see also Carlos Manuel Vázquez, "Laughing at Treaties," 99 *Colum. L. Rev.* (1999) 2154.

250. Jordan J. Paust, *International Law as Law of the United States* (Durham: North Carolina Academic Press, 1996) 51.

251. John C. Yoo, "Treaties and Public Lawmaking: A Textual and Structural Defense of Non-Self-Execution," 99 *Colum. L. Rev.* (1999) 2218, 2255; see also John C. Yoo, "Globalism and the Constitution: Treaties, Non-Self-Execution, and the Original

Understanding," 99 *Colum. L. Rev.* (1999) 1955. For a critique of Yoo's historical analysis, see Martin S. Flaherty, "History Right? Historical Scholarship, Original Understanding, and Treaties as 'Supreme Law of the Land,'" 99 *Colum. L. Rev.* (1999) 2095.

252. Louis Henkin, *Foreign Affairs and the United States Constitution*, 2nd ed. (Oxford: Clarendon Press, 1996) 210 n.*.

253. Henkin, *Foreign Affairs and the United States Constitution* 211; see *Restatement (Third) of Foreign Relations Law of the United States* § 115.

254. For a detailed discussion of the *Breard* case, see Bradley, 51 *Stan. L. Rev.* 529.

255. Curtis A. Bradley & Jack L. Goldsmith, *Foreign Relations Law: Cases and Materials* (New York: Aspen Publishers, 2003) 354.

256. *Treaties and Executive Agreements*: Hearings Before a Subcomm. of the Senate Comm. on the Judiciary, 83rd Cong., 1st Sess. 862 (1953) (reprinting speech by John Foster Dulles at the regional meeting of the American Bar Association, Louisville, KY, April 11, 1952).

257. U.S. Const. art. VI (emphasis added).

258. Henkin, *Foreign Affairs and the United States Constitution* 185. But see Peter J. Spiro, "Treaties, International Law, and Constitutional Rights," 55 *Stan. L. Rev.* (2003) 1999.

259. "Email Paranoia: Is the UN Charter Equal to the Constitution?", at <www .citizensoldier.org/uncharterconstitution.html>. Even the "Citizen Soldier" recognizes that "[t]his email is false" under current Supreme Court doctrine.

260. See John R. Bolton, "U.S. Isn't Legally Obligated to Pay the U.N.," *Wall St. J.*, Nov. 17, 1997, at A27.

261. Louis René Beres, "Assassinating Saddam: A Post-War View from International Law," 19 *Denver J. Int'l L. & Pol'y* (1991) 613, 619 (although concluding that assassination is lawful under certain circumstances). Professor Beres' assertion is justifiable only if he is referring to the legality of assassination as a matter of international law, rather than United States domestic law.

262. For a detailed discussion of Missouri v. Holland, see Charles A. Lofgren, "Missouri v. Holland in Historical Perspective," 1975 *Sup. Ct. Rev.* 77.

263. David P. Currie, *The Constitution in the Supreme Court: 1888–1986* (Chicago: University of Chicago Press, 1990) 100.

264. For discussions in the academic literature of the extent to which federalism concerns (which underlie the Tenth Amendment) may restrict the treaty power despite Missouri v. Holland, see Curtis A. Bradley, "The Treaty Power and American Federalism," 97 *Mich. L. Rev.* (1998) 390; Curtis A. Bradley, "The Treaty Power and American Federalism, Part II," 99 *Mich. L. Rev.* (2000) 98; David M. Golove, "Treaty-Making and the Nation: The Historical Foundations of the Nationalist Conception of the Treaty Power," 98 *Mich. L. Rev.* (2000) 1075; and Edward T. Swaine, "Does Federalism Constrain the Treaty Power?" 103 *Colum. L. Rev.* (2003) 403.

265. Congressional Research Service, *Treaties and Other International Agreements: The Role of the United States Senate*, S. print 106–71, 106th Cong., 2d Sess. (2001) 39.

266. Bradley & Goldsmith, *Foreign Relations Law: Cases and Materials* 409; see also 1 Ronald D. Rotunda & John E. Nowak, *Treatise on Constitutional Law: Substance and Procedure*, 2nd ed. (St. Paul: West Publishing Co. 1992) 518–519 (identifying four types

of executive agreements; treating executive agreements based on prior and subsequent congressional approval as separate types).

267. Henkin, *Foreign Affairs and the United States Constitution* 217.

268. North American Free Trade Agreement, Dec. 17, 1992, U.S.-Can.-Mex., 32 I.L.M. 289 (chs. 1–9); 32 I.L.M. 605 (chs. 10–22).

269. *Restatement (Third) of Foreign Relations Law of the United States* § 102(2).

270. U.S. Const. art. I, § 8, cl. 10.

271. Henkin, *Foreign Affairs and the United States Constitution* 508 n.16 (concluding that the Supremacy Clause "does not easily include international law").

272. The Federalist No. 3 (Jay) (Jan. 1, 1788), in 13 John P. Kaminski & Gaspare J. Saladino, eds., *The Documentary History of the Ratification of the Constitution* (Madison: State Historical Society of Wisconsin, 1981) 555, 557.

273. Pacificus No. 1 (June 29, 1793), in 15 Harold C. Syrett & Jacob E. Cooke, eds., *The Papers of Alexander Hamilton* (New York: Columbia University Press, 1969) 33, 34.

274. *Restatement (Third) of Foreign Relations Law of the United States* § 111 comment d.

275. Bradley, 51 *Stan. L. Rev.* 545.

276. Peter J. Spiro, "The States and International Human Rights," 66 *Fordham L. Rev.* (1997) 567, 578 n.40.

277. Curtis A. Bradley & Jack L. Goldsmith, "Customary International Law as Federal Common Law: A Critique of the Modern Position," 110 *Harv. L. Rev.* (1997) 815; Curtis A. Bradley & Jack L. Goldsmith, "Federal Courts and the Incorporation of International Law," 111 *Harv. L. Rev.* (1998) 2260.

278. Gerald L. Neuman, "Sense and Nonsense About Customary International Law: A Response to Professors Bradley and Goldsmith," 66 *Fordham L. Rev.* (1997) 371, 371. For an overview of the debate, see Ernest A. Young, "Sorting Out the Debate Over Customary International Law," 42 *Va. J. Int'l L.* (2002) 365.

279. Harold Hongju Koh, "Is International Law Really State Law?," 111 *Harv. L. Rev.* (1998) 1824, 1827.

280. For a comprehensive review, see Curtis A. Bradley, "The Juvenile Death Penalty and International Law," 52 *Duke L.J.* (2002) 485.

281. U.S. Senate Resolution of Advice and Consent to Ratification of the International Covenant on Civil and Political Rights, 138 Cong. Rec. 8071 (Apr. 2, 1992).

282. 138 Cong. Rec. at 8070.

283. Kevin C. Kennedy, "Conditional Approval of Treaties by the U.S. Senate," 19 *Loy. L.A. Int'l & Comp. L.J.* (1996) 89, 91, 97.

284. *E.g.*, Ex parte Pressley (Ala. 2000); Domingues v. Nevada (Nev. 1998).

285. Brief for the United States as Amicus Curiae, Domingues v. Nevada (1999) (No. 98–8327).

286. William A. Schabas, "International Law and the Abolition of the Death Penalty," 55 *Wash. & Lee L. Rev.* (1998) 797, 799.

287. Young, 42 *Va. J. Int'l L.* 370.

288. *E.g.*, State v. Tenace (Ohio Ct. App. 2003); State v. Odom (Tenn. Crim. App. 2002).

Bibliographical Essay

PART I: HISTORY

Primary Materials

The standard documentary resource for the Constitutional Convention remains 1–3 Max Farrand, ed., *The Records of the Federal Convention of 1787*, rev. ed. (New Haven: Yale University Press, 1937), and for the state ratification debates is 1–5 Jonathan Elliot, ed., *The Debates in the Several State Conventions on the Adoption of the Federal Constitution* (Washington: 1836). Searchable online versions of both Farrand and Elliot are available at the Library of Congress web site "A Century of Lawmaking for a New Nation: U.S. Congressional Documents and Debates, 1774–1785" <lcweb2.loc.gov/ammem/amlaw/lawhome.html>. The web site also includes extensive materials from the Continental Congress and the United States Congress. The Library of Congress "Thomas" web site includes a link to the Federalist Papers as well at <lcweb2.loc.gov/const/fed/fedpapers.html>.

The most complete source for primary materials on the ratification of the Constitution is John P. Kaminski & Gaspare J. Saladino, eds., *The Documentary History of the Ratification of the Constitution* (Madison: State Historical Society of Wisconsin) (multiple volumes), which includes volumes on the ratification debates generally as well volumes with materials organized by state. For Anti-Federalist writings not available in other sources, see 1–7 Herbert J. Storing, ed., *The Complete Anti-Federalist* (Chicago: University Press of Chicago, 1981). A convenient starting point for research on the Supremacy Clause is 4 Philip B. Kurland & Ralph Lerner, eds., *The Founders' Constitution* (Chicago: University of Chicago Press, 1987), which collects relevant excerpts from a wide variety of primary sources. The series is available online at <press-pubs.uchicago.edu/founders>.

Secondary Sources

From Independence to Ratification

A good overview of the idea of supremacy from the British and the colonists' perspectives can be found in Gordon S. Wood, *The Creation of the American Republic 1776–1787*

(Chapel Hill: University of North Carolina Press, 1969) and Martin S. Flaherty, "More Apparent Than Real: The Revolutionary Commitment to Constitutional Federalism," 45 *U. Kan. L. Rev.* (1997) 993. A useful reference on the Articles of Confederation generally is Merrill Jensen, *The Articles of Confederation: An Interpretation of the Social-Constitutional History of the American Revolution 1774–1781* (Madison: University of Wisconsin Press, 1940). References with a more direct focus on the question of federal supremacy under the Articles are Edward S. Corwin, "The Progress of Constitutional Theory Between the Declaration of Independence and the Meeting of the Philadelphia Convention," 30 *Am. Hist. Rev.* (1925) 511 and Edward S. Corwin, *National Supremacy: Treaty Power vs. State Power* (New York: Henry Holt & Co., 1913).

A pair of sources provide detailed descriptions of the evolution of the Supremacy Clause during the course of the Constitutional Convention. See Jack N. Rakove, *Original Meanings: Politics and Ideas in the Making of the Constitution* (New York: Alfred A. Knopf, 1996) and James S. Liebman & William F. Ryan, "'Some Effectual Power': The Quantity and Quality of Decisionmaking Required of Article III Courts," 98 *Colum. L. Rev.* (1998) 696. For an article that focuses on James Madison's proposal for a congressional negative, which was replaced by the Supremacy Clause, see Charles F. Hobson, "The Negative on State Laws: James Madison, the Constitution, and the Crisis of Republican Government," 36 *Wm. & Mary Q.* (1979) 215. Finally, for general sources tracing the ratification of the Constitution in the states, see Patrick T. Conley & John P. Kaminski, *The Constitution and the States: The Role of the Original Thirteen in the Framing and Adoption of the Federal Constitution* (Madison: Madison House, 1988) and Michael Allen Gillespie & Michael Lienesch, eds., *Ratifying the Constitution* (Lawrence: University Press of Kansas, 1989).

Foundational Cases

A number of Supreme Court histories provide interesting insights on the foundational cases decided by the Court. The first volume of Professor David Currie's two-volume set on the history of the Court provides a concise overview. David P. Currie, *The Constitution in the Supreme Court: The First Hundred Years 1789–1888* (Chicago: University of Chicago Press, 1985). The published volumes in the series on Supreme Court history sponsored by the Oliver Wendell Holmes Devise provide a more in-depth review: 1 Julius Goebel, Jr., *Antecedents and Beginnings to 1801* (New York: Macmillan Publishing Co., 1971); 2 George Lee Haskins & Herbert A. Johnson, *Foundations of Power: John Marshall, 1801–15* (New York: Macmillan Publishing Co., 1981); and 3–4 G. Edward White, *The Marshall Court and Cultural Change, 1815–35* (New York: Macmillan Publishing Co., 1988). In addition, the editorial notes in Charles F. Hobson, ed., *The Papers of John Marshall* (Chapel Hill: University of North Carolina Press) (multiple volumes) are uniformly excellent in setting the Marshall Court decisions in their historical context. For articles and books that focus on specific cases, see the notes to the text accompanying the discussion of those cases.

Supremacy and States' Rights

Numerous sources are available on the history of the nullification crisis of 1832, the Civil War, and the Civil Rights movement. I found Professor William Freehling's histories of the period from the nullification crisis leading up to the Civil War to be most helpful.

See William W. Freehling, *Prelude to Civil War: The Nullification Controversy in South Carolina, 1816–1836* (New York: Harper & Row, 1965) and 1 William W. Freehling, *The Road to Disunion: Secessionists at Bay 1776–1854* (New York: Oxford University Press, 1990). Until volume 2 of *The Road to Disunion* is available, one will have to make do with Professor Freehling's Weil Centennial Lecture on "The Slaveholders' (Amazing) Theory of Secession and the Renewal of U.S. Constitutional History," which was delivered on Feb. 20, 2003, at the University of Texas School of Law, and which can be viewed at <www .utexas.edu/law/depts/media/Reels/Louisiana/louisiana1.ram>. As for the legal history of the Civil Rights movement, several chapters in Lucas A. Powe, Jr., *The Warren Court and American Politics* (Cambridge, Mass.: Harvard University Press, 2000) chaps. 2, 3, & 7, are of particular interest. Finally, a good overview of the legal issues underlying nullification, secession, and interposition can be found in Robert B. McKay, "'With All Deliberate Speed': A Study of School Desegregation," 31 *N.Y.U. L. Rev.* (1956) 991.

PART II: ANALYSIS

Most sources address only one of the several doctrines that have developed under the Supremacy Clause, rather than examining those doctrines in their entirety. Exceptions are the leading treatises on constitutional law. Most useful is 1 Laurence H. Tribe, *American Constitutional Law*, 3d ed. (New York: Foundation Press, 2000), which contains detailed discussions of each of the substantive doctrines considered in this volume.

The Supremacy Clause and the Courts

The bicentennial of Marbury v. Madison (1803) in 2003 seemingly has prompted a recent outburst in writings on judicial review. An excellent overview of the issues, which relies heavily on the Supremacy Clause in making the case in favor of judicial review, is Saikrishna B. Prakash & John C. Yoo, "The Origins of Judicial Review," 70 *U. Chi. L. Rev.* (2003) 887; see also Bradford R. Clark, "The Supremacy Clause as a Constraint on Federal Power," 71 *Geo. Wash. L. Rev.* (2003) 91. For contrary views, which argue that the Framers viewed the Constitution as fundamental law not enforceable in the courts, see Sylvia Snowiss, *Judicial Review and the Law of the Constitution* (New Haven: Yale University Press, 1990) and Larry D. Kramer, "Foreword: We the Court," 115 *Harv. L. Rev.* (2001) 4. A classic critique of the doctrine of judicial review is Alexander M. Bickel, *The Least Dangerous Branch: The Supreme Court at the Bar of Politics* (Indianapolis: Bobbs-Merrill Co., 1962). For a variety of perspectives on the subject, using *Marbury*'s bicentennial as the jumping off point, see "Judicial Review: Blessing or Curse? Or Both? A Symposium in Commemoration of the Bicentennial of *Marbury v. Madison*," 38 *Wake Forest L. Rev.* 2003 313–838.

The duty of state courts to enforce federal law usually falls within the subject of "federal courts" at law schools. Hence, treatises on the law of federal courts, such as Charles Alan Wright & Mary Kay Kane, *Law of Federal Courts*, 6th ed. (St. Paul: West Group, 2002), address the topic. Law school casebooks for classes on federal courts likewise discuss the subject. A classic casebook, which has a detailed overview of the duty of state courts to enforce federal law, is Richard H. Fallon, Jr., et al., *The Federal Courts and the Federal*

System, 5th ed. (New York: Foundation Press, 2003) (also dealing with judicial review). Although addressing whether Congress has the power to regulate state court procedures for state law claims, Anthony J. Bellia, Jr., "Federal Regulation of State Court Procedures," 110 *Yale L.J.* (2001) 947, provides a nice summary of the law as to claims based on federal law as well. Finally, for competing views on the source of a congressional power to "commandeer" state courts, see Evan H. Caminker, "Printz, State Sovereignty, and the Limits of Formalism," 1997 *Sup. Ct. Rev.* 199 (relying on Supremacy Clause as a whole) and Martin H. Redish & Steven G. Sklaver, "Federal Power to Commandeer State Courts: Implications for the Theory of Judicial Federalism," 32 *Ind. L. Rev.* (1998) 71 (relying on Article I of the Constitution).

Federal Preemption of State Law

Perhaps it used to be true that, "as a topic, preemption has largely been ignored by constitutional law scholars." Stephen A. Gardbaum, "The Nature of Preemption," 79 *Cornell L. Rev.* (1994) 767, 768. But that no longer is the case. Since Professor Gardbaum's article was published, a number of scholars have engaged in a thoughtful reexamination of federal preemption doctrine.

The standard source on federal preemption (which predates Gardbaum's criticism) is a report prepared by the Appellate Judges Conference of the American Bar Association, with former judge and Clinton special prosecutor Ken Starr as the lead author. Kenneth Starr et al., *The Law of Preemption* (Chicago: American Bar Association, 1991). The report provides a detailed overview of preemption doctrine, while arguing in favor of a "clear statement" rule for federal preemption. Professor Caleb Nelson has undertaken a creative historical reexamination of preemption doctrine and the Supremacy Clause, which also supports a significant curtailment of the doctrine. See Caleb Nelson, "Preemption," 86 *Va. L. Rev.* (2000) 225. Other useful critiques of current doctrine can be found in Viet D. Dinh, "Reassessing the Law of Preemption," 88 *Geo. L.J.* (2000) 2085 and Mary J. Davis, "Unmasking the Presumption in Favor of Preemption," 53 *S.C. L. Rev.* (2002) 967. Among the constitutional law treaties, the section on preemption in Erwin Chemerinsky, *Constitutional Law: Principles and Policies* (New York: Aspen Law & Business, 1997) Section 5.2, is straightforward and particularly helpful. An empirical study of Supreme Court decision making in preemption cases, which this book updates, is David M. O'Brien, "The Supreme Court and Intergovernmental Relations: What Happened to 'Our Federalism'?", 9 *J.L. & Pol.* (1993) 609.

Of course, numerous authorities discuss the scope of preemption under particular federal statutes. For an overview of preemption under the Federal Arbitration Act, see Christopher R. Drahozal, "Federal Arbitration Act Preemption," 79 *Ind. L.J.* 393 (2004). Leading authorities on arbitration law generally, each of which discusses preemption issues, are 1 Ian R. Macneil et al., *Federal Arbitration Law* (Boston: Little, Brown & Co., Supp. 1999) ch. 10 and Stephen J. Ware, *Alternative Dispute Resolution* (St. Paul: West Group, 2001) 26–43.

Federal Immunity from State Law

Beyond the constitutional law treatises, federal immunity from state law has received relatively little attention in the legal literature. The one exception is federal immunity from state taxes, where the leading text is 2 Jerome R. Hellerstein & Walter Hellerstein, *State Taxation*, 3rd ed. (Boston: Warren Gorham & Lamont, 2001) ch. 22. Because of the book's focus on state and local taxes, not surprisingly it does not deal with federal immunity from state criminal laws. For that topic, see the essay by former Solicitor General Seth P. Waxman, "Federalism, Law Enforcement, and the Supremacy Clause: The Strange Case of Ruby Ridge," 51 *U. Kan. L. Rev.* (2002) 141 and the subsequent article by Waxman and Trevor W. Morrison, "What Kind of Immunity? Federal Officers, State Criminal Law, and the Supremacy Clause," 112 *Yale L.J.* (2003) 2195.

Treaties as the Supreme Law of the Land

Much has been written about international law and federal supremacy in recent years. A classic work from an "internationalist" perspective (supporting the incorporation of international law into domestic law) is Louis Henkin, *Foreign Affairs and the United States Constitution*, 2d ed. (Oxford: Clarendon Press, 1996). The black letter rules are stated in the *Restatement (Third) of the Foreign Relations Law of the United States* (St. Paul: American Law Institute Publishers, 1987), which also has an internationalist flavor. A helpful source that collects many of the relevant materials and sets out the issues in a manner designed for law students but readily accessible to a more general audience is Curtis A. Bradley & Jack L. Goldsmith, *Foreign Relations Law: Cases and Materials* (New York: Aspen Publishers, 2003). International law challenges to the juvenile death penalty are evaluated in detail in Curtis A. Bradley, "The Juvenile Death Penalty and International Law," 52 *Duke L.J.* (2002) 485.

For a sample of the academic debate on when treaties are self-executing, see John C. Yoo, "Globalism and the Constitution: Treaties, Non-Self-Execution, and the Original Understanding," 99 *Colum. L. Rev.* (1999) 1955 (contending that treaties addressing subjects that fall within Congress' Article I powers should be non-self-executing, relying on a detailed historical analysis of the treaty power); Martin S. Flaherty, "History Right? Historical Scholarship, Original Understanding, and Treaties as 'Supreme Law of the Land,'" 99 *Colum. L. Rev.* (1999) 2095 (criticizing historical analysis in Yoo article); Carlos Manuel Vázquez, "Laughing at Treaties," 99 *Colum. L. Rev.* (1999) 2154 (arguing that Yoo thesis is inconsistent with the text of the Supremacy Clause and the structure of the Constitution); and John C. Yoo, "Treaties and Public Lawmaking: A Textual and Structural Defense of Non-Self-Execution," 99 *Colum. L. Rev.* (1999) 2218 (rejoinder to Flaherty and Vázquez critiques).

For a sample of the debate over whether customary international law preempts state law, see Curtis A. Bradley & Jack L. Goldsmith, "Customary International Law as Federal Common Law: A Critique of the Modern Position," 110 *Harv. L. Rev.* (1997) 815 (arguing that customary international law is not federal common law and does not preempt state law); Harold Hongju Koh, "Is International Law Really State Law?," 111 *Harv. L. Rev.* (1998) 1824 (critiquing Bradley & Goldsmith argument); Gerald L. Neuman, "Sense and Nonsense About Customary International Law: A Response to Professors Bradley and Goldsmith," 66 *Fordham L. Rev.* (1997) 371 (same); Curtis A. Bradley & Jack L. Goldsmith, "Federal Courts and the Incorporation of International Law," 111 *Harv. L. Rev.* (1998) 2260 (responding to criticisms of the argument); and Ernest A. Young, "Sorting Out the Debate Over Customary International Law," 42 *Va. J. Int'l L.* (2002) 365 (providing overview of the issues).

Table of Cases

C

D

E

F

Felder v. Casey, 487 U.S. 131 (1988)
Federal Energy Regulatory Comm'n v. Mississippi, 456 U.S. 742 (1982)
Fidelity Federal Savings & Loan Ass'n v. de la Cuesta, 458 U.S. 141 (1982)
First Agricultural National Bank v. State Tax Comm'n, 392 U.S. 339 (1968)
First National Bank v. Bartow County Board of Tax Assessors, 470 U.S. 583 (1985)
Florida Lime & Avocado Growers, Inc. v. Paul, 373 U.S. 132 (1963)
Foster v. Neilson, 27 U.S. 253 (1829)
Freightliner Corp. v. Myrick, 514 U.S. 280 (1995)

G

Gade v. National Solid Wastes Management Ass'n, 505 U.S. 88 (1992)
Geier v. American Honda Motor Co., 529 U.S. 861 (2000)
Gibbons v. Ogden, 22 U.S. 1 (1824)
Gillespie v. Oklahoma, 257 U.S. 501 (1922)
Glassroth v. Moore, 229 F. Supp. 2d 1290 (M.D. Ala. 2002), aff'd, 335 F.3d 1282 (11th Cir. 2003)
Glassroth v. Moore, 275 F. Supp. 2d 1347 (M.D. Ala. 2003)
Goodyear Atomic Corp. v. Miller, 486 U.S. 174 (1988)
Graves v. New York ex rel. O'Keefe, 306 U.S. 466 (1939)
Green Tree Financial Corp. v. Bazzle, 539 U.S. 444 (2003)
Gregory v. Ashcroft, 501 U.S. 452 (1991)
Guaranty Trust Co. v. United States, 304 U.S. 126 (1938)

H

Hancock v. Train, 426 U.S. 167 (1976)
Harper v. Virginia Department of Taxation, 509 U.S. 86 (1993)
Harris v. Roderick, 126 F.3d 1189 (9th Cir. 1997), cert. denied, 522 U.S. 1115 (1998)
Helvering v. Mountain Producers Corp., 303 U.S. 376 (1938)
Herb v. Pitcairn, 324 U.S. 117 (1945)
Hillsborough County v. Automated Medical Laboratories, Inc., 471 U.S. 707 (1985)
Hines v. Davidowitz, 312 U.S. 52 (1941)
Hisquierdo v. Hisquierdo, 439 U.S. 572 (1979)
Hodel v. Virginia Surface Mining & Reclamation Ass'n, 452 U.S. 264 (1981)
Hodges v. Abraham, 253 F. Supp. 2d 846 (D.S.C.), aff'd, 300 F.3d 432 (4th Cir. 2002), cert. denied, 537 U.S. 1105 (2003)
Howlett v. Rose, 496 U.S. 356 (1990)
Howsam v. Dean Witter Reynolds, Inc., 537 U.S. 79 (2002)
Hylton v. United States, 3 U.S. 171 (1796)

I

Idaho v. Horiuchi, 1998 U.S. Dist. LEXIS 7667 (D. Idaho May 14, 1998), aff'd, 215 F.3d 986 (9th Cir. 2000), rev'd, 253 F.3d 359 (9th Cir.) (en banc), vacated as moot, 266 F.3d 979 (9th Cir. 2001) (en banc)
In re Compliance with Writ of Injunction of the United States District Court for the Middle District of Alabama, Order No. 03–01 (Ala. Aug. 21, 2003), available at <news.findlaw.com/hdocs/docs/religion/glsrthmre82103alsc.pdf>

In re McShane, 235 F. Supp. 262 (N.D. Miss. 1964)
In re Neagle, 135 U.S. 1 (1890)
In re Stanford, 537 U.S. 968 (2002)

J

James v. Dravo Contracting Co., 302 U.S. 134 (1937)
Jefferson County v. Acker, 527 U.S. 423 (1999)
Johnson v. Fankell, 520 U.S. 911 (1997)
Johnson v. Maryland, 254 U.S. 51 (1920)

K

Kentucky v. Long, 837 F.2d 727 (6th Cir. 1988)
Kern-Limerick, Inc. v. Scurlock, 347 U.S. 110 (1954)
Keystone, Inc. v. Triad Systems Corp., 971 P.2d 1240 (Mont. 1998)

L

Leslie Miller, Inc. v. Arkansas, 352 U.S. 187 (1956)
Livingston v. Van Ingen, 9 Johns. 507 (N.Y. 1812)
Lorillard Tobacco Co. v. Reilly, 533 U.S. 525 (2001)
Louisville & Nashville R.R. v. Stewart, 241 U.S. 261 (1916)

M

Marbury v. Madison, 5 U.S. 137 (1803)
Martin v. Hunter's Lessee, 14 U.S. 304 (1816)
Mastrobuono v. Shearson Lehman Hutton, Inc., 514 U.S. 52 (1995)
Mayo v. Dean Witter Reynolds, Inc., 258 F. Supp. 2d 1097 (N.D. Cal. 2003)
Mayo v. United States, 319 U.S. 441 (1943)
McCulloch v. Maryland, 17 U.S. 316 (1819)
McDermott v. Wisconsin, 228 U.S. 115 (1913)
McKnett v. St. Louis & San Francisco Railway Co., 292 U.S. 230 (1934)
Medtronic, Inc. v. Lohr, 518 U.S. 470 (1996)
Memphis Bank & Trust Co. v. Garner, 459 U.S. 392 (1983)
Mesa v. California, 489 U.S. 121 (1989)
Mescalero Apache Tribe v. Jones, 411 U.S. 145 (1973)
Minneapolis & St. Louis R.R. v. Bombolis, 241 U.S. 211 (1916)
Missouri v. Holland, 252 U.S. 416 (1920)
Missouri ex rel. Southern Railway Co. v. Mayfield, 340 U.S. 1 (1950)
Moe v. Confederated Salish & Kootenai Tribes of the Flathead Reservation, 425 U.S. 463 (1976)
Mondou v. New York, New Haven & Hartford R.R., 223 U.S. 1 (1912)
Morgan v. California, 743 F.2d 728 (9th Cir. 1984)
Moses Lake Homes, Inc. v. Grant County, 365 U.S. 744 (1961)

N

New York v. Federal Energy Regulatory Comm'n, 535 U.S. 1 (2002)
New York v. United States, 505 U.S. 144 (1992)

New York State Conference of Blue Cross & Blue Shield Plans v. Travelers Insurance Co., 514 U.S. 645 (1995)
Norfolk Southern Railway Co. v. Shanklin, 529 U.S. 344 (2000)
North Dakota v. United States, 495 U.S. 423 (1990)
Northwest Central Pipeline Corp. v. State Corp. Comm'n, 489 U.S. 493 (1989)

O

Ohio v. Thomas, 173 U.S. 276 (1899)
Oklahoma Tax Comm'n v. Texas Co., 336 U.S. 342 (1949)
Oklahoma Tax Comm'n v. United States, 319 U.S. 598 (1943)
Osborn v. Bank of the United States, 22 U.S. 738 (1824)

P

Pacific Gas & Electric Co. v. State Energy Resources Conservation & Development Comm'n, 461 U.S. 190 (1983)
Panhandle Oil Co. v. Mississippi ex rel. Knox, 277 U.S. 218 (1928)
Penn Dairies, Inc. v. Milk Control Comm'n, 318 U.S. 261 (1943)
Pennsylvania v. Nelson, 350 U.S. 497 (1956)
Perez v. Campbell, 402 U.S. 637 (1971)
Perry v. Thomas, 482 U.S. 483 (1987)
Phillips Chemical Co. v. Dumas Independent School District, 361 U.S. 376 (1960)
Prima Paint Corp. v. Flood & Conklin Mfg. Co., 388 U.S. 395 (1967)
Printz v. United States, 521 U.S. 898 (1997)
Public Utilities Comm'n v. United States, 355 U.S. 534 (1958)

R

Ragsdale v. Department of Revenue, 895 P.2d 1348 (Or.), cert. denied, 516 U.S. 1011 (1995)
Ray v. Atlantic Richfield Co., 435 U.S. 151 (1978)
Reid v. Covert, 354 U.S. 1 (1957)
Retail Clerks International Ass'n v. Schermerhorn, 375 U.S. 96 (1963)
Rice v. Santa Fe Elevator Corp., 331 U.S. 218 (1947)
Rush Prudential HMO, Inc. v. Moran, 536 U.S. 355 (2002)
Rutgers v. Waddington (N.Y. City Mayor's Ct., Aug. 27, 1784) (unpublished opinion)

S

Schneidewind v. ANR Pipeline Co., 485 U.S. 293 (1988)
Shaw v. Delta Air Lines, Inc., 463 U.S. 85 (1983)
Sheehy v. Public Employees Retirement Div., 864 P.2d 762 (Mont. 1993)
Silkwood v. Kerr-McGee Corp., 464 U.S. 238 (1984)
Simmons v. Miller, 40 Miss. 19 (1864)
South Carolina v. Baker, 485 U.S. 505 (1988)
Southland Corp. v. Keating, 465 U.S. 1 (1984)
Sprietsma v. Mercury Marine, 537 U.S. 51 (2002)
St. Louis & San Francisco R.R. v. Brown, 241 U.S. 223 (1916)
Standard Oil Co. v. Johnson, 316 U.S. 481 (1942)

Stanford v. Kentucky, 492 U.S. 361 (1989)
State v. Odom, 2002 Tenn. Crim. App. LEXIS 871 (Tenn. Crim. App. Oct. 15, 2002)
State v. Tenace, 2003 Ohio App. LEXIS 3143 (Ohio Ct. App. June 30, 2003)
State ex rel. Dawson, 39 Ala. 367 (1864)
State ex rel. James v. ACLU, 711 So. 2d 952 (Ala. 1998)
Sterling v. Constantin, 287 U.S. 378 (1932)

T

Takahashi v. Fish & Game Comm'n, 334 U.S. 410 (1948)
Tennessee v. Davis, 100 U.S. 257 (1880)
Testa v. Katt, 330 U.S. 386 (1947)
Texas v. White, 74 U.S. 700 (1869)
Thompson v. Oklahoma, 487 U.S. 815 (1988)
Thorpe v. Rutland & Burlington R.R., 27 Vt. 140 (1854)
Ticknor v. Choice Hotels International, Inc., 265 F.3d 931 (9th Cir. 2001), cert. denied, 534 U.S. 1133 (2002)
Toll v. Moreno, 458 U.S. 1 (1982)
Trinityfarm Construction Co. v. Grosjean, 291 U.S. 466 (1934)

U

United States v. Barnett, 346 F.2d 99 (5th Cir. 1965) (en banc)
United States v. Belmont, 301 U.S. 324 (1937)
United States v. Boyd, 378 U.S. 39 (1964)
United States v. City of Detroit, 355 U.S. 466 (1958)
United States v. County of Fresno, 429 U.S. 452 (1977)
United States v. Georgia Public Service Comm'n, 371 U.S. 285 (1963)
United States v. Locke, 529 U.S. 89 (2000)
United States v. Manning, 215 F. Supp. 272 (W.D. La. 1963)
United States v. Mississippi Tax Comm'n, 421 U.S. 599 (1975)
United States v. New Mexico, 455 U.S. 720 (1982)
United States v. Percheman, 32 U.S. 51 (1833)
United States v. Pink, 315 U.S. 203 (1942)
United States v. Township of Muskegon, 355 U.S. 484 (1958)
United States ex rel. Drury v. Lewis, 200 U.S. 1 (1906)

V

Volt Information Sciences, Inc. v. Board of Trustees of Leland Stanford Junior University, 489 U.S. 468 (1989)

W

Ware v. Hylton, 3 U.S. 199 (1796)
Washington v. United States, 460 U.S. 536 (1983)
Weston v. City Council of Charleston, 27 U.S. 449 (1829)
Whitney v. Robertson, 124 U.S. 190 (1888)
Wisconsin Public Intervenor v. Mortier, 501 U.S. 597 (1991)

Index

ABOUT THE AUTHOR

CHRISTOPHER R. DRAHOZAL is a Professor of Law at the University of Kansas School of Law.